Victorian Country Parsons

Brenda Colloms

VICTORIAN COUNTRY PARSONS

University of Nebraska Press

Lincoln and London

Publishers on the Plains

UNP

Copyright © 1977 by Brenda Colloms
Printed in Great Britain
First published in the United States of America
by the University of Nebraska Press, Lincoln, Nebraska 68588
Library of Congress Catalog Card Number 77–82027
ISBN 0–8032–0981–9

Dedication

For Martin and Marianne Colloms

Contents

Illustrations

Acknowledgements

A book of this nature could not have been written without the encouragement and assistance of a number of people, many of them related to the parsons and their families described in this volume.

I wish to thank all of them, and especially those who are more particularly mentioned in the references appertaining to the individual chapters.

Historical Introduction

Amid the diverseness of Victorian life the English country parson, by character, career and preoccupations, shines forth in infinite variety. Like all professional men, the village clergy responded to the pressures and possibilities of that age, and since the period 1840 to 1900 saw prodigious changes in social attitudes and technological development it naturally witnessed corresponding changes in the views and activities of churchmen. Before considering the nineteenth-century parson in detail, we should perhaps spare time to trace his antecedents. Most historians agree that the system of the village church and village priest grew up more or less spontaneously when the Saxon Lords of the manor were converted to Christianity by Irish and Roman monks on their evangelizing missions to England. The newly Christian lord set aside some of his land to farm the glebe for his priest; he had a church built at his expense; and he appointed the priest, who would then look to the glebe for a part of his income, to the dues and offerings of the parishioners, but most importantly to the tithe, one tenth of all that the parish land had produced in a year. The tithe was a humble offering in essence made to God; in practice to His servant, the priest.

These Saxon priests were often well educated men whose status and function were similar to those of the eighteenth-century 'squarson'. The effect of the Norman conquest on this parochial system was detrimental because it directed many benefices towards the great monastic houses, and these institutions made use of the incomes from the benefices without giving much heed to whether the parish was still being properly cared for by a suitable priest. Not unexpectedly, those years saw a steep decline in the status and living standards of the parish priest, until the situation became so scandalous that in 1215 (the year that King John was forced to grant the barons their Magna Carta) a canon of the Lateran Council granted the vicar his freehold and guaranteed him a living income. These two changes were fundamental, for they made the priest independent of his patron once he was appointed. Seven years later it was decreed at the Council of Oxford that a vicar must have been admitted to Holy Orders and must reside constantly in his vicarage.

In spite of these reforms there continued throughout the next century and a half persistent abuses of the kind which William Langland criticized in his *Vision of Piers Plowman*, a warning signal indeed of social unrest which surfaced in 1381 with the Peasants' Revolt. Some country priests, notably John Ball, upheld the peasants' cause. Throughout the Middle Ages we can find examples of these simple, forthright men, part priest part worker for the most, living on the same level as the majority of the villagers and therefore aware of the miseries and joys of their lives. Such men appreciated the hardships imposed by the spread of sheep farming and by the enclosure system in the fifteenth and sixteenth centuries. Those innovations produced the rapacious Tudor landed gentry on the one hand and the embittered 'sturdy beggars' on the other.

The political Reformation of Henry VIII entirely changed the life of the priest in that he was allowed to marry and raise a family. A general increase in the prosperity of the country, including especially improvements in agriculture, rendered the glebe and the tithes more profitable. By the eighteenth century a village parson could reasonably aspire to live in the style of a country gentleman. A family which owned a clerical living (and some families owned more than one) was very likely to direct a younger son into the church, and he certainly did not have to be 'the fool of the family'. The son of a parson might well follow his father in such a family living and act as curate to his father until he 'inherited', as it were, on his father's death or retirement.

The little parish of St Michaels-on-Wyre in Lancashire was served—and well served—from 1789 to 1919 by 'squarsons' of the Hornby family, who were paternalistic vicars and humane landlords in their little community, shielding it from most of the vicissitudes of 130 years. The would-be parson went as a matter of course to Oxford or Cambridge before taking Holy Orders, and so by upbringing and background he was a 'gentleman' and thus regarded by the class-conscious villagers. So we come to Victoria's reign which, in Dr Hart's pleasant phrase, 'witnessed the golden summer of the parson's progress'.[1]

Because nearly every village and hamlet still has its parish church, the English countryside seems closely connected with the Anglican Church. Most people, asked to visualize a village scene, automatically place a church in the setting. In many cases the existing church covers the site of an early pagan place of worship, a fact which underlines the old bond between earth and spirit, village and church—tenuous though this bond has now become. Our great occasions, public or private, are carried out within a solemn framework of ecclesiastical ritual, but however dramatic and photogenic these rites may be, they have lost their true meaning so far as the majority of spectators or even participants are concerned, and for all practical purposes the link between Church and community is increasingly brittle. In spite of this obvious fact, or possibly just because of it, many people hark back nostalgically to some idyllic country existence which provided clearly defined social patterns and real job satisfactions (an existence which they glamourize and sentimentalize beyond all reality) wherein the country parson goes his tranquil way in an impossible blend of 'poor parson' and 'squarson'.

Chaucer's 'poor parson' continues to exert a pull even in the twentieth century—the man of God, schooled in the Bible; unworldly, devoted to his pastoral duties; a man of the people among the people, set apart only by his religious learning and humility. Centuries later the Rev. George Herbert limned a not too dissimilar village priest—simple, dignified, lovable—and it was an ideal to which many of the best country parsons aspired.

The particular character of the Anglican Church and its relationship with the State was shaped both by Henry VIII's political Reformation and by a quirk of history which saw English nationalism burgeon simultaneously with the growth of Lutheran Protestantism in Europe. In the sixteenth century the Protestant English Church was the sole patriotic and national church when England's enemy was Roman Catholic Spain, and also in the

seventeenth and eighteenth centuries when Roman Catholic
France was the enemy, and those years set a permanent seal of
suspicion upon the Roman Church. During the French Revolution
the English Church became a patriotic bulwark against an atheist
enemy. Successive Acts of Parliament assured the ascendancy of
the Anglican Church over other Protestant groups, making it
mandatory for all people in positions of power—from the monarch
to Members of Parliament, local councillors and higher civil
servants including the military—to belong to the Established
Church.

In the eighteenth century the Anglican clergy often seemed to
conform altogether too meekly to the materialistic and rational
ethos. Not that all the livings were lucrative, at least for country
parsons, since another legacy of the Reformation had been unequal
benefices, with the result that although the Church as a whole was
wealthy, and some clerics were amazingly well paid, others were
very poor and unjustly blamed for not carrying out their duties
adequately. The abuse of plurality, whereby one clergyman held
more than one living, was sometimes an inevitable consequence of
poor livings.

Politically the English country clergy from the eighteenth
century onwards stood squarely behind the Tory party, and promotion was usually a matter of wearing the right party badge. A
tract entitled *How to rise in the Church* gave sound advice:

> Vote for the True Blue next election, and you may steal all the
> horses in the parish; or light your cigar with the whole Thirty-
> Nine Articles, and you will dine with the Bishop once a fort-
> night, and be a prosperous gentleman with a leash of fat livings
> in the course of a short time. Does the prospect not please you?[2]

One of the eighteenth-century parsons whom we know well
because he kept a detailed diary, the Rev. James Woodeforde of
Weston Longeville in Norfolk, has given us a model of such a man
and, rightly or wrongly, we tend to take this as a norm. Parson
Woodeforde was a scholar and a gentleman, and attended to his
clerical duties in a rather skimpy fashion. Assuming that his diary
reflects his priorities, these were food, social visits, amusements
and holidays. Church matters appear to lag behind. He did rather
well on his income of £400 from the living (Oliver Goldsmith's

country parson was 'passing rich on £40 a year'), and he thought
nothing of calling on the Bishop to solicit an appointment as
Cathedral preacher. '24 October 1783. After breakfast I dressed
myself in my best Coat and Waistcoat and then walked down in my
Boots and had a long conversation with the Bishop abt. many
things . . .'[3]

During the French Revolution and the Napoleonic Wars the
super-patriotism of Anglican clerics, born of alarm lest French
atheism should invade English shores, was strongly and fervently
displayed and led to a surge of popularity for the Church of
England. Nevertheless, this same alarm accompanied a set of
rigidly orthodox Anglican views, devastatingly High Tory political
attitudes and an utter lack of sympathy for any radical or reform-
ist opinions, to such an extent that even mere suspicion that a man
agreed with any of the revolutionary ideas which continued to
hover over Europe after 1815 was enough to brand him as a man
having dealings with Satan. This exaggerated taunt did not imply
literal devil worship or black masses but was merely a highly-
coloured assertion that God's pattern for English society was a
highly-stratified one under the control of the landed gentry and
the Tory party. The word 'Fascist', when used in its common loose
manner, is probably today's equivalent of that early nineteenth-
century 'Satanist'. The Rev. John Mitford (discussed later)
suffered from this smear.

Clergymen whose formative years were spent prior to the 1830
decade of reforms inclined to look backwards rather than forwards,
resembling Metternich at Vienna, and showed little sign of the
moral earnestness, deriving from Samuel Taylor Coleridge and Dr
Arnold, which was later to characterize the Victorian age. That
acute, witty and pessimistic commentator upon the world, the Rev.
Sydney Smith, who believed in competition for unequal benefices
to keep the parsons up to scratch, remarked to W. E. Gladstone in
1835, 'Whenever you meet a clergyman of my age, you may be
sure he is a bad clergyman.' Even as late as the 1860s the bishops
possessed such wide patronage that Anthony Trollope indulgently
called it a privilege having in it 'much of the sweet medieval flavour
of old English corruption'.[4]

All the same, reform was on the way, and comprehensive reform
at that which covered religious as well as secular life. Jeremy
Bentham's concept of utility became a convenient yardstick for all

jobs, including clerical ones. Partisan journalism drew attention to injustices and abuses in all walks of life and the Church came in for its due share. First published in 1820 under the title *Corruption Unmasked,* and then reprinted in various forms up to 1835 under the title *The Extraordinary Black Book,* an attack upon the Church by a Benthamite radical called John Wade enjoyed big sales. His criticisms, which were more or less founded on fact, reflected broad public opinion in their distaste for pluralities and for certain instances of conspicious consumption on the part of bishops. The material for these criticisms came chiefly from diocesan returns and reports drawn up by the Church in 1827 and 1829, which showed less than 42 per cent of Anglican incumbents lived in their parishes, 24·6 per cent of these having permission to reside outside. The Rev. W. W. Andrew could not find a suitable house to rent within his Norfolk parish and so had permission to live a few miles over the boundary. A particularly zealous Low Churchman, this parson certainly did not use it as an excuse to slack. The Rev. O. Pickard-Cambridge, as a curate, was forced to lodge some miles away because the chief landowner in the parish was a Roman Catholic who refused to let Anglicans rent his property.

The abuse of pluralities, and the attempts to reform this, sometimes had odd results. There is an account of one minister who had charge of three churches and lived at a point central between the three. He certainly officiated at one Sunday service at each church and managed it by giving a service at the central church, and an alternate morning or evening service at the two outlying churches. In effect, the parson rode out to a further church for the morning service, paused midway to give a noonday service at the middle church, and reached the third church for an evening service. Suddenly his bishop ordered that the middle church should also have an alternate morning and evening service. The parson rose to the new demand. One Sunday he arrived at the middle church early and began the service at five minutes to noon—the morning service. The next Sunday he arrived later, and began the service at five past—the evening one.[5]

In spite of the widely-held belief that all clerical pluralists were wealthy, the truth was that some parsons were compelled by poverty to hold more than one living. Men with private incomes could usually manage on one living and after the end of the French Wars a surprising number of ex-Army and Navy officers, retired on half-pay pensions, entered the Church. At that time about 80 per cent of livings produced less than £400 a year. Robert Stephen Hawker (1804–1875) of Morwenstow in Cornwall was an eccentric, autocratic poet-parson. The value of his living was £365, which prompted him to compose the following verse which he affixed to the porch of his vicarage:

A house, a glebe, a pound a day
A pleasant place to watch and pray:
Be true to Church, be kind to poor,
O minister for evermore!

Curates fared much worse. Their average stipend was £81 per year and more than 4,000 of them served parishes where the rector resided elsewhere. Resident clergy apparently had more tender consciences than non-resident clergy, for they paid their curates on average seven pounds a year more than the non-resident clergy did.

But the answer to the problem of inadequate stipends was more complex than most lay critics imagined, and if all the incomes from benefices had been pooled and an average reached this would have amounted to only £285 a year. The matter of tithes, too, was a very thorny one, and might or might not add much to the income, while the glebe varied in value so greatly from parish to parish that it merely increased the inequalities.

When the 1830s opened, the Anglican establishment had become thoroughly unpopular and by contrast Roman Catholicism had received a boost through the 1829 Act which removed legal restrictions from Catholics. It was a decided point in favour of the Roman Church that it did not permit pluralities. The Whig reform campaigns of the 1830s were vigorously opposed by the Tories, amongst whose ranks the Anglican bishops were notoriously prominent, and the lower clergy was tarnished by the bigotry and selfishness of the proud prelates. Furthermore, it had been the Dissenters, not the Anglicans, who had provided the main Christian response to the poverty and uncertainties of the Industrial Revolution, so that in the industrial towns and even in many country villages newly-built chapels stood plainly as a visible reproach to the Church of England, tangible monuments to the Church's inadequacies, shortsightedness and selfishness. Certainly among town workers there had emerged an instinctive feeling that

the Church of England was 'them'—the Chapel was 'us'. The
sophisticated jibe that the Anglican Church was the Tory party at
prayer was countered by the retort that Nonconformity was Radicals singing hymns. The rustic poor, keeping their mouths grimly
shut in the presence of their landlords and their employers, frequently gave the appearance of ignorance and apathy. But did they
in actual fact accept peculiar or insensitive vicars as part of a divine
plan not theirs to question, or did prudence dictate their silence?

The Rev. G. A. Denison has a story which illustrates the capacity
of a congregation to put up with almost anything. He had (it was
1832) lately been ordained and was curate in charge at Cuddeson
whilst still retaining his tutorship at Oriel College, Oxford. He was
young and determined to be a new broom, and he ran the little
parish in high-handed fashion. The church had a central tower in
the space beneath which Denison installed a heating stove with a
complicated flue to take the fumes away out through the roof.

Christmas Day was bitterly cold, and Denison made sure that a
roaring fire was going so that the church was pleasantly warm. He
was well into the service when he became aware that the congregation, which had been trained to be extremely quiet and orderly,
was fidgeting and looking around uneasily. Finally Denison could
not ignore this strange behaviour and he turned to his clerk, who
sat immediately behind him.

'Mortimer, what is all this disturbance about?'

'Please, sir, if you don't stop reading we shall all be burnt alive.'

'Burnt alive? What do you mean?'

'Please, sir, the church be on fire.'

At this Denison hastily looked over his right shoulder to discover
that the part of the ceiling where the flue-pipe disappeared was
red hot. He announced calmly to the congregation, 'I see there
is a little accident, you had better go and get ladders and plenty of
water.' With permission given (but not till then) the villagers were
out of the church in a trice and shortly afterwards the roof burst
into flames, leaving Denison to muse that if he had not been told
what was happening, they would presumably have remained
obediently inside while the church burned.

All communities need a spiritual heart and in villages where the
Anglican minister failed to supply it, the Dissenter often succeeded.
Punch was happy to make the point about the sporting parson who
fell off his horse into the ditch—'Don't abandon the chase, let

parson stay there, he won't be missed till Sunday!' Traffic in advowsons, which as private property were advertised for sale like any other private property, supplied further kindling for scandal, especially when advowsons were described in advertisements for sale as 'situated in fine sporting country', or 'with plenty of game' or 'a pack of staunch fox-hounds kept in the neighbourhood'.[6]

The spread of enclosures which accompanied the Agricultural Revolution in the eighteenth and early nineteenth centuries changed the life of the countryman permanently and tragically. Prior to that time the yeoman-farmer who owned or rented a plot, and employed no labour apart from his family, lived much as his ancestors had done, with a garden where he grew food for the family, the village common to graze his donkey, pigs, geese or hens, and access to wood for winter fuel. He frequently augmented his sub-sistence farming by part-time work at village crafts. The richer yeoman-farmer who could employ labour and rise to the social niceties of a gentleman's life managed to survive the enclosures, but the poorer yeoman was uprooted and deprived at a parlia-mentary stroke of his ancient grazing rights. The peasant poet John Clare mourned:

> Then came Enclosures—ruin was its guide
> But freedom's cottage soon was thrust aside,
> And workhouse prisons raised upon the site.

The small yeoman had no real choice; he could hire himself out as a farm labourer, or he could emigrate. The big farmer, now with plenty of men to pick and choose from, could and did hold agricul-tural wages down to starvation levels. The man with the hoe was allowed to breathe, but he could not be said to live:

> A thing that grieves not and that never hopes,
> Stolid and stunned, a brother to the ox.

Sydney Smith was doubtless thinking of another side of life when he said jestingly, 'Country life is very good, in fact the very best—for cattle.' The introduction of machinery led to resentment and redundancy on the farms as it did in cottage industries. John Denson, a dignified and articulate Cambridge labourer, whose ancestors were English yeomen, wrote feelingly in 1830 of 'Your

infernal thrashing machines . . . those parents of poachers, convicts
and Poor's Rates . . .'.

But the passing of the small yeoman-farmer changed village
life in a more subtle way also. He had possessed the instincts of the
good steward. His family had lived off and with the soil, without
exploiting it, renewing its goodness, building for posterity. A fence,
a gate, a cottage, was meant to last for years. The acquisitive
society might be accepted in the industrial town where both
Church and Chapel preached the personal values of thrift and
industry, which were essential elements for an acquisitive society,
but these values were wrong for the country. When the yeoman
was driven from the village, or when he lost his personal dignity
and became a hired hand, the squire too was the loser, for the
change broke the long and durable social relationship between
yeoman and squire.

New social barriers erected upon wealth and the employer-
employee relationship gradually eroded the life of the village. The
squire moved from his house in the village to an imposing mansion
secluded in the midst of an ornamental park, and the village
church seemed transformed into an annexe of the Big House instead of being the old communal place of worship. This point was
even more clearly demonstrated when the squire had a gate cut
into the wall dividing church land and his own so that he and his
family could slip discreetly into church without having to mix with
the villagers, who were by that time usually their tenants or em-
ployees or both. To make the situation even more explicit, the
squire sat in a high panelled pew, safely hidden from prying eyes,
pampered by cushions and footstools, even a fire. If the church
had a three-decker pulpit, the parson could see over the pew walls
and check on the behaviour of its occupants, although whether he
would have the desire or the nerve to rebuke the squire was quite
another matter.

R. S. Hawker had considerable difficulty at Morwenstow when
he was modernizing the interior of the church and started taking
down the curtained family pews. He received consent from all but
one of the owners, this last being a wealthy yeoman farmer who
insisted that he had a faculty right to the pew and refused to give
it up. Sunday after Sunday he barricaded himself inside until his
was the only remaining pew.

Finally, the impetuous rector could tolerate it no longer and gave due notice that on a certain day at a certain hour he would pull down the pew himself. The farmer arrived, ready to defend his property, but was so taken aback at the sight of Hawker striding up the aisle with a large axe that he remained motionless and the rector smashed the pew to bits and flung the pieces outside the church. It says a good deal about the piety of that farmer and the personality of that parson that the farmer continued to attend church in spite of Hawker's arbitrary behaviour.

When young John Sterling, a Cambridge intellectual, called the parsons the 'black dragoons' of the villages employed by the ruling powers to keep their parishioners in subjection, he expressed the views of many early Liberals. Revitalization of the Church had to come if the Church were to survive, and it had to come from within. It occurred on two fronts; from Cambridge, through the Evangelical fervour of Charles Simeon, Fellow of Kings and minister of Holy Trinity Church; and from Oxford, not long afterwards, from the romantic Christianity of John Keble, E. B. Pusey and John Henry Newman. These low and High Church movements were at opposite poles, and usually deeply suspicious of each other. An enthusiastic young High Churchman, eager to bring saintliness into everyday life, once wrote to his Low Church bishop a letter headed, 'The Rectory, St Timothy's Day', to which his uncompromising bishop replied with a letter headed, 'The Palace. Washday.' Bishops liked to feel that they were a law unto themselves. Dean Hole tells of a young vicar who dared to argue with Bishop Blomfield and quoted St Ambrose as his authority. Back came the reply from Fulham Palace—'Sir, St Ambrose was not Bishop of London. I am.'

Alfred Tennyson, who was an admirer of the moderate, conciliatory F. D. Maurice, wrote in 'Maud' of listening to a High Church clergyman 'until I heard no longer The snowy-banded, dilettante, Delicate-handed priest intone. . .'. Low Church parsons, clear descendants of seventeenth-century Puritans, ran their parishes with an iron grasp of spiritual discipline, insisting that the most important thing in life was to meet death in the correct submissive frame of mind, and that life on earth was but the prelude to the more welcome life hereafter. Such men placed particular emphasis upon conversion. The Rev. W. W. Andrew, patiently trying to bring Squire Boileau, a lonely widower, sincere Christian and public-minded man, round to Andrew's austere views, noted in his diary with something like triumph that the squire had given up reading Charles Kingsley and was reading the evangelical Roberts of Wood Rising instead.[7]

The religious picture of England in the 1820s was a dreary one and the inadequacy of the Church of England and her officers merely underlined the lack of warmth and inspiration. Major poets and moralists like Wordsworth and Coleridge touched upon emotions whose roots were quasi-religious, but these writers were not revivalist Christians. The task of influencing half a century of decent men and women in the Anglican Church fell to the quiet, unassuming Oxford don who became a country parson, the Rev. John Keble, and he performed it not by stumping the country and holding dramatic meetings, but by publishing anonymously in 1827 a collection of poems to be read as daily spiritual refreshment under the title of *The Christian Year.*

There is almost always a market for comforting 'Thoughts for the Day' to cheer people along their path and to sustain them in times of personal unhappiness, and Keble's book proved by its immense sales (over a hundred editions by the year he died, 1866) that it filled a genuine need. The poems could be read in the privacy of the bedroom or study, or read aloud to the family. Middle-class women especially found comfort in them and the influence of the poems on the menfolk may have come first through the wives and daughters. Thackeray's Pendennis read the poems to his doting mother: 'Faint, very faint, and seldom in after life Pendennis heard that solemn church music: but he always loved the remembrance of it.'

Keble's life as a country parson testified to his shining goodness and people who came in contact with him went away feeling that his ideas and actions had to be correct because he was manifestly such a saintly man. The Rev. F. D. Maurice, an entirely different man in other respects, had a similar effect on people and for similar reasons. Isaac Williams, a brilliant Oxford scholar and a very gentle soul, met Keble one afternoon in a country lane near Horseley, and the encounter affected him like revelation from on high. He felt that until that moment he had been a sinner of the worst kind but that henceforth he would live righteously.

Keble moved and worked like a man in constant communion with God. He was one of the first parsons to hold daily church services. He taught for an hour every day in the village school and on Sundays he taught for an hour in the morning and for another hour in the afternoon. He was very serious about careful preparation for confirmation, and he was a conscientious cottage visitor. His parishioners valued him as their village priest without realizing that he was a national Church leader. Although he was correctly associated with the Oxford Movement he was not aggressive enough in intellect or temperament to storm the country, and he was equally reluctant to look into the future and recognize the trend of national thought and beliefs. He left it to his early friend, Dr Thomas Arnold, who represented the broadly liberal Anglican tradition, to carry the banner of Christianity against the agnostic forces which followed on Darwin's theories of evolution.

In some ways the Oxford Reformers were as unworldly as the Evangelicals, but they were fascinated by ritual and they proclaimed the historic development of the English Church from the Roman one. One of their least controversial features was an interest in church architecture, as evidenced by the Camden Society (formed in Cambridge in 1839) which encouraged successive waves of amateur antiquarians with a passion for medieval churches and brass rubbings. Beauty both inside the church and outside, handsome robes, and disciplined music, were other signs that as the century wore on some at least of the ideas of the Oxford Movement were seeping into the body of the Church.

Two legislative reforms of the 1830s had a special bearing on the lives of Anglican parsons. The first was the Poor Law Amendment Act of 1834 which set up state apparatus for welfare work and relieved the parson of some of the charitable work which had always been part of his service to the parish—what Dean Hole called 'a sweet, simple Christian charity'.[8] This, did the parson but realize, was the start of a long process by which the social work which underpinned his pastoral influence would be taken over by state agencies, making his own position in the parish increasingly anomalous.

The second was the Tithe Commutation Act of 1836. No longer would a disgruntled parishioner be tempted to pay his tithes in scrawny hens, along the lines of the harvest song in Dryden's *King Arthur*:

We've cheated the parson, we'll cheat him again
Why should a blockhead have one in ten?

The tithe was henceforth computed on a monetary basis and the heaviest burden fell eventually upon the main landlord who was both better placed to pay it and more willing to do so. The practice of the parson holding tithe dinners was kept up, often taking on the character of village feasts. A well attended and happy tithe dinner was an excellent straw poll indicating the parson's popularity. Parson after parson records in his diary how the tenant farmers came early and went late, understandably resolved to eat and drink the value of the tithe payment they had just made. Sensible parsons accepted this as in the nature of things and reckoned to retain their tithe-payers' respect and loyalty by their work in the parish.

The 1830s and 1840s were years of painful agricultural depression and the government was sufficiently concerned to set up the Royal Agricultural Society in 1838, charged with the task of persuading farmers to use fertilizers, to select better varieties of seed and to improve their animal husbandry. It presupposed that farmers had capital to finance these improvements, and it did nothing to improve the lot of the poorer tenant farmers for whom the repeal of the Corn Laws in 1846 was an additional burden. The erstwhile yeoman farmers as a class were virtually wiped out. By contrast, well-to-do farmers benefited, enlarged their holdings, and put many more acres into permanent pasturage. When the agronomists and the great landowners talked smugly and volubly of the advantages to the nation of the new 'high farming' they ignored the individual human tragedies which accompanied it. The country parson, if he were a good man who understood the realities of his parishioners' lives, was well aware of these tragedies and did all he could to alleviate them, although he could not affect the root causes. He could and did provide tickets for free coal, for meat and for clothing, and gallons of specially nourishing broth were made at the vicarage for collection by needy families. Some parsons saw emigration as the solution and worked in organizations which sent country families to new lives overseas. But often all that they could do was continue their endless rounds of cottage visiting, especially to the chronic sick and bedridden, visits which gave the patient's family a much needed spell of rest and cheered or soothed the patient. People were grateful. There is an old story of a little girl whose recovery from illness was ascribed to the good offices of the parson; her father said:

'I can't afford to pay you anything, but I'll poach you a little rabbit.'

All these activities comprised a welfare aspect which was increasingly carried out by socially conscious parsons, especially those from the 1850s onwards who were influenced by the Broad Church movement, amongst whom F. D. Maurice and Charles Kingsley were perhaps the best known. Little publicized, this important side of the parson's work cemented good human relationships between himself and the villagers. Like an M.P., the best parson tried to help all who lived in his village whether they were of his flock or another's, and there were many jobs, such as writing formal letters or helping to draft wills, where the literate parson was greatly in demand as an adviser. Unlike the modern career state or municipal welfare worker who moves from district to district, the Victorian country parson often spent most of his working life in the same parish, building up over the years an invaluable body of knowledge and trust in his community.

Relatively few parsons supported the country labourers when they organized under the leadership of Joseph Arch in the early 1870s, although men like Canon Edward Girdlestone and Lee Warner of Tarrant Gunville came out boldly on the side of the men. The Rev. J. W. Horsley, then a young curate at Witney, sympathized with the Oxford labourers who earned only ten shillings a week. Arch found fertile soil at Witney. Horsley commented that apart from his friend Leigh at Leamington (later to become Dean of Hereford) he knew of no clergyman who was Arch's friend.

Girdlestone faced opposition from the local farmers who were a powerful body in vestry meetings and could make it next to impossible to raise a church rate. Some of them, incensed by his support of the labourers, went so far as to desert the Anglican Church and join the Wesleyans in a mass protest. An earlier country parson who had faced opposition from the farmers was the Rev. J. S. Henslow, rector of Hitcham, who in the 'hungry forties' and 1850s divided his glebe into allotments and rented them to the labourers. His respectable farmers complained that possession of an allotment made a labourer too independent, but Henslow continued, unafraid and unrepentant, and when he died in 1861 there were 150 allotment holders in his village.

A country parson who gave evidence in the 1860s before a Royal Commission on rural conditions was blunt:

Bread was dear, and wages down to starvation point; the labourers were uneducated, underfed, underpaid—their cottages were
often unfit for human habitation, the sleeping and sanitary conditions were appalling. Naturally they took colour from their
environment.[9]

Such parsons however were exceptional, and Joseph Arch's
personal observation of country life convinced him that the distribution of parish charities was so arranged by agreement between
parson, squire and local landlord as to be an indirect weapon of
political pressure. His father was an Anglican but his mother was
'a Dissenter by nature' and Arch himself became a lay preacher of
the Primitive Methodist Church. It was practically inevitable that
Arch would conclude that in most country areas the parson was a
pillar of an unjust Establishment.

But from the 1870s onwards there came upon the scene a new
breed of parsons, products of the reforming zeal of the 1830s and
1840s and of the church legislation initiated by Sir Robert Peel.
With the State assuming increasing responsibility for people's
lives, and with the parson thereby edged out of so many of his
traditional village tasks, these new clergymen began to devote
more time to church improvements, both of the structure of the
building and the quality of the services. Much certainly needed
doing to the church buildings, many of which were in a parlous
condition, and with graveyards that were a positive disgrace. Even
as late as 1856 the churchyard of Chipping Norton was assessed for
parish rates as grazing land let to a local butcher for his sheep.
(Not that this appealed to all the customers. One old lady confessed she refused to buy mutton which had been grazed in the
churchyard because she thought it gave the meat 'a deathly
taste'.) Up to the 1850s however many churchwardens and also
parsons had habitually used the area as pasture for cows and
horses, and one rector had even sowed his churchyard as if it were
an ordinary allotment.

Repairs and modernization to the interior of the churches became the order of the day, and archdeacons sent out peremptory
instructions to brighten up the church. Parsons with private
incomes or wealthy relatives or friends were not upset by this, but
some parsons were poor. P. H. Ditchfield tells a story of one
such impecunious rector, who was commanded to make the church

interior more attractive, but lacked the money to do so. His wife was a determined and capable soul, as indeed she had had to be, and she went to the village wheelwright and bought up his stock of farm wagon paints, these being cheap and serviceable. They were in the usual country folk art colours of brilliant red, blue, green and yellow. Thus equipped, she painted all the woodwork in the church, pulpit, pews and doors, until the church was quite literally 'brightened up' as the archdeacon had directed!

Another important matter was village education, which also usually necessitated financing the building of a new school or the enlargement of an existing one. The parsons spent as freely as they could of their own time and money, and shamelessly solicited subscriptions from their relatives and friends. Through teaching, overseeing the classes, and serving as governors, they dominated village education, whether in the primary school (nearly always a Church school), the Sunday school or adult evening classes; and also through Penny Reading evenings and through the Lending Library. These last three amenities were frequently run by the ladies of the rectory, with any friends who could be roped in to assist. It is not commonly recognized that England owes a considerable debt of gratitude to these parish priests for the contribution they made to literacy in those years.

It was of course also true that the school became the 'parish priest's right hand', for through this medium his influence, if he had a strong personality, could permeate village thought and behaviour as one generation after another remembered him as teacher and examiner, and retained a certain awe and respect for him in that capacity, quite apart from any other influence he wielded through family connections or through some position of authority, such as Justice of the Peace.

Towards the latter part of the nineteenth century, when village populations had begun to dwindle and the attractions of nearby towns became more accessible through better public transport, these pioneering and initially successful adult educational projects based in the village petered out, and when institutions like the Workers Educational Association took up the task at the start of this century they had to begin the pioneering work all over again.

As the village became more secularized and the economic hold of the landowners lessened, so the parson's position inevitably shrank in importance. He would try to enter into communal projects, but often the work he did was disproportionate to its effect. Richard Jeffries has a touching vignette of just such an average parson in the 1870s, seen through the eyes of his devoted, equally well-meaning and somehow also ineffectual wife:

> But the work, the parish, the people, all seemed to have slipped out of her husband's hands. . . . But surely his good intentions, his way of life, his gentle kindness should carry sway. Instead of which the parish seemed to have quite left the Church, and the parson was outside the real modern life of the village. No matter what he did, even if popular, it soon seemed to pass out of his hands.[10]

Unless the parson possessed charisma or was a demon fund-raiser so that village church affairs prospered, there was always the likelihood that at best he would be tolerated and at worst he would be denounced (in private) as a Jesuitical Protestant. The unkindest cut of all was that as the century progressed the expenses of maintaining the parsonage increased, while the income from the glebe or its tenants was likely to decrease, so that the parson faced a future of genteel poverty. He would make whatever personal economies he could, while wondering what he would do when he became too old to work. He would hope to die in harness.

Some idea of the decrease in income from tithes can be gauged from the Rev. Edward Bligh, who was appointed rector of Rotherfield, a large prosperous parish in the gift of his father-in-law, the Earl of Abergavenny. Around the early 1860s Bligh in a good year expected to get in £1500 from his tithes, for which he paid £100 a year to a solicitors' firm in Lewes for collection. He paid another £100 towards another Church for which he was responsible, and a further £150 a year for a curate, and he paid agricultural rates of six shillings in the pound. He would be left with about £800 or £900 from the tithes. However, when the agricultural slump began to be felt from about 1875 onwards, the income from that same tithe slumped correspondingly, and in the 1880s Bligh estimated that the same tithe would bring in net only about £300 a year or less.

Whatever the Anglican minister's income might be, the Dissenters still placed him in a higher social grouping than themselves. Michael Home, recalling memories of a Primitive Methodist home in East Anglia in the late 1880s, remarked that 'The Church then, as I saw it, was a kind of superior form of worship and the peculiar property of those with power and money and of those immediately dependent on them.'

By the last quarter of the nineteenth century a change could be perceived in the type of men who entered the Church. Dean Hole, reflecting upon the difference between parsons in 1850 and parsons in 1900, says, 'The priest and his patron had in many cases been at the same school and university, and a much larger proportion of the clergy belonged to the higher grades of society . . . there were more gentlemen among the clergy in the conventional meaning of the word.' The career reforms of Gladstone's first ministry opened new professions to merit through the examination system and the Church lost its advantage as a premier attraction. In addition, there was general agreement that it was desirable for a priest to have a genuine vocation—never a particularly common thing, and becoming less so as a result of the battering which belief in the infallibility of the Bible had received from the new scientific theories of the 1860s and onwards. Sons of the parsonage, still dutiful, educated and hard-working, now entered the services, the higher civil service and the universities, which offered respectable scales of pay and assured retirement pensions, and they did very well in those fields. The Church sought to redress the balance by establishing theological training colleges which young men could enter without taking a university degree first.

The priest thus trained tended to have a narrower, more specialized outlook than his old-style predecessor, who had been broadened by three years at university, and in some instances Sydney Smith's unforgettable quip (that there were three sexes—men, women and curates) appeared to have come to fulfilment. When priests like these went into the villages, especially the remoter ones where traditional social mores persisted, they discovered it was quite impossible to achieve the social or intellectual ascendancy which the earlier parson had been granted as his due. The parson of this later period found that his sphere of activity was circumscribed, limited to work and decisions connected with church clubs and services but no longer extending over the parish as a whole. Important men in the Church like Edward King, who became Bishop of Lincoln and who was for several years principal of a theological training college set up by Bishop Wilberforce at

Cuddeson, knew exactly what effect a parson's personality could have in a country village. 'I do hope we never lose in England the true manly independent spirit which our clergy have,' he wrote in a letter of advice to a young parson.

The agricultural depression was meanwhile continuing and deepening and it hit the hired farm labourers worst. Some, whose spirit was not entirely quenched by deprivation, joined Joseph Arch's union, an act which prompted the more reactionary farmers to lock-out their labourers and sit stiffly through a period during which their farms fell into even greater decay. In 1884 a new parliamentary reform Act enfranchised the country worker, but it came too late to improve the living standards of the labourers, even though Joseph Arch was elected to the House of Commons. Government economic policies which made Britain a world exporter of manufactured goods also made her a world importer of cheap food, and British farmers could not compete with the low prices of large-scale foreign agriculture.

The Church, by and large, had no answer to this problem as it showed itself in the farming villages, and an informal agnosticism arose, particularly among the men, which oddly enough often accompanied a broad toleration of all Christian creeds, so that in one village the same people might attend both church and chapel on different occasions. There were after all few entertainments, especially in the winter, and good singing, a visiting preacher famous for his exciting sermons, or special Church festivities, would draw a larger congregation than usual. On the great holydays the church, lovingly beautified with flowers, was filled, and although Dissenters would not be confirmed or attend Holy Communion, they might go to the Anglican Church—it was their village church, when all was said and done—for christenings, marriages and burials. Most vicars held the churchyard to be the village burial ground to be shared by all, whether Anglicans, Dissenters or agnostics. This easy-going attitude towards organized religion was well expressed by Coggan, drinking his ale in *Far From the Madding Crowd*— 'There's this to be said for the Church, a man can belong to the Church and bide in his cheerful old inn, and never trouble or worry his mind about doctrines at all.'

But if Church doctrine were to be ignored, was the same to be true about its moral teaching? The country parsons of this later Victorian period were still largely imbued with the moral earnest-

The Rev. Richard
Chichester

Mrs Chichester

The Rev. Octavius Pickard-Cambridge with his wife and family

The Pickard-Cambridge family orchestra

ness of reformed public school and university teaching, with principles which were beginning to look old-fashioned. The nation's moral and cultural standards were being set not, as for so long, by an entrenched landed aristocracy, but by a thrusting, educated, ambitious middle class whose leading members did not open their Bibles to find a blueprint of a better world, either on this planet or elsewhere. In these circumstances, how much real influence could the country parson exert?

W. H. Hudson recounts a story of a Hampshire village parson who was locked out of his church for three Sundays in a row because he had dared to criticize publicly his churchwardens for spending more on themselves on market day than they paid their ploughman for an entire week's work. Churchwardens, of course, were invariably well-to-do farmers or tradesmen, hardly ever labourers. Yet if the village parson did not possess the independent spirit and social conscience to fight for the labourers, who at the turn of the century was left to be their champion?

A village usually had a pretty clear idea of the value of its minister. There is a famous Scottish story of the minister who was asked to visit a sick man, and dutifully went to the bedside of this stranger. Afterwards, he could not resist asking why the minister of the man's own church had not been sent for. 'Na, na,' was the rebuke. 'We wouldna' risk him. Do you no' ken it's a dangerous case of typhoid?'

With approximately ten thousand country parsons to choose from any selection must of necessity be personal and random, so the men described in this book are those who appealed to me from my reading and researches as representing certain types or trends within the Anglican Church during the nineteenth century. I decided to confine myself to men who remained country parsons, with the result that many clerics who did their stint in the villages but who later moved to towns or who gained promotion in the Church were regretfully placed on one side. As the manuscript progressed it became woefully apparent that for every lesser known minister whom I had picked there were dozens of equal interest and equally worthy of inclusion. Any readers of this book who have a country parson two or three generations back in their family are bound to criticize my list for failing to include their favourite parson. I can only apologize for such omissions and point out that it is manifestly impossible either to know or to include everyone.

Some of these men, by reason of their talents and their careers, seemed to me to demand more space than others; again, this is a personal judgement and I do not pretend to have said the last word on any one of them nor would I argue with readers who can make out a case for alternative choices. Let them write their own book.

Among the scientifically-minded parsons were the Rev. T. T. Lewis, modest and retiring, a geologist who was immensely helpful to young Roderick Murchison in his monumental book about the Silurian system, and the Rev. Octavius Pickard-Cambridge, Dorset 'squarson' and father of a British school of arachnologists. The Rev. Sydney Godolphin Osborne, the redoubtable 'S.G.O.' of *The Times*, stood for the crusading parson. A black sheep, or perhaps merely a dark grey one, was the Rev. John Mitford, a noted literary editor of whom his friend, Samuel Rogers, said that he was 'no more fit to be a parson than I am to be the Archangel Gabriel'. Poetry and parsonry frequently went together, as demonstrated by the Rev. William Barnes, the Dorset poet, and the Rev. Charles Tennyson Turner, brother of the Poet Laureate and a sonneteer of great merit. The Rev. Patrick Brontë, cruelly misrepresented in literary legend, was a distinguished minister of a parish already distinguished in Wesleyan history, and he certainly deserves to be better known in his own right, not simply as 'the father of the Brontës'. In almost total contrast to Brontë was the Rev. Francis Kilvert, who was content for many years to be a curate but who finally matured into a hard-working country parson, whose fascinating and revealing diaries resurrect a vanished age.

Nevertheless, to describe only exceptional characters, no matter how entertaining they may be, would be to give a distorted picture of the Victorian country parson, and to keep the balance right I have included others who, while not possessing the immediate appeal of a Barnes or a Kilvert, must be held to represent the generality of country clerics over this period. How could one disregard, for instance, the Rev. Jack Russell and his famous terriers? Or the Rev. William Kingsley, friend of Ruskin and Turner, and still a working parson on his hundredth birthday? Or the Rev. R. W. Dixon, 'impressible' poet and historian, whose friends ranged from the Pre-Raphaelites to Gerard Manley Hopkins? My second chapter is deliberately low-key, describing the more humdrum lives of a number of minor country parsons.

Earlier books than this one have described different Victorian parsons and it is clear that a rich vein of English social history is by no means exhausted. Black sheep there were, for parsons were human after all, but the percentage of criminous clerks was remarkably low. One has to search hard to find many cases like Burgoyne v. Free, D.D., where the minister was accused of seducing a succession of maidservants, as well as drinking, using profane language, owning an immoral book, demanding payment before conducting baptisms and funerals, and even selling the lead off the church roof! For the most part, Victorian village clergymen lived quietly, had time for contemplation, and busied themselves with a variety of tasks and responsibilities bearing directly upon human problems. Their daily work needed to be its own reward since recompense in a worldly or financial sense was not reserved for them. In retrospect, they can be seen as a group of men who, like Battle of Britain pilots, responded to a particular situation and then vanished permanently from the scene along with the special circumstances which had shaped their lives. The aims and optimism of the Victorians are so far out of step with the political cynicism and material wealth of our Western world that the folk hero of Tom Hughes' best seller is no longer Dr Arnold's disciple, Tom Brown, but his rebel, Flashman the Cad. Before all trace of the Victorian country parsons disappears, therefore, let us pause in friendly tribute and grant their memory a moment at least of appreciation.

2

A Clerical Mixed Bag

When the old-fashioned parson and the old-fashioned peasant
lived in harmony with each other, the parson's private life was his
own affair provided that he carried out his public duties. This
situation was well illustrated by the country gentleman who said
to an acquaintance of his from the next village, 'And how's your
parson? I hear he's rather odd,' knowing full well the clergyman
was said to be addicted to drink and to what Dr Johnson called
'the lighter vices'. 'Odd, sir, odd?' retorted the neighbour indig-
nantly. 'There's nothing odd about our parson, barring his character!'

But after the liberal reforms of the 1830s the country parson's
status became more nebulous and he had to be careful of his position.
Bishops began to ask embarrassing questions about hunting.
Young William Hornby was interrogated about the nature of his
leisure pursuits by John Bird Summers, Bishop of Chester. 'Hunting and shooting in a small way, my lord,' replied Hornby. 'These
of course you intend entirely to give up after ordination, at least
hunting,' prompted the bishop, and when Hornby, taken aback,
denied that such was his intention, the bishop declared roundly
that he would not countenance hunting in any way and would
hesitate to introduce a hunting man into the Church. At that broad
hint, Hornby decided to renounce hunting as soon as he became a
priest. He came of a clerical family and ordination was a serious
matter. '. . . ordained, & now I write under a new character,' he
confided to his diary.

As the nineteenth century wore on, hunting parsons became scarcer, and those who followed the hounds tended to do so as much in the nature of protest against religious narrowness and bigotry as for love of the sport. The Rev. Joseph Arkwright, however, was a devotee of hunting pure and simple. He became famous in Leicestershire as a horseman and judge of horseflesh, and when in 1850 he resigned his living of Latton in favour of his son, Julius, and purchased Mark Hall, near Harlow in Essex, he went to a county which was proud of its hunting traditions. The Essex Hunt had unfortunately deteriorated under an indifferent Master, so in 1857 the Mastership was offered to Arkwright who had the money to support it, having inherited a fortune from his grandfather, Richard Arkwright, the inventor of the spinning frame.

Arkwright's first season was so unsuccessful that a fellow cleric and hunting fanatic, the Rev. Frederick Fane, was moved to write a malicious criticism for publication in the *Chelmsford Chronicle* under the signature of 'Now an Old Fox'. Fane and Arkwright soon learned to dislike one another cordially.

Fane's passion for hunting and his outspoken manner often led him into altercations. He was conspicuous in a famous run of the Essex Hunt in 1866 when he took his young daughter with him, and in his eightieth year he was among the leaders of a formidable run which lasted for three hours. He was still hunting in the year of his death in 1894. Outside the hunting field, 'Parson' Fane was an active and public spirited man. He was an early supporter of the Volunteer movement; for many years he chaired the meetings of the Ongar Board of Guardians, and he was in great demand as an extempore preacher. He held the living of Norton Mandeville from 1855 until 1890 when he resigned it at the age of seventy-nine.

The best-known occasional guest of the Hunt during the Arkwright period was the writer Anthony Trollope, who was then living at Waltham House on the borders of Essex and Middlesex. He used to travel the twenty miles to Harlow either by cab or by the Great Eastern Railway, and in his autobiography he described his immense enjoyment of the Essex meets in spite of being already too heavy, too stiff with age and too blind to ride well or even to be certain whether he was riding at a fence or a ditch.

Members of the Essex Hounds took their sport very seriously. One elderly farmer even asked the parson to refuse to administer the Sacrament to a dying lady because she had killed a fox.

However, the archetypal Victorian hunting parson must assuredly be the Rev. John Russell, 1795–1883, better known as 'Jack' Russell, and today commemorated not only in West Country hotel rooms and bars but also in the breed of fierce little terrier dogs named after him, all originating from a dog he purchased when a student at Oxford.

Russell's father was a Devonshire hunting parson who trained his sons to be keen followers of all field sports. Young Russell kept hounds as a schoolboy, spent a few happy years at Oxford, mostly in the hunting field, and never considered any other career than the Church. He obtained his B.A. degree in 1818, was ordained deacon in 1819 and priest in 1820, and was appointed curate at Nympton near South Molton in Devonshire.

It was not long before he met the notorious Rev. John Froude of Knowstone. Russell admired Froude's hunting skill and his cavalier way with bishops, nor was he overawed by Froude if we can believe the story that he once tried to sell Froude a blind horse. After Froude's death the living of Knowstone went to a man who was almost exactly Froude's opposite, and the new parson alleged that his predecesser had been guilty of almost every crime in the calendar, too broad a generalization to be true but very tempting to make.

Critics of 'Jack' Russell's way of life professed to recognize him as Parson Rambone in Richard Blackmore's novel *The Maid of Sker*, just as Froude was certainly Parson Chowne, but Russell's loyal friend and biographer, F. J. Snell, asserted that according to Blackmore himself it was the Rev. John Radford, the brutal rector of Lapford, and not Russell, who was the model for Rambone.

Russell acquired money when he married Penelope Bury, daughter of an admiral and an heiress, and he was to need all of her fortune in order to realize his ambition of breeding an ideal pack of hounds. The newly married pair moved to Iddesleigh, where Russell became his father's curate, and since his responsibilities there were not onerous he had time to build up his foxhounds— the 'wild red rovers of Devonshire'. Within five years Russell had become famous for his endurance in the hunting field, the boxing and wrestling rings and the cricket field. As an example of his physical strength there is an account he gave a friend of how he spent three days. First he rode twenty miles to Iddesleigh, found a fox and killed him in a thunderstorm, then rode to Ash to dine and dance until one in the morning. He slept for two hours, then rose early at three so that he could ride fifty miles to Bodmin to hunt with a friend, then ate dinner, and spent the remainder of the day resting except for walking a few miles to and from a country fair. At three a.m. on the third day he rode back to Iddesleigh, took out the hounds, found a fox at Dowland, killed him near Chawleigh twelve miles away, and then rode twenty miles to Tordown to sit down to dinner again at six o'clock.

Russell was an abstemious man who did not drink spirits or smoke, who ate in moderation and normally went early to bed. Doubtless he owed his extraordinary stamina to those simple rules of health.

In 1832 he was appointed 'Perpetual Curate' of Swymbridge and Landkey, and remained there until 1880. It was a poorly paid living with a stipend of only £180, out of which he paid a curate (possible only because of his wife's money). The incumbency brought him within the jurisdiction, although hardly under the control, of Henry Philpotts, one of the new reforming bishops who disliked hunting. It was Philpotts who, happening to see a run from his coach on his arrival in the West Country, was so struck by the number of black-coated huntsmen that he concluded that there must have been an epidemic to put so many men in mourning! Inevitably there were many anecdotes about Russell and his bishop. When Russell once complained that it was common talk that Philpotts objected to Russell's hunting, the bishop replied with deceptive mildness that his only objection was that Russell did not appear to do anything else! There came the time when the bishop felt driven to insist that Russell must give up his hounds, and was astonished to find that the parson agreed to do so. Then Russell, a truthful man, felt forced to add, 'But I think it only right to tell you, my lord, Mrs Russell will keep the pack for me.'

Russell popularized stag-hunting in Devonshire and in 1855 helped inaugurate a hunting tournament at Dulverton which became an annual two weeks' event. At its greatest, his hunting tract stretched from Torrington to Bodmin. His hunting prowess made him a popular parson and Swymbridge basked in reflected glory. The parson's favourite mount for years was a bay pony called Billy, and when it died the hide, legs and hooves were used to make an armchair. Two other horses, Cottager and Money, were granted similar immortality and one can imagine the equestrian jokes which were bandied about when the parson invited his cronies to sit in the horse chairs.

But there was more to Russell than hunting. He was a greatly sought-after visiting preacher and a successful fund-raiser for charitable institutions, particularly the North Devon Hospital of which he was an honorary governor. He spoke with a strong West Country burr and his conversation was laced with salty humour. He carried out his pastoral duties in bluff, pragmatic fashion and had no truck with fine points of religious doctrine. None the less, during his incumbency he carefully restored the interior of Swymbridge Church and built two small daughter churches at Travellers' Rest and at Gunn. He summed up his accomplishments at Swymbridge:

> When I was inducted to this incumbency there was only one service here every Sunday—morning and evening alternately with Landkey, whereas now, I am thankful to say, we have four services in Swymbridge every Sunday alone.

In November 1875 he wrote to a friend:

> I am worked to death at this season of the year: going about from church to church on working days as well as Sundays, preaching and begging for the N.D. Infirmary and finding when I come home heaps of letters to answer.

He worked for the Royal Agricultural Society and met the Prince of Wales through those activities. The prince, who had already heard much about the extrovert parson, took an immediate liking to him and Russell was twice invited to Sandringham. On one occasion he preached in Sandringham Church and on another, in 1873 when he was seventy-seven, he led the Princess of Wales out to dance at the Sandringham New Year Ball.

After his wife's death the parson's financial situation changed drastically and he could no longer afford to stay in Swymbridge. When Lord Poltimore offered him the richer living of Black Torrington he was forced to accept it although he grieved to say goodbye to his parishioners. 'How can I leave my own people with whom I have lived in peace and happiness for half a century?' His parishioners were as regretful as he was and presented him with a testimonial and £800, a contribution towards his outstanding debts. It was their honest tribute to a well-liked pastor.

The tall, gaunt old man remained rector of Black Torrington until he died, four years later, on 28 April 1883 at the age of eighty-eight. He was buried at Swymbridge, next to his wife, and it was estimated that over a thousand mourners attended his funeral, including many famous Devonshire personalities and most of the population of Swymbridge and Landkey. Among the lesser known mourners was his distant cousin, the Rev. Richard Chichester.

The Rev. Richard Chichester, 1838–95, came from a Devonshire family which traced its origins back to Henry I's reign, and his branch lived at Hall, near Barnstaple. As a younger son Richard was destined for the Church, and his first appointment, as a curate in Leicestershire, showed that he had the makings of an effective country parson. Indeed, he was so well liked by his rector and his parishioners that Mrs Chichester became alarmed in case her son settled permanently in Leicestershire. Accordingly the Chichester parents purchased the presentation of the living of Drewsteignton in Devonshire, the price having been reduced from an unacceptable £11,000 to an acceptable £5,000 when the elderly incumbent's curate suddenly deserted him and Chichester promised to take his place without delay.

On 25 July 1869 Chichester arrived in Drewsteignton and preached the following Sunday to a half empty church. That was both bad and good; bad because it was disconcerting, but good because it showed that he would not be following a popular man. Not even the most sanguine of curates could have expected to inherit within two weeks of arrival, but such however was the case. On 1 August 1869, Chichester noted in his diary, 'Poor Mr Ponsford died at 5 a.m.' As he had barely been acquainted with the late rector, Chichester saw no disrespect in hunting two days afterwards. 'Up early, went out on Banker to see buck killed. G. Snow [hit] it directly, went on round bottom of Park by Woolstone to Halmestone, saw a chestnut mare and rode it for trial.' Chichester was always ready to be talked into buying a horse.

He quickly took charge of the parish. The rectory was painted and the orchard pruned. Chichester taught in the school, organized bell ringing groups and supervised choir practice. He also compiled the list of parish events. 'Wrote out fair copy of circular. Mr

Widgery, artist, had a bad attack of bleeding piles just before 12, which kept me up rather late. He got better after taking some brandy.' Christmas gave Chichester some notion of the state of religion in Drewsteignton. There were thirty-seven communicants and 19*s*. in the offertory plate, not very encouraging for a village which numbered about a thousand. But when Druston Common caught fire the villagers turned naturally to their parson to lead in stamping it out. John Ponsford, nephew of the late rector, was squire of Drewsteignton but he lived outside the village and the leadership role of squire fell naturally to Chichester.

Meanwhile his matchmaking mother had plans for him. He was introduced to Miss Jessie White, his sister's friend, and he commenced an extremely unromantic but none the less productive courtship of the young lady. Six months after meeting her he recorded in his diary, 'Walk by the River, then up into the Wood with Jessie White. We became engaged to be married. Saw her Father & Mother, who were willing.' The wedding was fixed for the following January.

At Christmas 1870, Chichester counted his communicants again. This time there were forty-four and the offertory was 19*s*. 4*d*, still not very much to show for a year's hard slog. However, the village concert on 27 December was better attended. They had Hand Bell Ringing, Singing and Reading, and Chichester's latest recitation, a humorous poem entitled 'Grumbling'. He was a popular performer at Penny Readings, more especially because he would get on his horse and gallop through all kinds of miserable weather to participate in these village entertainments.

In January 1871 Chichester was married, and the bridal pair went to the Isle of Wight for their honeymoon. It was wet and chilly and the bride caught cold and stayed in the hotel, leaving her husband to tramp the beaches on his own. He was relieved when they joined his mother and sister at Exmouth and he could call in a good Devonshire doctor to attend his wife. On 27 January the rector took his bride home. The vicarage and all the cottages were decorated in their honour and the schoolchildren were neatly lined up in a ceremonial welcome.

Their first year passed quickly. August saw the school treat, an important village date, with races in the vicarage field and a bazaar in the vicarage garden, where two of Devonshire's prettiest girls held court at their stall under the deodar tree. A few days later there was a heatwave, bringing the fear of typhus and cholera, and Chichester sped around the parish disinfecting drains with chloride of lime and carbolic acid. It became noticeable that as a mature and married man Chichester had less and less time for hunting and shooting. On 23 January 1872 Jessie Chichester gave birth to their first son at an Exeter nursing home where her husband visited her and read *Barchester Towers* aloud to make her smile. His days were full and satisfying.

February 19, 1872. Looked in at school, smallpox at New House, Howard family. Collected for Clothing Club, £2.8.2, gave out Library books. Went out to Cross to see about men at Front Garden, put a 2nd lock on Cellar Door. Put on riding boots & rode to Gibouse, Furlong, and visited all at Sandypark and Parford Showers. Masons doing drains.

When the daffodils were out the church was decorated with the golden blooms. Chichester had candles fixed so that the church could be lit. He said thanksgiving services for the recovery from illness of the Prince of Wales and noted with approval that these congregations were larger than usual. The Chichesters frequently visited London, when the parson usually managed to go to the races and look at horses at Tattersalls. He was not a man to make speculative or philosophical comments. Once he made a considerable detour to visit Stonehenge but his diary entry was merely factual: '. . . nearly 16 upright stones on outer edge, said to be antediluvian' —very different from the reverent reaction of the Rev. Francis Kilvert who visited it around the same time. We have a clue to Chichester's real interests when we read that he was so anxious about his two favourite dogs, Vic and Bess, which had been badly bitten, that he completely forgot to attend a special village meeting organized to protest against a new scheme of the Charity Commissioners!

For all his energy the village remained obstinately untouched by religious fervour, taking his pastoral work for granted. A compassionate squire might have done as much. Christmas after Christmas the number of communicants remained obstinately low. Drewsteignton was a village in decline, losing about two hundred of its number every census. Sometimes the parson's most altruistic efforts were thwarted. Take, for instance, the matter of the new schools. Chichester had set his heart on building new schools for the village and he engaged an architect to draw up plans. He took it for granted that the school board would see things his way, but one member proved contrary, protested against the designs, and persuaded the village to protest against having new schools. The architect, aware of the Gilbertian situation and insulted by it, gave notice to the school board that when the buildings were completed he would not formally hand over the keys unless the board signified its acceptance. The board stubbornly refused, the architect held on to the keys and the board felt impelled to take the extreme step of breaking a window in order to effect entrance! Fortunately tempers cooled with time, the schools, being finished, were accepted, and some months later there was a ceremonious opening, with Jessie Chichester leading the school children from the old schools into the new, and the parson saying a brief prayer. In the evening the church bells rang out in celebration, if not triumph.

When Richard Chichester looked back over his first ten years in Drewsteignton he was, on the whole, satisfied. The tithe dinner was 'a good muster, all well paid'. The school was 'in good order under George Smith'. The parson had perfected his sermon style. It was short and pithy. 'All sin and lying found out', was a typical theme. He had long forgotten that as an idealistic young man he had aimed at rousing the congregation to solemn and religious thoughts. Even the 1880 election was under control since the two Conservative candidates had been duly elected.

The parson began to take a greater part in district affairs beyond the confines of the parish. He joined in discussions over the boundaries for the new divided parishes Act. He campaigned against the proposed Affirmation Bill being introduced by Bradlaugh, the atheist M.P. for Northampton. Drewsteignton was every bit as Conservative as its parson and when Bishop Temple was billed to lecture in the village one of the elders recalled *Essays and Reviews* and in righteous indignation had posters put up proclaiming that 'Bishop is Atheist in Disguise'. That was really going too far and Chichester hurried round the village taking the posters down before the bishop's arrival.

Sometimes Chichester felt like a clerical Canute trying to hold back the waves of a new and unpleasant age. He tried to deter the Radicals in the election of 1885 by refusing to let the school be used for political meetings, but in spite of his endeavours a Radical was returned for Mid-Devon and Chichester felt further depressed when his brother informed him that all the workmen at Hall were Radicals in their speech and thinking. The parson began to note items from the national press which dealt with social unrest and the emergence of radical parties. 'Reading paper, unemployed in London holding meetings.' 'Social Democrats to be prosecuted', and so on.

But when the parson turned his gaze to his large and happy family, so many now that the rectory had been enlarged by the addition of a new storey, he felt considerably happier. The older boys were doing well at Sherbourne School. Jessie Chichester was deep in parish organization and the rectory was always lively with guests. The Rev. Richard Chichester was contented with his place in life, a Devon man tending a Devon parish, and he hoped there were many years remaining to him. In the event, however, he died relatively young. He was taken suddenly ill with acute appendicitis in April 1895 and two days after his collapse he was dead.

The sheltered existence of a country parson which Richard Chichester had so appreciated did not always operate to the advantage of the incumbent, particularly if he were a gifted man. Take, for instance, the Rev. Robert Eyres Landor, 1781–1869, who lived his last forty years in obscurity at Birlingham near Worcester, and is today recalled, outside that parish, only as the younger brother of Walter Savage Landor.

Robert Landor followed his brilliant and arrogant brother to Oxford, obtained his B.A. degree in 1801 and his M.A. degree in 1804, and being a younger son took Holy Orders, although it was his fervent wish to emulate his brother and live by his pen. At university he had helped edit the *Oxford Review* and was the anonymous author of a scurrilous lampoon on Oxford dons entitled 'Guy's Porridge Pot' which was attributed to Walter Savage Landor, to the latter's discredit.

The Rev. Robert Landor became curate of Wyke Regis in Dorsetshire, remaining there until the end of the Napoleonic War made it possible to travel abroad, whereupon he resigned his curacy and embarked upon a Grand Tour. As a student his republican views had once earned him the title of 'Citizen Landor', but the passage of time and a year of European travel changed all that. He visited museums, galleries and churches, perfecting his French and Italian so that he could study the art history of France and Italy. He visited his brother, Walter, and sister-in-law, Julia, who were then living at Tours, submitting a bundle of family documents for Walter to sign, much to that individual's disgust. Walter and Robert had been very friendly in the past but the visit provoked bitter quarrels which did not abate when Robert took Julia's side against Walter. The estrangement between the two brothers lasted for the next twenty years.

On returning to England the Rev. Robert Landor was appointed vicar of St Michael's at Hughenden in Buckingham, and remained there until 1824. During that period, but for a very brief time, he was Chaplain in Ordinary to the Prince Regent, an honour which either the Prince or the parson rapidly decided was quite unsuitable, and it may have been that fleeting insight into the royal household which contributed to the extraordinary hostility he displayed towards Queen Caroline. From the safety of his Hughenden parsonage he published in 1820 and 1821 some letters in the *Courier*, signed 'Laternarus' and addressed to Lord John Russell, which were so vituperative that the government threatened the paper with a libel suit. Landor explained his motives in a letter written in 1820 to his brother Henry. '. . . the country is in danger, that a set of scoundrels have undermined the Government, abused the Church, and calumniated all honest men. . . . If I can make the base more contemptible, and the infamous more notorious, it is doing good.'

He still hoped to make his name as a writer and published a play, *The Count Arezzi*, also anonymously. When its authorship was flatteringly attributed to Lord Byron, Landor claimed the piece for his own and published a lengthy poem, 'The Impious Feast', under his own name. That work was poorly received, but nevertheless Landor resigned his living to spend five unsuccessful years as a literary man until, thoroughly disheartened, he returned to the security of the Church. In 1829 he was appointed vicar of Birlingham where he would remain, a country parson, until his death forty years later.

He was a religious man by upbringing with a deep sense of moral purpose. In his early days at Birlingham he used to walk into Worcester and back every Saturday, a total of sixteen miles, composing his sermons on the road to be written out in his study in the evening on his return. In the words of one of his obituaries, 'His inspiration was ascribed to exhilaration from exercise, because his sermons were breezy.' How breezy we shall never know because on his express instructions they were all destroyed after his death. He lived on his small private income, and devoted his stipend to parish charities and the maintenance of the church, these expenses sometimes accounting for half his total income in a year. He never married, and lived in very comfortable style in the vicarage, apart from being a martyr to gout, probably attributable to his fine cellar. He was a passionate art collector and covered the rectory walls with paintings, most of them remarkably good.

His quarrel with Walter was healed in 1840, and thereafter whenever the latter visited England he spent several days at Birlingham Rectory—'a most delightful place'. Robert, declared Walter, was noted for keeping 'a capitally good table' and the rectory garden was a gem. In 1841 Robert Landor published three dramas: *The Earl of Brecon, Faith's Fraud* and *The Ferryman*, only to receive bad reviews yet again, and in great chagrin Landor bought up as many copies of his books as he could find and burned them. Very few had been sold, and still fewer have survived. When Eric Partridge searched for them in 1924 in the Bodleian Library he noticed that the pages of *Faith's Fraud* and *The Ferryman* were still uncut. All three plays were heavily moralistic and excessively dull, although their author plaintively insisted that they were 'as merry as I could make them'.

We must conclude that forty years of rustic seclusion and the security of a private income hampered his literary development. Certainly he possessed the talent and industriousness of a writer, and had in overwhelming measure a craving to be praised as an author. In 1846 there appeared *The Fawn of Setorius*, an historical novel set in classical times which he had completed several years earlier. He reverted to his practice of publishing anonymously, and the critics, recognizing a Landor style, guessed that the author was Walter Savage Landor. For once the vicar had good reviews. The *Literary Gazette* praised the novel; the *Athenaeum* called it 'vigorous and remarkable' and the *Examiner* thought it was a 'graceful tale'. So the parson published another novel, of similar kind, *The Fountain of Arethusa*, also anonymously, and that novel was even better received than the first. The *Eclectic Review* declared that the author must be 'a man of independent mind; thoughtful, inventive, humorous, polished, discursively learned, sparkingly acute, and pervaded by deep moral feeling'.

Here was balm at last to the sensitive parson, and it might have been expected that he would thenceforth press forward to consolidate his literary reputation. Nothing of the kind. Although he lived over twenty more years there was virtual silence at Birlingham. In his writings the classical scholar had always been neatly dovetailed into the good Christian neighbour and in the end the Christian won out. In his last years the parson devoted himself exclusively to his ministry.

The Rev. Robert Landor's greatest problem was Walter Savage Landor, who had never had to doubt his literary brilliance and who had paid scant attention to contemporary critics because he was prepared to write for posterity alone. The vicar of Birlingham yearned for plaudits in his own lifetime and lacked the self-confidence to devote himself entirely to literature. Unlike Walter Savage Landor, the Rev. Robert Landor had managed to warm only one hand before the fire of life.

Representative of many hard-working country parsons in the mid-Victorian period was the Rev. Francis Macaulay Cunningham, 1815–98, who held benefices at different times in Hampshire, Oxfordshire and Berkshire. He was virtually born into the Church, his father being rector of Harrow, Middlesex, for over sixty years. Cunningham sent his sons to public school and took paying pupils to pay the fees: 'September 17, 1861. Beautiful day, but alas our last of liberty, 5 of the boys back after the holydays. 3 still to come, which is 2 too many for comfort.' At that time Cunningham was rector of East Tisted, a small agricultural village near Petersfield in Hampshire, his first living and one very much to his taste. He was a reserved and pessimistic man who neither sought nor gained that type of spontaneous affection which was offered to men like the Rev. Francis Kilvert. When sentiment crept in it manifested itself primly. 'In evg. a v. pleasant teadrinking at the school. It was got up entirely by the villagers—we had nothing to do with it, but were there only as *guests*. It was intended as an act of respect and regard by our people, and as such was v. pleasant. After tea I made a short speech & they had some singing, the magic lantern and ended up with a fire balloon. There were upwards of 90 people present, and all seemed v. much to enjoy themselves.'

He differed from many country parsons in commenting strongly in his diaries upon national and world events. He waxed indignant when the Northern government of the United States in 1861 boarded the British ship *Trent* in mid-Atlantic to remove some Southern agents. It was, he considered, a 'tremendous outrage on our flag' and must 'I fear, lead to some v. serious results, and certainly bring us to the very verge of war with America, unless they apologise, wh. is very unlikely.' Nor did Cunningham mince his words when the Prince Consort died. 'No greater misfortune cd. have happened to us—and it has evidently produced a feeling of gloom throughout the whole country, for nobody cd. have filled his position more admirably than he has . . . One almost feels as if it wd. have been better for us if the Queen herself had been taken, and he left to guide his son in a new reign, for both mother and son are v. unfit to rule without him.'

Church organizational meetings outside the parish sorely tried his patience. 'Thurs. Jan 2 1862. To Winchester for Diocesan Bd. of Education, I went by train and found it a most expensive business, & as the meeting was utterly unimportant I was vexed enough that I went.' It was however quite another matter when it came to his pastoral work. He was meticulous about visiting the sick, often changed their surgical dressings and was constantly being reprimanded by the doctor for visiting infectious cases like smallpox. During unhealthy summers when scarlet fever and typhus ravaged the villages, taking an especial toll of the children, Cunningham rearranged the school classes and lessons were held in the airy rectory and its rambling garden instead of in the stifling, cramped school rooms.

In December 1863 when he was offered the important living of Witney in Oxfordshire he hesitated, believing himself too old at forty-six. His wife persuaded him to make the change, but it was a wrench to leave East Tisted. 'Before luncheon I drove round in the rain to say goodbye to the people. . . . It was v. upsetting indeed.'

Witney was a country market town and too large for one man to manage on his own. There were two curates, Harrison and Mills, of whom Harrison had already tendered his resignation, so one of Cunningham's first tasks was to find a replacement. That proved difficult. 'Much disap. last night by the non-arrival of a curate whom I hoped wd. have done for Wood Green. The negotiation quite broken off, I fear.' He did not take to Mr Covey, another

applicant. '. . . his sermon was dull enough to send the most lively
to sleep. It was all I cd. desire in point of doctrine, but he is evidently far from being a brilliant man—however, if he will really work
among the poor, he will do great service in the parish.' A Mr
Henderson arrived who was much better but he finally declined
the job. Months passed and still the curacy was not settled. 'I
question whether either of them will do', wrote the harassed
rector after interviewing two more candidates. 'One is too weakly,
& the other not enough of an evangelical for me.' He travelled to
Oxford to meet a man who had advertised his availability in the
Guardian but swiftly decided that that man 'wd. not do at any
price'.

His worries were compounded when Mills also resigned. Cunningham felt he might well have to put up with Mr Chope.

> Mr Chope preached aft. & evg. & put me in a regular perplexity to
> know what to decide. His sermons were very clever, but not in
> the least to my taste. They were regular rhapsodies, & delivered
> as rhapsodies. The one in aft. was certainly very impressive, &
> made the people listen most attentively—but to my mind it was
> rather trying in its effects, & made me smile when it was all over.
> The evg. sermon was also very clever, but miles over the people's
> heads & exceedingly wanting in arrangement. I don't think I
> shall be very sorry if he declines the curacy. His great beard &
> moustache are especially odious to me.

Mr Chope did indeed decline the position and Cunningham in the
end engaged two decent young men who did their best but were
certainly not the towers of strength he had hoped for.

Concurrently with the curate problem was the matter of the
church choir and the organist, all of whom were on the point of
resignation. 'I feel to be standing on a volcano, & am losing Mills &
Harrison together, & seem quite friendless. I must hope for the
best, pray much, & work to the utmost.' Such was his simple rule
of life and generally speaking it served him well.

Being an evangelical, Cunningham believed that his pastoral
work among the poor was just as important as church services,
and he rated his curates according to their effectiveness in the
deprived areas of Witney. In his latter years in the parish Cunningham was very fortunate to have an active and idealistic young

curate, the Rev. J. W. Horsely, later to become Bishop of London. In 1879 Cunningham moved for the last time. His new living was at Brightwell near Wallingford, not far from Witney but across the Oxford border. It was a felicitous move for a man in his mid-sixties who had always acted older than his years. Brightwell was a tiny village in the shadow of the Chilterns and only a mile or so from Chalgrove Field where John Hampden had been wounded fighting for Parliament in the Civil War. Cunningham could indulge once again in his old pleasures of country walks, antiquities, gardening and caring for a simple parish where he did not become irritable because so many people had views contrary to his own.

He mellowed into a benign and patriarchal figure with a flowing white beard, the very picture of a country parson of the old school. When his grandchildren were old enough to play in the rectory garden he won their unfailing admiration by his amazing trick of doubling money. Each child was given a halfpenny to plant under the weeping ash, and next day, when the coins were dug up, lo and behold! faith was justified: all the halfpennies had been mysteriously transformed into pennies!

The country parson with eyes in his head had to admit by the 1890s that times were changing. During the 1892 General Election many country labourers voted for the Liberals, alleging that the squire and the parson were no less than tyrants holding back the villagers. Among those parsons who resented the title was the Rev. Edward Miller who in 1868 became parson of a remote Warwickshire living with a gross income of about £150 and only twelve acres of glebe land. Miller could have made many times that income from teaching and tutoring, but his heart was in pastoral work and he could not resist the idea of living in Shakespeare's Warwickshire.

A man like Miller, with no family links with the squirearchy and with a background in education, was bound to pay particular attention to the village school. He soon uncovered a far from satisfactory situation—an inefficient schoolmistress who took the classes in her own cottage. He longed to improve the school overnight, but being a strong believer in village participation he took no steps until he had won the approval of the village elders to sack the schoolmistress and engage a new one. He then obtained the promises of the local gentry to finance a school building, while in the meantime a farmer lent his barn as a temporary schoolroom. Miller underwrote the initiatial expenses and called a village meeting to sanction the new school.

> All in the parish did something. The chief landowners contributed largely, the farmers supplied most of the haulage; the Government and the National Society shook hands over the matter, if not for the very first time, yet nearly for the first; friends of the vicar gave their aid; and the 'village tyrant', there being no resident squire, contributed more than his share at the beginning, and made up the deficit at the end when all the fountains of help had run dry.

Miller had secretly hoped to use the school in the evenings as a reading room but dropped the idea when he realized that the adults had so little schooling that only one man was likely to join.

The parson next turned to allotments, the provision of which interested many country clergy at that time as a means of alleviating agricultural hardship and allowing the men to add to their wages by growing vegetables. Some thirty years earlier, during the 'hungry forties', a former vicar of Miller's parish had divided one of the glebe fields into allotments, but over the years the system had become disorganized. Some villagers had more than one allotment, and in some instances it was impossible to gain access to one without crossing another. Other villagers complained that they had been waiting years and in vain for an allotment. So Miller called a second big parish meeting to discuss the allotment question and the plots were amicably redistributed. When two years later a second glebe field fell vacant, a deputation of villagers asked the vicar to divide that one into allotments as well, which Miller was very willing to do. The enthusiasm for allotments was part of a general feeling that nearly all agricultural poverty would be eradicated if only labourers could have a few acres of their own. Countries like New Zealand were at that time conducting official propaganda compaigns with promises of free land to attract settlers, and the new glebe allotments officially called 'Parson's Woolland', or woodland, were unofficially dubbed 'New Zealand'.

At first the scheme went swimmingly, so much so that an elderly farmer, desirous of dividing up his land, offered small-holdings varying from six to thirty acres for rent and saw them eagerly snapped up. Unfortunately these small-holdings quickly failed, mainly because the tenants gave up their steady employment and tried to live exclusively off their allotments. Sadly, by the end of ten years, many of the parson's allotments were also in ruins and at least half reverted to the parson. Finally, only two remained, both badly managed, and allowed to remain in existence merely through Miller's indulgence.

He wanted the village to help run the church as well as its secular affairs and drew up plans for a church council, obtained his bishop's approval of it, and presented the idea, rather proudly, to the parish. To his surprise and disappointment he was informed that everyone would prefer to leave decisions to him, as usual. Discouraged but not entirely deterred, the vicar persevered and tried to form a village committee to support home and foreign missions. Much as in the case of the allotments, that committee functioned well for some years, and then disintegrated amid a welter of committee jealousies, so that in the end Miller buried his brain-child in private and did the committee work by himself.

By long tradition, squire and parson were expected to pay for their privileged positions by constant outlay on the church and its services, on the school and on the poorer members of the parish. Where there was no resident squire a double burden fell automatically upon the parson. Miller was fortunate in that the church had been largely restored by his predecessor, but nevertheless when he left that parish after eleven years he computed that he had spent four years' income on completing or maintaining the church and school.

When a richer living was offered him in 1879 he accepted it, although regretfully, and moved to a parish which was materially better and spiritually worse than his Warwickshire one. Once more Miller applied himself to a reading room project, to be run by a village committee, but although he managed to get it started, it disintegrated after three or four years. Miller opened a lending library, maintaining control himself, and some time later he extended it by opening a reading room. This time, although he disliked having to do so, he ran the reading room himself in order to ensure its continuance—the 'village tyrant' *malgré lui*.

Each winter, as the agricultural depression showed no sign of abatement, he deliberately made work for the men—repairing village paths, clearing drains, landscaping the rectory garden. He followed the example of John Keble in finding enjoyment and satisfaction in his work with children. 'The best way to a parent's heart is through the children. If a parish priest is loved by the children, he is sure to be loved by the parish', he wrote, and through his teaching of the catechism to the Anglicans and his teaching of the Bible to all the children in the school he grew to know them and to joke with them.

By the end of the century life in the villages was changing faster than ever. Young men and women sought more interesting and better paid work in the towns. The traditional acts of charity, such as distributing tickets for coal and blankets, became resented and refused by some of the villagers. Indeed, as a new class of parson became more widespread, without a private income or a well-connected family in the background, the vicarage charities in an age of rising prices were often beyond a parson's means. Even a sermon which lived up to John Ruskin's ideal of 'thirty minutes to raise the dead' was not sufficient to draw a large congregation.

Miller was an end-of-the-century parson who could see quite clearly into the next century. The Rev. Edward Boys Ellman, 1815–1906, was a nineteenth-century Sussex parson who looked backwards over his long life and did not peer into the twentieth century. Ellman went to school at Lewes in the days when so many parsons lived in that pleasant town and commuted by horse or carriage to their parishes that Lewes was called 'The Rookery', because of its black-costumed inhabitants. Ellman had hoped to remain at Oxford after graduation and enjoy the life of a mathematics don, but unknown to him his father purchased the advowson of the Sussex parish of Berwick and Ellman was too meek to protest. He remained rector of Berwick for over sixty years, a model parson with a gift for pastoral work. 'A house-going parson makes a church-going people,' he used to say.

Only a few days before his death, on hearing a favourite clock outside his bedroom door strike midnight, Ellman told his daughter: 'Eighty-seven years ago tonight was the first time I remember hearing midnight strike. I woke up in the old Firle nursery and heard the nursemaid Philly read aloud to the nurse the account of King George III's death, which had taken place that day.'

In spite of having had his path in life decided without consulting him Ellman had no regrets. 'I sometimes think,' he told his daughter as he lay dying, 'I have much to be thankful for in having led this quiet life. I have not had the temptations other men have had. Looking back, I can't remember ever having wilfully committed sin. No, I cannot ever have had the temptations of other men.'

The Rev.
Octavius Pickard-Cambridge
Parson and Naturalist
1828-1917

A country parson whose senses were attuned to Nature was in an ideal situation to pursue the hobby of naturalist, and nineteenth-century natural science in its broadest aspects owes a good deal to the patient industry of these cheerful, unpaid research assistants. In this field the Church can boast of an extremely eminent clerical roll of honour from the seventeenth century onwards. Outstanding was the Rev. Charles Butler, sometimes called the 'Father of British Bee-Keeping', who profited sufficiently from his bees to give his daughter, his 'sweet honey girl', a very useful dowry, and a century later his great-great-grandson, the Rev. Gilbert White, wrote a classical book on the Hampshire parish of Selborne and its 'Natural History and Antiquities'. In the early nineteenth century the Rev. Dr Kirby's book on natural history set a new standard, as did *A Synopsis of British Land Birds*, published in 1841 by that pioneer of British ornithology, the Rev. John Mossop of Lincolnshire.

Among these esteemed names we must place the Rev. Octavius Pickard-Cambridge, rector of Bloxworth in Dorset, who may fairly be described as the 'Father of British Spiders', although he did not limit himself to spiders but interested himself in all insects and flora. The fame of this Dorset clergyman was worldwide in his lifetime and his work is still recognized as being of permanent value. Dr W. S. Bristowe, naturalist and author believes that we know more about British spiders and their habits than people of any other country in the world, and he attributes this to the work and

influence of Octavius Pickard-Cambridge. 'With advancing knowledge there have of course been alterations in schemes of classification and some of his species new to science have been recognized
as synonyms of species, often inadequately described by earlier
workers in a foreign language without good illustrations. His work
was chiefly with preserved specimens so he scarcely devoted himself to habits and behaviour. For specimens he depended on those
he could collect himself by bicycle or on walks on his beloved
Bloxworth Heath and collections sent him from all over the world
by his numerous correspondents.'[1]

Octavius was born in 1828, the eighth child and fifth son of a
family of fifteen. His father, the Rev. George Pickard, was both
rector and squire of Bloxworth, and rector of the neighbouring
hamlet of Winterbourne Tomson. 'Squarson' Pickard was also a
J.P. and made use of his gamekeeper as unpaid and unofficial
village constable. There is a story that on one occasion a local
offender was ordered to appear before the magistrates at Blandford.
The accused objected, and the rector told his gamekeeper to take
the largest wheelbarrow, and a length of rope, and if need be to
wheel the offender through the village. The threat was enough,
and the unfortunate man decided to 'go quietly'.[2] Pickards had
been squires in Bloxworth for generations, usually living in Bloxworth House which, with its estate, provided employment for
practically the entire village.

Bloxworth House had been first built in the late Elizabethan
period by the Savage family, which sold it to the Trenchards. It
later came into the possession of the Pickards, who had family
connections with the Trenchards. Among the manor's historic
treasures was a Jonah Goblet, a trophy from Henry VIII's cavor-
tings at the Field of the Cloth of Gold, and also portraits of Philip
and Joanna of Spain, given by them in payment of hospitality
offered by an early Trenchard when the Spanish royal ship was
storm-driven into Weymouth harbour. The nineteenth-century
Pickards grew up in the secure knowledge that they and their
forbears had played a significant part in local history for centuries.

Family pride does not add to the bank balance and an exuberant
family of fifteen had no opportunity to be spendthrifts. The
Pickards spent their holidays at Weymouth which was then embarking upon a career of genteel prosperity as the Victorian middle

class took to the seaside. For the rest of the year Bloxworth was world enough, and the mere size of the family, without counting house guests and servants, created a home atmosphere full of bustle and companionship.

The Pickards were encouraged to be musical, and nearly every member could play at least one musical instrument, or sing. Octavius loved music all his life. He played the violin well, had an excellent singing voice, and throughout his long life proclaimed the joy of music, making sure that his own children enjoyed music and could play instruments. As a very young man he organized elaborate family concerts, often conducting as well as performing. He insisted upon semi-professional standards, but kept a sense of fun and proportion, and had posters privately printed to advertise 'unrivalled talent' under 'Herr Octavius, famed foreign violinist and conductor'. Later on, back in Bloxworth as rector, he was tireless in promoting Dorset musical societies.

His formal education was patchy, a plan to send him to Winchester having fallen through upon the sudden death of his sponsor, so he stayed at home, applying himself to his books in a fairly haphazard way. However, he spent two years at the Dorchester school run by the remarkable William Barnes. Nobody quite knows how this came about, although family legend has it that one day Octavius merely rode off to Dorchester and enrolled himself—an inspired gesture, for Barnes was a sensitive, amusing and gifted man, and certainly the greatest of all Dorset poets besides being a self-taught scholar, artist and antiquarian. He taught his pupils to be geologists and fossil-hunters, among other things, taking advantage of the excavations made locally by the railway company as it dug cuttings. Barnes hoped that the boys would develop life-long interests in the natural sciences, a hope which was amply realized in the case of Octavius. In a memorial written on Barnes's death, Octavius declared that Barnes's great gift as a teacher had been not only to make his pupils understand what was taught, but to love it as well. In the 1840s William Barnes was a pioneer in giving the sciences such a prominent place in his curriculum. He also placed great importance on English and drawing, and Octavius acknowledged the debt he owed to that school in both these subjects. Frederick Smith, the music teacher, further developed the boy's musical bent, and a generally well-rounded and happy attitude to life was fostered by Barnes.

In 1848 a branch of the Pickard family—the Cambridges—died out, and the Cambridge estate was left to the Rev. George Pickard with the proviso that he thereafter linked the Cambridge name with his own, a condition which no father of fifteen was likely to cavil at. If the Cambridge blood had thinned and finally run out, the reverse seemed then true of the newly-named Pickard-Cambridges. They were thick on the ground in Dorset and you could hardly cross the street in Wareham without stumbling over at least one of them. Later on, the balance of sexes changed. Only daughters were born in succeeding generations and today there are only two male Pickard-Cambridges, father and son, neither living in England, let alone Dorset. Bloxworth House is no longer in Pickard-Cambridge hands. Bloxworth Church is part of a united benefice whose rector lives in another village. Only the churchyard mutely testifies to the enormous hold of the Pickards and Pickard-Cambridges over that village for two hundred years.

Octavius attained his majority without having decided on a career. He lived the ordinary life of a carefully brought up, not very rich, young man in the country. He loved outdoor sports, especially shooting; he enjoyed the social rounds and endless dinner parties of gentry life. The most unusual thing about him was his habit of keeping careful nature diaries which he lovingly illustrated with accurate, sensitive line drawings. He had collected butterflies from the age of seven. He shot birds and had them stuffed for his collection. He was a keen and active gardener. Nothing about him or his interests suggested any particular career, so the family packed him off to London in 1849 to study for the Bar, that most popular of solutions for middle-class young men of slender means.

Two years were sufficient to prove conclusively that the law was not for him nor he for the law, so another family conclave was held and the soothing conclusion reached that Octavius should succeed his father in the family living of Bloxworth.

He went to live with a tutor in Somerset so that he could pass the university entrance requirements, and in between cramming sessions he rode about Somerset making pencil sketches of churches and the countryside. In 1852 he revealed his true interest when his first naturalist paper was published, in the *Zoologist*, and at the same time he began a lifelong friendship with Frederick Bond, one of Britain's leading specialists on insects. From 1854 onwards Bond was to be a constant guest at Bloxworth, and he and Octavius made regular collecting expeditions in the New Forest.

The young man, twenty-seven years old, was now ready for university and he went to University College, Durham, where some twenty years earlier a fine religious department had been opened. The Professor of Divinity in Octavius's day, Dr Henry Jenkyns, was an excellent lecturer, much admired by his students. Octavius enjoyed every moment of his time at Durham, remained immensely proud of his university and included Durham College banners in all Bloxworth processions after he became rector.

Durham offered both music and sport to this friendly, eager and unassuming young man. He acted as steward at university steeple-chases; he joined the Boat Club, to which in after years he presented a challenge cup, and—naturally—he joined the University Choral Society, eventually becoming its president. But his main purpose was first to obtain a degree and then to take Holy Orders, and he applied himself conscientiously to his studies. No intellectual high-flyer, he needed to check over the day's lectures with his friends each evening and to write out as close a verbatim account as he could before going to bed. This grind was rewarded in 1859 when he received his M.A. degree and was ordained priest, and his first appointment was as curate of Scarisbrick in Lancashire at a stipend of £60 a year.

1859 also saw the publication in the *Zoologist* of his first article on spiders, a foretaste of things to come. His interest in spiders had been aroused through reading a book by John Blackwall, of Llanwrwst in North Wales, who was a leading spider authority. Octavius became friendly with the older man, and some years later collaborated with him on a monumental book devoted to spiders.

Scarisbrick was a daunting parish, particularly for a young curate, partly because the chief landowner was a Roman Catholic who refused to permit the new Anglican curate to take lodgings anywhere on his estate. Octavius had to find rooms in Southport and suffer the long walk into Scarisbrick. Nor did he find his Anglican colleagues congenial, for they were unbendingly orthodox and incensed by the evolutionary theories recently propounded by Charles Darwin. Octavius supported the Darwinian ideas and speedily became unpopular with all the local clergy; especially after he declared loudly at a public meeting that critics who denounced Darwin, Lyell and others ought to have read their books and articles at the very least!

It was a devastatingly lonely experience for a young man who until that time had always lived with lively and affectionate companions. He filled his time with solitary collecting expeditions and listed Southport spiders in another scientific paper published in the *Zoologist*. In 1860 he very thankfully shook the Southport dust off his shoes and returned to Bloxworth to become his father's curate.

He moved into a cottage near the rectory and took up his duties, which were hardly onerous, since Bloxworth was a small parish and his father was a resident, full-time rector. The curate accordingly had ample leisure to continue collecting insects, among which by this time spiders had begun to predominate, partly because news had spread in scientific circles that he was helping Blackwall in his work, and partly because spiders enjoyed only a minority appeal and naturalists were delighted to find a young man willing to specialize in them. Octavius's stipend was small, but his needs were few and his scientific pursuits not financially demanding.

Of course his expenses would increase upon marriage, unless his wife had money, and Octavius's spider speciality did not inhibit him from taking a lively interest in young ladies, although those whom he found most attractive usually hoped for a better match than an impecunious curate with a predilection for spiders.

He was now thirty-five with a fast growing international as well as national scientific reputation. He arranged to go abroad on a modest and scientific version of the Grand Tour, at the only possible period, i.e. before he married and before he had to take over from his father. Two trips to Europe, Egypt and the Holy Land were planned, the first to be in preparation for a second, more extensive one. He was accompanied by O. Bradshaw, a young pupil, who assisted him with preparing specimens, and the pair sailed from Southampton bound for France on 30 December 1863.

They stayed at the Hôtel du Louvre in Paris: 'very good but very expensive', as the frugal Octavius noted. Two days later he jotted down a much more significant detail—'A lady and 2 daus. in Hotel—English obviously fr. having an *Urn* at breakfast.' One of the girls, Rose Wallace (they were in fact nieces, not daughters) was the girl Octavius would marry, although on that particular day he had no idea that he would ever see the trio again.

Octavius and Bradshaw raced on to Egypt where a careful itinerary had been mapped out and a host of friends, acquaintances, and acquaintances of friends had been alerted by letters from England to expect courtesy visits from Octavius. His travel diary was largely an inventory of birds, scorpions and spiders, and only rarely did a more aesthetic note creep in. 'Had long tramp in desert—found but little animal life. Shot white and black chats. Views of Nile and rocky islands near Cataracts very striking and beautiful.'

The birds were stuffed and sent back to England, and Octavius set the insects himself and made meticulous sketches. Spiders are classified by the hairs on their bodies, position, length and thickness of hairs being important points for identification, so that Octavius's artistic skill and infinite care were crucial for success in his field. Around 1880, when it was generally acknowledged that he would be Blackwall's successor, the Royal Society had a binocular microscope constructed specially for him and gave it to him on long loan. Today the camera has superseded such drawing skills and we can only marvel at the delicacy and accuracy of his sketches.

Most of the initial collecting of the first trip was completed by May, and the young men were free to return to Europe and enjoy the sights like regular tourists. Octavius was not sure he quite approved of Venice. 'Hotel de la Ville *very* dear ['very' was underlined three times!] and not first rate so next day moved to Hotel Barbesi.' But the city was by no means a total loss for they met the Wallaces again and noted 'R.W. quiet, good-tempered but deep feeling.' The Wallaces were, not unexpectedly, bound for many of the same historic centres as Octavius and Bradshaw and the young curate both hoped and feared the outcome of more meetings. His mixed feelings resulted from an existing but unsatisfactory relationship with a young lady in England, and he did not consider that in all honour he was free to follow his heart, assuming it led him to Rose Wallace. His diary speaks for itself:

Friday May 27. . . . did not see W's in Breakfast room—disappointed—hardly knew why—saw W's at Table d'Hote! Plucked up courage to waylay R.W. & shake hands in Reading

Room. They go away tomorrow. I must not think any more of her for my heart & faith are pledged to D. tho' that other had behaved so wickedly, yet my duty to her is clear.

Sunday May 29. To Ch. twice—R.W. too much in my thoughts —Sure she is as good & high principled as her smile is sweet & deep.

Monday May 30. Left for Como—reached Como at 5 p.m. To P.O. A letter there wh. nearly drove me mad, from D. directed by J.S. Nearly distracted—almost paralysed—prayed fervently for help—wrote to Cal. & utterly exhausted went to bed. After having torn D. from my heart, shd. be unworthy of name of a man if I'd kept her there after this last disgusting insult. I forgive her truly. May God do so too & enable me to forget her, but life seems now of no use.

Help, however, was on the way to cure Octavius's wounded heart and his next entry was more cheerful.

Tues. May 31. Went to Bellagio at 8 a.m. raining nearly all day. Went to Hotel Grand Bretagne—full—& so to Hotel Grazzini— first persons I saw there were the W's who wd. have gone early today but for the rain—talked to R.W. & went to Villa Nebzi with them—almost forgot my misery, with her—so simple & un- affected—went in Boat with them after luncheon. Wed. June 1. Raining hard—W's will not go today. Glad of it. God forgive me if I am doing wrong but D. is dead & gone to me now. Oh if R.W. shd. be destined to take her place in my poor heart. In every- thing but looks & studies D's superior, but she cannot care for me and I am only preparing more misery for myself—thought much & deeply of her and we were together much today & everything in her mind & character seems good and lovable & her quiet smile makes me thrill with pleasure—heard her reading the Bible to her Aunt at night my room being next the W's.

Rose Wallace *did* care for him and the June 3 entry was ecstatic.

. . . Got to Lugano. Hotel du Parc, at 3.30 p.m., first persons we met were W's & Mr and Miss N. just starting to go up Monto

Salvadore, went up with them. R.W. rode up part of the way. Oh the bliss of that ascent & descent. Heaven grant that the unmistakeable proof R.W. gave is sincere. I am a gone loon now. No earthly power can save me. Every interview reinforces my first opinion of her worth & excellence. They go to Lago Maggiore tomorrow & of course I go too.

Octavius was indeed 'a gone loon'. On the following Sunday he knelt beside her at the Anglican service held in the hotel. 'God of his mercy prosper my love and intentions. Else how can she care for me and yet I feel she does.'

The Wallaces had a set tour which they were following and he was in agony as to whether to follow brazenly, or let them go and risk never seeing her again. But the aunt, and Rose too no doubt, conspired to help him and the young couple were left alone for the first time 'intentionally or God knows', mused Octavius. This did not stop him from using the opportunity to beg permission to write to her '& so declared my love & the joy—found it in some measure returned. She is an angel of goodness and sense. Told her candidly of my former love and engagement and near marriage to D. Walked with her towards Stresa. Oh the bliss of that walk. Spoke to her aunt and wrote to her mother.'

Confirmed in every way, the young man's affection deepened. 'I love her better every hour.' The lovers were temporarily parted. 'Oh how desolate it seemed without R.—but she is mine in heart & soul & if it please God & her mother consents she will be mine irrevocably ere long—God enable me to love her better and care for her happiness and make her happy. She will make me so I fear not.'

Mrs Wallace's letter came, also a letter from Rose—'*All right*', noted Octavius exultantly. It all seemed too good to be true. 'I can hardly believe that I am loved by and allowed to love so dear a little soul as my Rose . . . her Mother's letter is everything that is kind, honourable and sensible . . .'

The Wallaces then continued their itinerary and Octavius and Bradshaw applied themselves to sightseeing—galleries, museums, churches, cathedrals. In Munich Octavius commented with wry humour—'a regular *bellyful* of it—Nothing like a good dose while you are about it.'

When Octavius and Bradshaw returned to England at the end

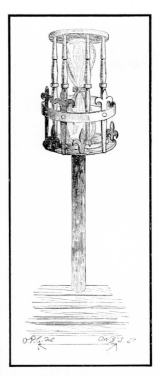

*Two drawings by
the Rev. Octavius
Pickard-Cambridge*

The Rev. Patrick Brontë

of October the Wallaces were already home. Mrs Wallace was the
widow of a headmaster who had taken Holy Orders. She now lived
in Oxford where she took in pupils, the most illustrious of whom
was John Wordsworth, an eventual Bishop of Salisbury. The
Wallaces were a High Church family in comfortable circumstances,
pious, living very retiring lives in the university city. Their pattern
of existence was in almost complete contrast to that of the Pickard-
Cambridges in Dorset. Rose was shy and modest, tiny in stature,
resolute in spirit and twelve years Octavius's junior. It was no
easy task for a young girl of Rose's quiet nature to prepare to be a
wife in the Pickard-Cambridge clan, knowing that one day she
would have to run a large household and be an efficient hostess for
her husband's scientific friends as well as clerical associates, not
counting the Dorset relatives and friends. But her love for Octavius
and her steadfast character saw her through all difficulties. She
proved an excellent parson's wife, deeply loved by her husband,
and adored by all her children.

The wedding was not planned until after Octavius and Bradshaw had returned from their second, and more serious, collecting
trip abroad, an elaborate expedition which filled the whole of 1865.
These two foreign journeys provided unforgettable memories for
Octavius and inaugurated many friendships with foreign scientists
who corresponded with him thereafter and often visited Bloxworth
in later years.

Travel in the mid 1860s often presented difficulties. Crossing
the Alps, for instance, entailed first diligences and then sledges.
The two men spent a couple of months in Palestine and Syria,
where Octavius was as much fascinated by the antiquities as by
the insect life. He despised the commercialism which he saw in the
holy places.

Quite enough for us, as for the Apostles and their successors for
300 years, to know that all these scenes of our Lord's life took
place at Jerusalem, thus sanctifying the whole place . . .; while
to be told as certain facts about the spots in the Church of the
Holy Sepulchre, and to see unsightly buildings, tawdry orna-
ments and bad pictures heaped up over them, takes away all
interest, and rouses in one a spirit of scepticism and incredulity.

The Christian associations held more appeal for him than the

c

Egyptian tombs and temples and he made dozens of sketches of
places and objects in the Holy Land. When he returned to England
it was with a sense of mission accomplished and eager expectations
of his new life with Rose.

They were married in Oxford on 19 April 1866 and spent the
honeymoon (as did so many other serious-minded clerical couples)
touring the cathedrals of England. From then until his death in
1917, Octavius's travels were confined almost exclusively to
Dorset apart from occasional trips to London to lecture on natural
history or to attend scientific conferences or visit museums.

The newly weds began living in Bloxworth in late May and in
1867 their first child, a son, was born. In January 1868 the Rev.
George Pickard-Cambridge died unexpectedly, a shock for the
entire family and especially for Octavius who recorded the anni-
versary sadly in his diary each year. Octavius became rector and in
August he, Rose and the baby moved into the rectory.

The 1860s were years when it was remarkably fashionable to
restore country churches, usually at the expense of the rector and
his friends, or at the behest and expense of the squire, although
the Church of England had some funds available for this purpose.
Frequently the expenditure was considerable and some wealthy
squires spent a fortune on churches. Sir Tatton Sykes, of Yorkshire, fifth baronet, reckoned he spent about a million and a half
pounds restoring or building some twenty Yorkshire churches.[3]
All over the country old features and furnishings were ripped out
of the churches, sometimes sold, sometimes discarded, and the
taste and teachings of John Ruskin were made abundantly manifest as Victorian Gothic rose on every side.

Octavius was exceptional in that he had long been seriously
interested in church architecture and he was determined to restore
Bloxworth Church with dignity and restraint. It was the first
major rebuilding of the church since the seventeenth century and
the Pickard-Cambridge family intended it to be a loving memorial
to the late rector. The fourteenth-century Early Decorated chancel
was rebuilt as an exact replica, although slightly enlarged. Two
original windows were retained and two others copied exactly, but
also enlarged. The Dorset county surveyor donated his services, a
Blandford firm did the work, and Octavius was an ever-present,
all-seeing supervisor. Flint and stone was carefully matched into
the exterior; Corsham Down, Bath and Doulting stone, soft and

easy to carve, was used for the windows, doors and arches; polished Irish marble formed the columns and the reredos was of tiled mosaic. The new east window (which everyone admired) was a stained-glass copy of the sketch which Octavius had made in Jerusalem of the tomb of Jesus.

Rebuilding began in September 1869 and was completed the following July, a tribute to Octavius's organization and to the important social and economic position which the family occupied in Bloxworth. Octavius was delighted and wrote and illustrated a pamphlet detailing the history of the church, which ended with a characteristically humorous reference to an earlier rector, who had later become Cardinal Morton, but who was better known in village history as 'The Fighting Parson of Bloxworth'.

The Wallaces contributed to the church furnishings, not caring to be outdone by the Pickard-Cambridges, and Rose's aunt gave a harmonium. Octavius had very definite ideas about improving the quality of church music and the harmonium was only the first step. The use of music to produce a more spiritual atmosphere in services was another indirect result of the Oxford revival and was welcomed, along with better lighting and heating, by many parsons who would have hesitated to introduce doctrinal changes.

In many villages the installation of a harmonium or an organ spelled the end of the long-established village orchestras and choirs, whose members took it hard when they were ousted by mere machines. Grandfather Dewey, in Hardy's *Under the Greenwood Tree*, castigated harmoniums and barrel-organs as 'miserable dumbledores'. No such problems arose in Bloxworth, however, and the harmonium was used until 1872 when Octavius found an organ whose tone satisfied his high standards. It was installed in the church and for forty years Rose Pickard-Cambridge played this instrument at services.[4]

The grand reopening of Bloxworth Church in July was attended by many local notables, and Octavius held a special morning service. A marquee was erected in the rectory's spacious garden and a fine luncheon with some excellent strawberries served for the honoured guests. The villagers and school-children were segregated, as was the normal custom, and made do with a tea later in the day in another part of the rectory grounds. Octavius officiated at a special evening service for the benefit of people who worked in the day and had been unable to attend the morning one.

One more change was needed before Octavius could feel that he
had a truly modern parish—a new school to replace the cottage on
the village green which served as school. He canvassed his friends
again and raised the money to buy land and build a school half-way
between the rectory and the church. A trust deed made it the
property of the rector and churchwardens and it was run as a
Church of England school, Octavius being for all practical purposes the sole manager until extreme old age forced him to resign.
Schools, of course, were being built or improved all over the country
as a consequence of the new Education Act by which the State for
the first time took responsibility for the elementary education of
the population.

Incidentally, it was at about this time that Thomas Hardy was
writing *Far From the Madding Crowd* in instalments for the *Cornhill Magazine*. He did not make Bloxworth the village of his novel,
but when the book was filmed almost a century later it was Bloxworth House which was chosen as Bathsheba Everdine's house,
and Bloxworth churchyard where Fanny Robin and Sergeant Troy
were buried.[5]

The historical background and social pattern of this small
Bloxworth community meant that Octavius could keep a firm
grip on parish affairs without recourse to a more formal apparatus
of parish clubs, although Rose ran the Clothing Club and the
Lending Library, kept an eye on the Slate Club and taught in the
Sunday School, and Octavius was always available in the rectory.
None the less, the village loyalty granted to him was his by family
inheritance. Bloxworth born and bred, and an active, resident
curate or rector for over fifty years, during which time he taught
most of the villagers, confirmed them, married them, christened
their babies, buried their elders and knew practically all their
secrets, he was unquestionably the leading 'person' of the village.
Being the fifth son he had not become squire, but for the greater
part of his incumbency there was no resident squire in Bloxworth
and the villagers looked to him to fulfil the dual function of squire
and parson.

If a labourer missed one or two Sunday attendances at church,
Octavius would be at the cottage door demanding to know the
reason why, and if he thought poorly of the excuse he would tell
the man to mend his ways or he'd have his cottage. And he meant
it. Nor did the rector always wait to be asked for his advice on a

parishioner's personal life. As his long beard whitened with age, a patriarch he looked and as a patriarch he behaved. Octavius had not come into money at his father's death (he had, after all, inherited the living) but Rose had some money and it was her private means which allowed them to keep hospitable open house to friends and scientists.

Many Anglican parsons had problems with Dissenters and although Bloxworth included one or two, these were not numerous enough to form any organized opposition. Octavius made a distinction between Dissenters as a group—to be gravely mistrusted—and Dissenters as individuals, who when all was said and done were Bloxworth folk needing his ministrations as much as anyone else.

Octavius and Rose regarded themselves as hard-working, up-to-date workers in the church, doing good in the village, keeping up with the times, trying to ensure that the church was not only the centre of community life but a beautiful centre at that. Octavius began the practice of holding special services at Easter, when the ladies decorated the church with primroses and daffodils against a background of trailing ivy. The service of Holy Communion was held more frequently than before, and Octavius personally trained a mixed choir to make sure that the musical background to the services would be as good as possible. Bloxworth choir soon acquired an enviable reputation, and it travelled regularly to choir festivals, either to listen or to participate.

The rector was not of the temperament to shine, nor indeed would he have wished to shine, at extempore preaching, and he invariably prepared his sermons beforehand and read them out. This practice had the additional advantage that sermons could be used more than once, after suitable revision. They were plain and reasonably short. If he wished to time himself, he had only to glance at the fine Jacobean hour-glass by the Jacobean pulpit. The pulpit, alas, became visibly unsafe by 1887 and had to be removed, but the hour-glass was cherished. By the end of the century Octavius's sermons sometimes sounded old-fashioned, even apocalyptic, but the villagers were accustomed to their parson, and those of his dwindling congregation who still attended regularly would never consider it their place to complain of parson's preaching.

The rector of Bloxworth also had responsibility for the parish of

Winterbourne Tomson, two miles distant. This was a decayed hamlet of less than twenty souls with a minuscule church producing a minuscule income to match. Across the fields stood a much larger church belonging to another parish, and those from Winterbourne Tomson who bothered to attend service at all usually found it more convenient and sociable to go there. Frequently Octavius would arrive to find his church completely empty. Once his sole congregation was a mild-tempered donkey. Nevertheless he dutifully strode over the fields every Sunday until 1890 when his bishop finally agreed that the church could be closed. Octavius used to assert that as curate and rector he had walked 7,000 miles in his duties at Tomson alone, setting out in all weathers, with his long step and coat-tails fluttering in the wind.

Bloxworth remained a surprisingly self-contained village. A man who had travelled as far as Poole, all of nine miles, was a traveller of note. He had seen the world. The villagers looked to the Tinkers Fair up on the hill in late September for their annual shopping spree. The gentry bought hunters and riding horses; the farmers bought their shire horses; the women bought their household china; and everyone bought new clothes. It was the highlight of the year, the main chance of meeting old friends and making new acquaintances, a flurry of excitement and merrymaking to colour the monotony of agricultural life.

Christmas was another grand festive occasion, and the rectory came into its own as the natural centre of hospitality for the village. Carol singing was held in the rectory drawing room, which was a large room capable of seating sixty people. Over the years this was the scene of many private concerts, and Octavius finally had a permanent platform built at the end of the room. All the rectory children were taught to play at least one musical instrument. Octavius had kept up his musical interests and he often played in concerts at Bere Regis, where there was a keen musical group. He was a prominent member of the Dorset Orchestral Association from the late 1880s, and was its president during the last ten years of his life. He composed a little, and wrote some Anglican chants and one or two hymn tunes. His taste was classical, and it was his keenest joy to popularize Beethoven, Haydn, Mozart and Schubert through the concerts he played in. He was proud of his violin, which was made by Vuillaume on a model of Guarnerius Del Gesu, and he usually played second violin in the more important concerts.

He and Rose took especial pains over the education of their children. Rose taught them herself until they were old enough to go away to school at Weymouth. Octavius showed them how to develop the naturalist's observant eye wherever they went. He made sure the boys were grounded in zoology, botany, geology and archaeology, and each one was expected to specialize also in at least one branch of knowledge. Throughout their lives they would send back to their father reports and specimens, so that Octavius— observing, classifying and drawing away in his 'Den'—had a constant stream of news and specimens.

The chief rectory sport was cricket, although Octavius's daughter took up archery. Octavius gave the boys their first cricket lessons and spent hours bowling underhand to them as soon as they could hold a bat. The whole village was drawn into cricket as the rectory boys became old enough to play in a team, and Octavius coached them so effectively that they shone in West Country competitions. When the rectory boys grew up, they took over responsibility for cricket coaching. Any cricket fixture in Bloxworth was a popular village occasion, and the rector took a hand in erecting the tents for the entertainment of the visitors. Cricket, music and their parson's spiders were beyond doubt Bloxworth's claims to fame, and most villagers would have put them in that order.

Politics played a minor part in Bloxworth life. The villagers took their cue from their rector, whose politics reflected his social background—he was a Tory of the old school who voted conscientiously at elections. Sometimes these occasions were less than peaceful. Octavius noted in his diary about the 1880 election: 'To Bere with Bertie to see Drax [Drax was the Tory candidate for Wareham]. With him to the Poll—a regular scrimmage with sticks etc. and a few heads cracked.' The 1880 election was rather a violent one. Riots took place in several places where the police force was not strong enough to control them.[6] Octavius became an active member of the Primrose League and was made a Knight Almoner in 1886. Sometimes he neatly combined political allegiance with musical interest and promoted concerts in aid of the League.

Although spiders had become his prime concern as a naturalist, Octavius was fascinated by all birds and animals. He could watch squirrels from the rectory windows and he wrote one or two papers on their habits. There was always a high mortality rate among these unfortunate beasts, many of whom fell accidental victims to the crossfire of the young Pickard-Cambridge boys out shooting. Afterwards the squirrels were gathered up and taken round to the kitchen to supplement family meals. One day Morton Stuart (later Earl of Moray) dropped in expectedly to lunch when pot-luck that day consisted of squirrel pie. The family, long inured to this local delicacy, thought it excellent, but the good Mr Stuart had difficulty in finishing his portion.

Hunting was another rural sport. A diary entry in 1887 reads: '. . . the hounds brought a fox from Colwood, and killed it under the housekeeper's room window and ate it in the yard. The Hunt—about a hundred—were regaled on cider and sherry.' (Cider of course was the ale of Dorset.) All the meets at Bloxworth or at the 'Red Post' were noted down in Octavius's diary, taking their due place among the more frequent notations about running the glebe farm, dates of planting and gathering fruit and vegetables either there or in the rectory garden, and buying and selling pigs. Octavius was in effect a part-time farmer, so long as his dairyman, Daniells, was alive to help. When Daniells died in 1914, Octavius was then over eighty and the glebe farm had to be let to a tenant.

As a parson, Octavius was a practical man of commonsense rather than a theological or ritualistic innovator. For example, he expressed strong views on the need for church repairs to be shared between a central church fund and the local parson, a point on which he considered he could speak personally. He also argued that provision should be made for pensions for the clergy. There were too many cases where an elderly clergyman could not afford to retire even though he had become incapacitated through age or illness. Not many livings were lucrative enough to maintain the parson and his family and cover a curate's stipend, meagre though that might be, so a parish priest who was totally dependent upon his living was faced with a painful dilemma if infirmity overtook him. Either he stayed on for the sake of his family and his pastoral work was neglected, or he resigned and died in penury after watching his family starve.

Education was another of Octavius's favourite hobby-horses and for three years, from 1879 to 1882, he was a Diocesan Inspector for church schools of the Poole Deanery. Financial stringency forced him to give this up since he could not afford to hire carriages to take him from school to school, and the bishop was unable or unwilling to meet these travelling costs. A family which looked to windfall squirrels to eke out its diet had to watch its expenditures, and Octavius used his own experience as further support for his argument that indigent clergy needed more financial support. His own scientific researches and studies were carried out at virtually no cost, as he walked or bicycled around Dorset to get specimens, and his notes, drawings and classifications were made in a specially converted outbuilding of the rectory, christened the 'Den'. Family and friends were under standing orders to send to Bloxworth any interesting specimens. From the depths of his heart Octavius could sympathize with the problems of brother clergy unblessed by private means.

Those were the years when the amateur could make a genuine contribution to art and science and by 1880 Octavius had published almost eighty scientific papers on spiders alone, in addition to about forty on antiquarian subjects, on meteorology, mammals, reptiles, birds, lepidoptera and general entomology. He was now in his early fifties, vigorous in his parish work, dedicated to science, and for the following thirty years he maintained an unflagging correspondence with scientists all over the world, and willingly identified and classified other people's specimens, with the sole condition that he should be allowed to keep one perfect specimen for his own collection which was destined for Oxford University after his death.[7] He made that proviso because he had discovered very early that other collectors were frequently less careful than he in preserving their specimens intact over the years. Octavius had meticulously high standards, unlike some amateur scientists whom he sardonically called 'the goodness gracious scientists'.

His Christian faith was uncomplicated, and he did not find difficulty in reconciling it with Darwinian or other scientific theories. He corresponded with Darwin on the sexual selection and the sexual habits of spiders, about which he knew more than Darwin, and was not altogether satisfied with the hypotheses of his fellow naturalist in this regard.

Bloxworth was a small, nucleated village, its cottages clustered near the church and rectory, and Rose undertook some of the pastoral duties of cottage teaching. This gave her husband the time to go off collecting whenever the weather permitted. One minute he would be sitting down, the next he had glanced up at the clouds, remarked, 'It looks nice now', and he was away, usually taking one of the children with him.

He thought nothing of tramping six miles to a collecting haunt and six miles back and made light of sudden showers. The peculiar richness of the Bloxworth area for a naturalist lay in its combination of heath, clay and chalk. Bere Wood was his closest good hunting ground and a mine of treasures. Morden Park, Portland, and the glorious heath which stretched from Dorchester to the New Forest were other favourite haunts. He spoke of Dorset as a queen of counties, a veritable paradise for the naturalist and the artist. He believed deeply that detailed local studies of all kinds of fauna were the best means of building up a true picture of any locality, and his own Dorset surveys were models of what a perfectionist hoped to achieve. These accounts were enriched by careful drawings wherein even the most horrific spider was by the artist's grace transmuted into a miracle of Nature's art and ingenuity.

In 1889 and 1890 he was gratified at being appointed Chaplain to Sir Frederick Johnstone, the High Sheriff of Dorset. Octavius had been interested in prison reform for some time, ever since he had done duty as a prison chaplain. He greatly enjoyed the conversation and legal anecdotes of the visiting judges to the Dorchester Assizes. Occasionally, usually when involved with a cause which he took very seriously, his sense of humour deserted him, as with his first Assize Sermon. This was meant to support the concept of work programmes for prisoners, and was based on the text, 'Why stand ye here all the day idle?' It provoked some puzzlement among its hearers, which was hardly resolved by the text of his second sermon, 'It is good for us to be here'.

He was a founder member of the Dorset Natural History and Antiquarian Field Club, and present at its inaugural meeting at the Digby Hotel at Sherborne in 1875. He acted as its treasurer from 1882 to 1900, and from 1883 until his death in 1917 he was also vice-president. In those latter years he was an extremely picturesque figure at these meetings—tall and majestic, his full, flowing beard now snowy white, and with a white puggaree swathed round his black clerical hat to show that he was 'off duty'.

As he grew older he derived increasing satisfaction from his connections with learned societies. Distance, lack of time and of money, and severe rheumatism during the last twenty years of his life all combined to maroon him in Dorset so that the scientific recognition rendered him was almost entirely due to his public-ations and correspondence, and owed almost nothing to personal interchanges in London or the university world. He rarely left Bloxworth even for meetings of these national and international bodies, but always followed their proceedings avidly through their journals. He was proud to be a Fellow of the Zoological Society, and especially proud of course of being made a Fellow of the Royal Society in 1887. At one period he had, indeed, made efforts to go fairly regularly to London, but was disappointed at the lack of welcome and response from fellow naturalists in the museums. He was too shy to attempt to impose himself upon them; anyone less like a social climber in the scientific field could not be imagined. Each visit to London deepened his conviction that Dorset, his parish, his family, and the local societies, including the musical ones, were world-wide enough for him. If he wished for approbation, he had only to thumb through his correspondence for instant reassurance.

From time to time he had the assistance of a nephew, Frederick Pickard-Cambridge. This young man was a born naturalist and a gifted draughtsman, but he came of a generation which could not reconcile the scientific method with Christian dogma, and like a true Pickard-Cambridge, Frederick did not scruple to express his views plainly. The two men, sharing so many interests, thus had fundamental points of difference. Octavius had trained himself to a slow and careful scrutiny of each new idea, and Frederick was young and impatient, prepared to accept new ideas readily if they were superficially plausible. This proved another source of disagreement. But Frederick had his share of the family charm and capacity for fun, and it was a bitter loss to Octavius when Frederick died comparatively young.

He was of great help to Octavius in the latter's lengthy and disciplined contribution to the *Biologia Centrali-American*, a work which was spread over the period 1883 to 1902, and which followed the scholarly and authoritative *Spiders of Dorset*, which was published in two volumes, the first appearing in 1879 and the second two years later. That title was misleading, because in fact the work included all British spiders. The Dorset list led the way, demonstrating the rector's local patriotism.

The book was immediately recognized as an important volume, and Octavius was hailed as the natural successor to John Blackwall, who died in 1881 at the age of ninety-one, leaving his spider

collection to Octavius. Another leading arachnologist of the day
was Eugene Simon, a French naturalist who fled to England after
the siege of Paris in 1871, and settled there. He became a valued
friend, and Octavius was finally persuaded by Simon to adopt the
latter's system of classification of the Theridiidae family of spiders.
This was a radical decision which involved the revision and cor-
rection of almost all of Octavius's earlier classifications, but it was
characteristic of the man that once he was sure he had taken the
correct scientific position, he commenced, uncomplainingly, the
tedious and time-consuming task of revision, and continued at it
for years, working patiently and precisely.

As Octavius approached his seventies the countless hours of
exposure to all weathers began to tell, and the twinges of pain and
the aching joints which he had endured stoically for several years
settled into the painful and permanent pattern of severe rheumatism. He made light of it, hobbling out in 1901 for a last defiant
ramble through the much loved Bere Wood, but at last he had to
agree with the family that his collecting and hunting days were
over. He became increasingly crippled with arthritis in the legs.
At one stage in 1903 he had to give up all his clerical duties and
stay in bed while a friend and fellow naturalist, the Rev. H. S.
Gorham, filled in for him, but he struggled up as soon as he could
move and managed to attend the consecration of an addition to
the churchyard in July of that year; and every day, rain or shine,
he dragged himself across the flower garden to the 'Den' where he
sat at his desk, revising his classifications and answering letters.
Sometimes he was well enough to attend a practice night of the
Orchestral Association in Dorchester, and he continued to play
with the orchestra until 1905.

Each successive year, however, saw a failing of his powers. The
last day he was strong enough to make the journey to church was
28 June 1908, and thereafter his curate, the Rev. E. D. Benison,
took all the services, although Octavius remained available at the
rectory for parish business and visits from parishioners. His legs
might be paralysed but his mind was as alert as ever. Benison was
a dashing young man who owned a motor car, something never
before seen in Bloxworth. The first time he drove it slowly through
the village to church he was delighted by the stir it caused, and by
the crowd which followed his progress. As he hurried into church he
anticipated a larger congregation than usual. Alas, it was his car

not his sermon which the villagers admired and they remained outside exclaiming at the mechanical marvel parked there whilst Benison was inside preaching to his faithful few.

Rose fell ill in 1909, lingering for a distressing year before dying of cancer, and the heart of the family died a little with her. Octavius, although kindly, and genuinely fond of children, had become a slightly intimidating figure in his patriarchal way, and it was Rose, diminutive in black bombazine, whose sweetness won the instant trust and love of the children. The five Pickard-Cambridge boys were grown up and out in the world, and were very rarely, except at festive occasions like Christmas, all at home together.

The bereaved rector clung to his scientific studies like a drowning man to a beacon, patiently checking, classifying, revising, answering letters, reading articles and writing them, and publishing at least one scientific article a year. The days passed uneventfully. It was a matter of minor excitement when a particularly interesting insect entrapped itself at the window of the 'Den'. His glimpse of nature became constricted to the view through the rectory windows and he took an even greater pleasure in the changing flower beds with their messages of new seasons. His heart lightened when he saw the first spring bulbs appear, especially those which blossomed in such profusion outside the 'Den'.

1914 was a sad year. His dairyman, Daniells, died, and war broke out. One by one the young men put on uniform and disappeared from the village. A whole world was disintegrating and so, quietly, was the old rector. By 1916 his family could no longer ignore the signs. He set his last butterfly, recorded his last rainfall measurement, and then spent five months from October onwards simply growing weaker. He died in March 1917, just short of his ninetieth birthday.

The passing of their rector was yet another instance of the old ways disappearing. Nobody in Bloxworth could remember the village without Octavius, man or boy. For the older men and women he had symbolized an entire era. 'There, 'tis the end of all things to we,' commented one sorrowfully. The patriarchal relationship between rectory and village had been very strong, and its memories persisted. As late as 1951, when two of Octavius's sons stopped their car near Bloxworth to question their route, a local farmer— after gazing at the elder brother in silence for a moment—exclaimed,

'Why! If it isn't Master Arthur!' As the car moved on, the brothers reminisced. 'Yes,' said one, 'he was rather a handful, but we made him into a good cricketer.'

The rectory had served the village in many homely ways. At the back of the rectory stood the former malt-house, in which two vats, one at either end and separated by a partition, were used as baths. Here the water was heated every Saturday evening. The boys and girls of the Sunday School all had to take their turn so as to be spick and span for the coming Sunday.

At various times of the year there would be casual work available at the rectory, either in the house, or in the garden or helping with extra work on the glebe farm. This work was not always popular, because the rector made up the wages with 'truckle' cheese made at the rectory. Once this payment in kind was so much resented that a public protest was shown by using the cheeses to prop open the gates across the village road. The rector was unabashed, and a thrifty member of the family collected the discarded cheeses and took them back to the rectory for future use!

The rector had always managed to live by a simple philosophy and had made the most of his time and talent as a naturalist: he had led a busy and happy life within tightly circumscribed limits. The occurrence of the initials 'O. P-C.' after the scientific names of 115 species of spiders speaks for itself in establishing him as an accepted world authority among arachnologists.

He had once read a paragraph in a newspaper which gave a set of rules for life, and he was so taken with it that he had cut it out and pasted inside the prayerbook which was always on his desk: 'Look at your mercies with both eyes, at your troubles with only one; study contentment; keep always at some useful work; let your heart's window be always open towards Heaven.' In a letter to one of his sons he once wrote '. . . happiness is a very comparative article, and will in the end consist more in what you can cheerfully and gracefully give up than in what you can get.'

Octavius Pickard-Cambridge lies buried in Bloxworth churchyard, next to his wife. Inside the church, near the brass tablet which he erected for his father, is a similar one erected by his children. In simple dignified words it testifies to the things he was proudest of—his degree at Durham university, his rectorship, and his worship of God through the study of nature.

The Rev.
Patrick Brontë
Parson
with Literary Connections
1777-1861

It is an unhappy fact that the Rev. Patrick Brontë[1] has been the victim of literary myth-making following a process which began when, at his request, Mrs Gaskell undertook a biography of his daughter Charlotte, who had recently died. Brontë chose Mrs Gaskell because he admired her work and because she and Charlotte had been friends. When the biography was finished and published he was pleased with its success, although disconcerted by the several errors concerning himself. Some of those errors had arisen because Mrs Gaskell had placed too much credence on the gossip of an unreliable and resentful former servant of the parsonage, but some were in fact owing to misrecollections which Brontë himself had given Mrs Gaskell.

When the minister protested to Mrs Gaskell about certain statements she deleted the offending material, and in the next two editions a more balanced portrait of the 'Perpetual Curate of Haworth' emerged. Other people mentioned in the book had caused trouble for Mrs Gaskell, but Brontë was certainly ready to let the matter rest so far as he was concerned. As he wrote to her:

Why should you disturb yourself concerning what has been, is, and ever will be the lot of eminent writers. . . . You have had and will have much praise with little blame. Then drink the mixed cup with thankfulness to the great Physician of souls. It will be far more salutary in the end . . . than if it were all unmixed sweetness.[2]

The revised portrait was not as entertaining a picture as the original character, and so in later editions of the biography the mythical monster crept back, to survive thereafter in literary folk lore as an eccentric, selfish to his wife and cold to his children. He had caused their premature deaths from consumption by his refusal to let them eat meat. In addition, it was alleged, he had drunk in secret, had fired pistols off throughout the day and had kept his gifted offspring deliberately marooned in the bleak isolation of the Yorkshire moors instead of taking or sending them to more favourable surroundings where their genius could have flourished.

That notion of the wicked father, the 'Mr Barrett' of the parsonage, was the more memorable because everyone knew that the Brontë children did not go to Italy like Elizabeth Barrett but only to the early seclusion of the Haworth vault.

Reason suggests that the Brontë ogre must be largely fantasy and several writers, dating from soon after his death to the present day, have made this point forcefully, but the old legend has proved to be amazingly potent. In the bicentenary of his birth it is more than ever appropriate to examine Patrick Brontë, the man and the country parson, who spent over forty years of his life in a parish which was famous in Evangelical history long before the Brontës arrived.

His father was Hugh Brunty, a penniless Protestant Irish labourer who married a Catholic girl. She renounced her faith and their children were reared as Protestants. This resulted in a lack of friends for the children, since their Catholic neighbours regarded the offspring of a mixed marriage as little better than heathens. The eldest child, a boy born on St Patrick's Day 1777, was inevitably named Patrick, and began life in a two-roomed, mud-floored, thatched cabin in County Down. Soon, however, Brunty was earning enough to rent a tiny house, and there the rest of the family was born. He worked for himself, roasting corn in a kiln which at one time was located in the kitchen. He made extra money by hiring himself out for casual work on the roads or mending fences. There were ten children in the family and little enough money for food. They ate porridge and milk for breakfast; jacket potatoes for lunch; indigestible homemade bread and milk for tea; milk and potatoes, sometimes with a boiled egg, for supper. Patrick Brontë continued to eat a diet similar to this for most of his adult life, although he later added meat and Yorkshire pudding.

Hugh Brunty's corn roasting made him unusually aware of the danger of fire and he insisted that his children should wear woollen clothes because wool was the least flammable material. Fear of fire was instilled into his eldest son and become a phobia, although the Brontës were allowed to wear silk as well as wool.

The Bruntys were semi-literate, but they did possess four books: the Bible, the New Testament, *Pilgrim's Progress* and the poems of Robert Burns, and on these works young Patrick Brunty taught himself to read. He went out to work at twelve, helping the blacksmith who noticed the exceptional abilities of the lad and once said to a customer in the boy's hearing that young Brunty was 'a gentleman by nature'. The phrase electrified him and he recalled as an old man that it had a profound influence on him. Another stirring moment was when he glimpsed the great John Wesley at one of the open-air meetings during his Irish campaign.

At fourteen the boy changed jobs and was apprenticed to a linen weaver. This was well paid work which allowed him to buy books, and to read them at work, for he perfected the trick of weaving the cloth with a book propped up in front of him. He was always reading, even when strolling along country lanes. One day he met the Rev. Andrew Harshaw, a school teacher who was an ordained Presbyterian minister. Harshaw sensed a potential student in Patrick Brunty and gave him the use of his own library and taught the boy Latin and mathematics. Young Brunty's eyes became badly strained by the fine weaving and the incessant reading but he could give up neither, the one being essential for the family income and the other essential for his mental and spiritual development.

Harshaw next recommended Patrick, aged sixteen, for the post of assistant teacher at Glascar Hill Presbyterian School, and although Mrs Brunty's original Catholicism was a slight stumbling-block, the only other candidate withdrew, and Patrick was appointed after passing a qualifying test. He began attending Presbyterian services and continued his own studies. He was a hard-working young teacher. He lent books to those who would profit by them, started a night school, held classes for church singing and gymnastics, and accompanied the boys on nature study rambles on the mountains of Mourne.

When he had been at the school for five years he fell in love with one of his pupils, the precocious daughter of a farmer. Her family objected angrily to his attentions and the hot-tempered young man was equally angry in return. Matters might have turned ugly if fate had not removed him. It happened that the Rev. Thomas Tighe of Drumballyroney needed a tutor for his sons who could also teach at the parish school. The Tighes were Anglicans who followed the Wesleyan tradition and the minister was always alert for promising young men who would enter the Church in the normal way and gravitate thereafter to its Wesleyan wing, and he saw Patrick Brunty as a future minister of that type. He was accordingly offered the position and gladly went to Drumballyroney, ignorant of Tighe's hopes for him and merely aware that it represented a step forward. He could save money and he had access to another library, the minister's.

Strong, ardent, adventurous and ambitious, the young man enjoyed reading military and naval history best of all and envied the life of a professional officer. Tighe, however, very firmly guided the boy into theological fields. The new tutor learned to discipline himself. He saved twenty-five pounds, an enormous sum to him, and he was eventually persuaded by his mentor to study for the ministry. Coached and recommended by Tighe, who was a former graduate of St John's College, Cambridge, Patrick Brunty applied to enter that college and was enrolled in October 1802, his name appearing first as Patrick Branty, a tribute to his Irish brogue.

England was then in the middle of the long war with France, and Brontë[3] joined the Volunteers, which had recently been formed as a precaution against invasion by Napoleon; he trained alongside a fellow student, Lord Palmerston. Life was necessarily spartan again for Patrick Brontë and his only recreation was long walks in the country. He managed to exist and even to spare a few pounds to send home to the family in Ireland. He won an exhibition, which helped financially, graduated B.A. in 1806, and was ordained the same year. An Irish nobody had come to Cambridge; an ordained man appointed to a curacy in Essex was leaving it.

Before going to his parish of Wethersfield he returned to Ireland and enjoyed the admiration and respect of his family. He preached his first sermon—largely extempore—in Drumballyroney Church which was crowded for the occasion, and was satisfied it was a success. Then he said good-bye to his family and left for England. He never saw his parents again. His father died in 1808 and his mother died in 1822. He kept in touch by letter with his brothers and sent a few pounds when he could to his mother, and after her death to the others of the family. Ties between them inevitably were loose.

At St John's College, Brontë had followed the teachings of the Wesleyan disciple, the Rev. Charles Simeon, and throughout his life Brontë took the Evangelical side and was always ready to cooperate with Dissenters. His vicar at Wethersfield was the Rev. Joseph Jowett, Regius Professor of Civil Law at Cambridge, who was normally absent from the parish, leaving the work to his curate. Brontë had plenty to do, but he was accustomed to work and he carried out his duties satisfactorily. In December 1807 he was ordained priest. He fell in love with a Miss Mary Burder whose uncle and guardian, despising the curate's Irish accent, poverty and uncertain future, roughly forbade any continuation of the relationship. Furiously angry, consumed with self-pity, and disappointed that the girl had not protested more to her uncle, Brontë wrote a long diatribe to Miss Burder, which relieved his feelings somewhat, and then took steps to find a curacy away from Wethersfield.

He was appointed curate at Wellington in Shropshire where he met an influential woman, Mrs Fletcher, widow of the Rev. John Fletcher who had been a friend of John Wesley. Like Tighe, Mrs Fletcher was always pleased to meet a possible recruit to the Wesleyan group within the Church. She liked what she saw of Brontë and her recommendation assisted him to a better curacy at Dewsbury in Yorkshire. His new vicar was a friendly man who wrote devotional literature, an example quickly followed by Brontë who composed pious verse of moderate quality which he was inordinately proud to have published.

Patrick Brontë became a familiar figure in the town; he was tall, imposing, and always dressed in black with a snowy-white cravat; he habitually carried a stout stick with him. His experience as a schoolmaster made him doubly useful in the parish school. The success story of his curacy at Dewsbury was marred by a curious and worrying incident which took place one Sunday when, in the absence of the vicar, the Dewsbury bell-ringers began to practise their peals, a competition being in the offing. It had not occurred to them to ask permission from the curate, and they were astonished to discover that the sound of the bells aroused him to a terrifying and uncontrolled fury at what he considered to be profanation of the Sabbath. Trembling with anger he laid about him with his stick until he forced them to stop. It was a totally unexpected side to the man who had become something of a town hero when. although a poor swimmer, he had rescued a boy from drowning.

In 1811 he was appointed minister of Hartshead, a village four miles distant, that living being in the gift of his Dewsbury vicar. His church was usually full, some of the congregation being former pupils of his from the Dewsbury school who walked across the fields to listen to him. It was a busy life. He held cottage meetings. He tramped the lanes and moors, a dog at his heels, visiting the old and the sick, composing sermons and verses as he walked. He took an interest in the Luddite disturbances and in spite of his Tory politics he was personally acquainted with poverty and sympathized with the mill-hands, although he deeply disapproved of violent demonstrations and damage to property. Since the riots were exceptionally bloody in the Hartshead area, he prudently purchased a pair of pistols. He did not have occasion to use them, but he kept them by him for the rest of his life.

In 1812, when he was acting as a temporary examiner at the newly opened Wesleyan Academy at Woodhouse Grove, Patrick Brontë met his future wife, Maria Branwell, a pale, delicate girl whose parents had been well-to-do Penzance tradespeople and Methodists but were now dead. Miss Branwell was not penniless. She had an annuity of fifty pounds, almost as much as Brontë's stipend. They fell in love and we glimpse a transformed man through her letters to him. 'I love you above all the world.' 'I am certain no one ever loved you with an affection more pure, constant, tender and ardent than that which I feel.' 'Your ludicrous account of the scene at the Hermitage was highly diverting, we laughed heartily at it . . .' 'My heart tells me that it will always be my pride and pleasure to contribute to your happiness, nor do I fear that this will ever be inconsistent with my duty as a Christian.' Can 'My Dear Saucy Pat' really be the stern minister of legend? Maria had no doubts. In that same letter she wrote, 'I firmly believe that the Almighty has set us apart for each other. . .'.

There was a double wedding at Guiseley near Bradford in December 1812, for their friends the Rev. William Morgan and

Jane Fennell were also married on that day and the two ministers officiated for each other. The Brontës did not take a honeymoon. Either funds did not permit it or else Patrick Brontë did not consider it necessary. He rented a house, engaged a local woman as servant, and because the house stood a little apart from others at the end of a lane he left a loaded pistol in the house when he was away in case the two defenceless woman needed protection. Contentment encouraged his muse, and two more volumes of his verse were published by the time their first child, Maria, was born in 1813. Patrick Brontë would never be as happy again; success against considerable odds had been achieved and there were all the signs for a bright future. Another child, Elizabeth, was born in 1815, and he was appointed to a better living, at Thornton, west of Bradford. The family moved again, this time accompanied by Maria's elder sister, Elizabeth Branwell, who was Patrick Brontë's senior by one year, and who was staying with them to help her sister.

The family enjoyed five happy years at Thornton. The Brontës had friends, they went out and they invited guests to the house. In particular, Maria Brontë was friendly with young Elizabeth Firth of Kipping House, whose mother was dead. Brontë had time to continue his writing, and he produced a novel entitled *The Maid of Killarney* which contained a few forthright criticisms of social and religious life, but was in other respects a pleasant but run-of-the-mill story. The children were coming quickly, a dangerous burden for his frail wife, who had four infants during those five years. Years later Brontë would recall those days nostalgically— '. . . indeed I have never been very well since I left Thornton. My happiest days were spent there.'[4] Maria Brontë did not question her husband's right to rule the house. She had once written to him, '. . . nor do I fear to trust myself under your protection or shrink from your control. It is pleasant to be subject to those we love especially when they never exert their authority but for the good of the subject.'

In 1820 Brontë was offered the living of Haworth, high up on the moors near Keighley. He would have the title of 'Perpetual Curate', which in reality meant vicar; his stipend would be £200 and there would be a larger parsonage than at Thornton. Furthermore, Haworth had an irresistible history to any man who, like Brontë, was steeped in the Evangelical tradition. The famous Rev.

William Grimshaw had been an earlier incumbent and the village
bore a name hallowed in Wesleyan history.[5]

The circumstances of his appointment were full of difficulty and
public protest, but not of his making. The appointment was initially announced as a *fait accompli* by the Vicar of Bradford who
had overlooked the fact that by a deed granted in the reign of
Queen Elizabeth I, the Trustees of Haworth Church had the final
say in any appointment, a right which they treasured jealously.
They had already thought of Brontë as a possible choice but, being
good Yorkshiremen, the Trustees refused to have an outsider like
the Vicar of Bradford dictate to them. Brontë visited Haworth,
spoke to some of the Trustees and realized the dilemma. The
Trustees suggested that Brontë should resign, that the Vicar of
Bradford should admit the error of his ways and then the Trustees
would set matters right by officially appointing Brontë. Nothing
so simple and reasonable occurred, and finally Brontë resigned and
the Vicar of Bradford appointed a new man, a step which so
enraged the villagers that they erupted in a state of uproar which
drove the new minister away. Other appointees by the Vicar of
Bradford were no more acceptable, and from the pleasant parish of
Thornton the Brontës watched the events with amazement,
wondering if a move to Haworth would after all be a wise one.

The sixth and last Brontë was born at Thornton, a girl called
Anne, and soon after her birth the Haworth affair was settled
when the Vicar of Bradford met with the Trustees. In February
1820 Brontë was told his appointment, which would be permanent,
was agreed. He could not resist a thrill of anticipation at the
thought that he would be preaching in a church where John
Wesley and all the leading Evangelicals had preached, and where
in 1749 during a sermon by George Whitefield the excitement had
been so intense that two people had dropped dead.

Haworth was a large, scattered parish which included three
hamlets and numbered in all about five thousand souls. Brontë had
plenty of lonely moorland walking when he began his rounds of
cottage visiting, and he carried a loaded pistol which he tested
each morning by firing it out of his bedroom window over the
churchyard. The moors, grand and free, nature at her most in-
spiring, began at the parsonage's back door. Although the parsonage bedrooms were small and stuffy, there were five of them—
room enough for the family and servants.

Then in January 1821 his wife suddenly collapsed. The local doctor called in a Leeds specialist and both practitioners informed Brontë that his wife had terminal cancer. The minister tried to console himself with prayer, and as a practical step hired a woman from the village as a day nurse; after that there was little to do except wait for the end. Maria Brontë died that September, her last words being, 'Oh, my poor children!' She was buried by the Brontë's friend, the Rev. William Morgan, who had married the Brontës nine years earlier when Maria Branwell was twenty-eight.

Sorrows came in threes for Patrick Brontë. He had mourned the death of the Rev. Thomas Tighe a month before Maria Brontë's death, and a month or so after his wife died news came from Ireland that his mother was dead. The three adults to whom he felt his closest personal links were snatched from him in less than half a year.

He was relieved that Elizabeth Branwell, who had been helping to nurse her sister, promised to stay on in Haworth to look after the children. That was a considerable sacrifice on Miss Branwell's part for she hated Yorkshire and missed the warmth and friendliness of Cornwall. Nor did she share Brontë's faith, adhering to her own frightening, Calvinistic creed of salvation through election. Little Anne, who as the youngest became her aunt's special charge, was the child who suffered most from the fear aroused by Miss Branwell's gloomy religion. Like her sister, Miss Branwell had a small annuity, and she contributed this to the parsonage expenses, a very welcome addition since Maria Brontë's annuity had died with her.

Twice the widower tried to marry again. He asked Elizabeth Firth to be his wife, but she was already engaged to a clergyman, and he asked Mary Burder for the second time. Miss Burder had no desire to take on the burden of a difficult-natured, grieving widower with very little money, six small children and a life in a remote part of Yorkshire. She gave him a tart refusal, getting some of her own back. Miss Branwell accordingly became the children's substitute mother, resigned herself to exile from Cornwall, and the minister had to sublimate any lusty instincts he might still possess in pride in his children and devotion to the needs of Haworth.

He sent his four elder daughters to Cowan Bridge,[6] a Yorkshire boarding school opened recently for the daughters of poor clergymen. Brontë spent a day looking over the school, considered it suitable—he was doubtless in a state of mind to consider almost anything suitable—and the girls went there. A year later, in 1824, Maria fell ill and her father took her home where she died of consumption three months later. Next her sister, Elizabeth, fell sick of the same complaint and was sent home, and Brontë, fearful of the health of Charlotte and Emily, removed those two girls within days of Elizabeth's return. Elizabeth Brontë died less than a month after her return, and her father decided that the rest of the children should remain at home and gain their education there. His own schooling, after all, had been thoroughly unorthodox yet he had gone to university in the end. He tutored Branwell, his son; Charlotte taught Emily and Anne; and Miss Branwell forced the girls to learn the rudiments of sewing. They were so poor that they relied on parcels of cast-off clothes or material from friends like Elizabeth Firth. Release from drudgery lay only on the moors, in their father's library and in their imaginative games. Their father tried on principle not to interfere in their self-development, but he was convinced that they were no ordinary children. He made sure that they had books, he encouraged them to read his newspapers, and he took them to the Keighley Mechanics Institution to borrow books.

The girls all knew they would have to earn their livings as soon as they could, the profession of governess being the obvious one open to them, and they dreamed of opening their own school. All hopes centred around Branwell, who seemed brilliant, talented, and sociable, and who had such a talent for sketching that his sisters were convinced he would become a famous portrait painter, make his fortune and solve all their problems. The three girls were possessed by a writing demon, although they kept their writing jealously private, and their father was not aware of its extent or seriousness until they had become published novelists. Branwell too was ignorant of their novels.

Life and family inheritance made Brontë look older than his years and by his mid-fifties his hair was already snow-white. He was slightly hypochondriac, was prone to bronchitis and indigestion, ate and drank sparingly and retired early to bed. The household assembled for evening prayers at eight o'clock, after which he would go to bed although the children stayed up.

A parish as widely scattered as Haworth could not be managed properly by one man and Brontë employed a curate whose salary was met by a grant from the evangelical Pastoral Aid Society. Charlotte secretly surveyed the succession of curates scornfully, reserving some of her most biting comments for the kindly and handsome Willy Weightman. He came from the Lake District; he was amusing and flirtatious, but he had a serious side and was always ready to give time and sympathy to those in need. Brontë was well pleased with him, Branwell found him a true friend and Anne fell secretly in love with him.

It almost seemed as if life would run smoothly for the Brontës. Anne had left home and was a governess with the Robinson family at Scarborough. Charlotte and Emily, aged twenty-six and twenty-four, in pursuance of their aim to further their education in order to open a school, enrolled at the Pensionnat Heger in Brussels. Their father escorted them to Brussels. It was a first foreign trip for all three. Brontë was sixty-five and as excited as a young man at finding himself near the famous battlefield of Waterloo, to which he paid a reverent visit after seeing the girls safely to the Pensionnat. He spent a week or so in Belgium and northern France, visited Lille, Dunkirk and Calais, and reckoned up his expenses as just under £23.10*s*.

He returned to a year of troubles. It was 1824, and cholera ravaged the parish. Weightman, exposed to the disease through his parish duties, fell sick and died. He was only twenty-six, and Brontë had looked on him almost as an adopted son. Brontë's funeral sermon for Weightman set out his ideas as to how a clergyman should behave:

> In his preaching, and practising, he was, as every clergyman ought to be, neither distant nor austere, timid nor obtrusive, nor bigoted, exclusive, nor dogmatical. He was affable, but not familiar; open, but not too confiding. He thought it better, and more scriptural, to make the love of God, rather than the fear of hell, the ruling motive for obedience.[7]

That was Brontë's personal credo as a clergyman and there were many in Haworth who felt he, as well as Weightman, had lived up to it.

Very shortly after Weightman died it was the turn of Miss Branwell. She died in agonizing pain, to Branwell's infinite distress.

Still mourning for his friend Weightman, Branwell had to watch
his aunt-mother die. Mr Brontë resigned himself to Miss Branwell's
departure but the changed circumstances meant that one of the
three girls must return to Haworth to run the household. Anne was
earning money so she stayed in Scarborough; Charlotte was in love
with her schoolmaster, M. Heger, and wished to stay in Brussels;
but Emily was homesick for the moors and most thankfully
returned to Haworth.

Branwell joined Anne to tutor the Robinsons' son. This was a
fatal step for Branwell who became besotted with Mrs Robinson, a
bored, selfish woman seventeen years his senior. Mrs Robinson
led him on, persuading him that were she widowed she would
marry him. Branwell was destroyed by their relationship and lost
heart for anything except drink and opium. Mrs Robinson did in
the course of time become a widow, but she did not, of course,
marry Branwell. She waited until she could make an advantageous
match, and eventually became Lady Scott. Anne Brontë, disillusioned by what she saw of her brother and Mrs Robinson, and lonely
after the death of Weightman, began writing realistic novels about
the superficial world as she had observed it in Scarborough, and
relieved her deepest feelings in the composition of religious poetry.
Emily Brontë also wrote poems, which she kept intensely private,
and she drew her strength from a passionate communion with
nature. Patrick Brontë, toiling away as a parish pastor, knew little
of his children's personal lives and longings and asked less.

During his forty-one years as minister in Haworth he raised
money to buy the first organ and the first peal of bells which
Haworth Church had ever possessed. He raised money to build a
Sunday school and two daughter churches which were erected at
outlying hamlets. A good deal of petty crime was stamped out and
better prison facilities built; new roads were constructed, cottages
were white-washed as a health precaution against cholera, and a
number of cottages were built for the village poor. Brontë was
usually the leading spirit in getting these improvements carried
out. He was normally in the chair at parish meetings and he was a
tireless letter-writer.

His eyesight began to fail and he worried in case he should go
blind. Sometimes when he preached in church he could not recognize the people even in the front row. To be cut off from books was
unthinkable, and how would he manage his parish visiting over

the moors, with only a dog to guide him? His daughters, all short-sighted, readily understood his fears. Brontë began to think that he would never have as good a curate again as Weightman had been. His latest curate was an Irishman called Arthur Bell Nicholls, whose church views seemed almost Puseyite—very far indeed from Brontë's evangelical preferences.

Meanwhile, and unknown to him, Charlotte had chanced to read Emily's and Anne's poetry, and had taken the first step which would make the name of Brontë world famous. This was to add some of her own poems to those of her sisters and to have the volume published, of course under an assumed name. Only two copies were sold but the important start had been made. It then came out that all three girls had written novels as well, and under the masculine names of Acton, Currer and Ellis Bell—did their curate's name suggest 'Bell' to them?—their stories were published and immediately successful. They kept the news of publication from their father until they had enough enthusiastic reviews to prove that there would be no repetition of the poetry failure. Soon afterwards Charlotte accompanied her father to Manchester where he had a successful cataract operation.

By this time Branwell had given up all thought of making a living, and he stayed at home running up debts which his father and sisters had to meet. He would stumble home from the village pub drunk every night. Once there was even the shame of a visit from the Sheriff's Office about Branwell's debts. The consumption which had killed his sisters began to manifest itself in him and in 1848, at the age of thirty-one, he died. As Branwell grew weaker, his father insisted on praying at his bedside every night, much to Branwell's dislike, but at the very end the young man seemed to undergo a change of heart and his last word, in answer to his father's prayer, was 'Amen'. Patrick Brontë, greatly relieved, hoped that his brilliant but unstable son would be granted salvation by the grace of that word. Branwell died in complete ignorance of his sisters' books and fame.

Hardly was Branwell buried when it became clear that Emily, too, was in the final stages of consumption. Emaciated, racked with pain but determined to have no doctors, the twenty-nine-year-old girl died three months after her brother. The third victim was Anne Brontë, always delicate, whose grief over Emily was all the greater because she and Emily had been more like twins than ordinary sisters. Anne was at Haworth that winter, and both she and her father caught influenza. He recovered, while she weakened and soon showed the fatal signs of the last stages of consumption. Charlotte and her close and dear friend, Ellen Nussey bundled Anne up warmly and took her to the Yorkshire coast so that she might enjoy one last look at the sea which meant as much to her as the moors had to Emily. Anne died soon afterwards and Charlotte had her buried in Scarborough rather than bring the body back to be buried in the Haworth vault with the rest of the Brontës. The news of Anne's death brought grief but no surprise to her father or to the people of Haworth. They had watched the girls grow more delicate and the sexton declared that the girls had wrecked their health when they gave up their long moorland walks and shut themselves up in the stuffy parsonage rooms writing their books until past midnight.

Brontë turned to work as an anodyne, and there was plenty to do. There had been much sickness in Haworth in 1849 as a result of contaminated water, and the parson got up a petition to the General Board of Health in London, thereby initiating a local campaign for a better water supply. He had the satisfaction of seeing this effected in his lifetime, but it was 1858 before the battle was finally won. He campaigned to have the streets lit by gas, which took rather longer and indeed, did not come to pass until 1865 when he was no longer alive to see it.

Charlotte was now the one child left, and she looked after him, leaving Haworth only for visits to friends, or to London where she was somewhat lionized—Currer Bell having become identified with Charlotte Brontë. Strangers often visited Haworth, gazing round the village and even occasionally calling at the parsonage, to the annoyance of Brontë and of Charlotte. One day her father gave Charlotte a bundle of old love-letters—Maria Branwell's letters to him—and Charlotte was touched as she read them. 'I wish she had lived, and that I had known her.'

In July 1852 Patrick Brontë had an apoplectic seizure, and although it was brief and he recovered, at seventy-five years of age it was not something which one took lightly. Then his curate, Arthur Nicholls, very unexpectedly proposed marriage to Charlotte. Astounded, she promised to give him a reply the following day and told her father what had happened. The effect was cataclysmic, transforming her father before her eyes into a complete stranger. That young curate who had chastised the Sunday bell-ringers burst out of the frame of the half-blind old man. He could find a dozen reasons against the marriage. He would be left alone, deserted. Charlotte was delicate like her sisters and her mother, and motherhood would literally kill her. Nicholls was a Puseyite. She was gifted and famous and he was unworthy of her. His story of owning property in Ireland was all lies.

In great alarm, Charlotte assured her father that in any case she had planned to refuse Nicholls, but as she wrote later: 'If I had *loved* Mr Nicholls and had heard such epithets applied to him as were used, it would have transported me past my patience; as it was, my blood boiled with a sense of injustice, but papa worked himself into a state not to be trifled with . . .'

Brontë could neither forgive nor forget his curate's daring and he behaved coldly and meanly to Nicholls. The village knew all about the quarrel and in the beginning most people took Brontë's side although later on Nicholls, too, had his supporters. Nicholls applied to go abroad as a missionary, then withdrew his application, and finally resigned from Haworth, taking up another appointment as curate elsewhere. He still loved Charlotte and by keeping in touch with some of the villagers he continued to have news of her.

Charlotte wrote of her father in 1853 that his mind was as clear as ever and he was not infirm but he suffered from partial privation and threatened loss of sight. He was well enough to read, write and walk about, and he preached twice every Sunday, but he needed the help of a good curate and Nicholls's replacement, George De Renzy, was very little assistance. Mrs Gaskell visited Charlotte at the parsonage and noted unsympathetically the parson's pre-occupation with weapons and military matters. She did not realize that it had been a lifelong interest and that the international news, pointing as it did to a possible involvement by Britain and France in a war with Russia, was stimulating his military thoughts.

In the following months Charlotte was made aware of Nicholls's continuing devotion to her and they began to exchange letters without Brontë's knowledge. The possibility of marriage was in Charlotte's mind although she felt for Nicholls nothing approaching the shattering ardour which she had experienced as a girl towards Ellen Nussey. Still, if her father would agree to it, Charlotte was prepared to marry Nicholls, who would thus return to

Haworth, and in this spirit she broached the matter to Brontë. A
year and more had passed since that unforgettable scene over
Nicholls and the fires had died down in the old man. He still
worried that Charlotte would never be strong enough to bear a
child, but he agreed that the pair could see each other, and he
realized as keenly as his daughter that it would be a blessing to
have Nicholls back in the parish as curate.

Charlotte's engagement and marriage followed swiftly. The
ceremony was as quiet as possible with only three persons present.
Her father was not one of those, and although he had softened to
the point of promising to give her away, when the time came he
could not bear to do so, and accordingly her friend, Miss Wooler,
gave the bride away. Brontë did, however, attend the wedding
breakfast as he had promised, and 'behaved very well in his
grandiloquent manner'. There was a honeymoon in Ireland—
where Charlotte discovered that her husband did indeed own some
property—and then the Nichollses returned to the parsonage
which they were to share with Brontë, but living as separately as
possible. Nicholls was indeed a great help. 'Papa has taken no duty
since we returned—and each time I see Mr Nicholls put on gown or
surplice—I feel comforted to think that this marriage has secured
Papa good aid in his old age,' wrote Charlotte to Miss Wooler. It
was understood among all three of them that Nicholls was tied to
Haworth Parsonage so long as Patrick Brontë lived.

The next winter brought a series of heavy colds to Charlotte,
some of them the result of being caught in the rain. By January
1855 she was so ill that the doctor was called in. He diagnosed a
chill coupled with pregnancy, which accounted for her nausea. The
following three months brought no relief, only constant vomiting
with blood, and she wasted away until on 31 March she died. The
cause of death was certified as 'phthisis—duration two months'.
Her father was always convinced that the pregnancy had greatly
contributed to it, and he felt sadly vindicated in his fear that
marriage would kill her. In his bedroom he gave way to the grief
which he concealed in public. Only the servants were aware of the
depth of his sorrow. Mrs Gaskell was not told of Charlotte's illness
until it was all over. She blamed Brontë for not having given her
the chance to go to Haworth and nurse Charlotte, believing that
she might have saved her, since she had great experience in helping
women over difficult pregnancies.

Writing to Mrs Gaskell, Brontë was the formal minister: 'May we resign to the Will of the Most High. After three months of sickness, a tranquil death closed the scene—but our loss, we trust, is her gain. But why should I trouble you longer with our sorrows?' In a letter to Henry Garrs, however, brother of two former servants at the parsonage, and therefore a man more intimately connected with the Brontës than Mrs Gaskell was, Brontë struck a more human note: '. . . but my grief is so deep and lasting that I cannot dwell on my sad privation—I try to look to God, for consolation, and pray that he will give me grace, and strength equal to my day.'

He would need that strength once more in coming to terms with the picture Mrs Gaskell drew of him in her biography of Charlotte Brontë. The idea of a biography had been first proposed by Ellen Nussey in order to counter some memorial articles which were appearing in papers and periodicals. Arthur Nicholls objected vigorously to the entire notion, wanting no memorial of any kind to his late wife, but Brontë overrode him. He and Charlotte had each had their share of ambition and he enjoyed her fame, in life and in death, especially when tribute was paid to her by successful or titled men and women. He wanted his daughter splendidly memorialized and Mrs Gaskell was his choice for biographer.

He had no idea that Mrs Gaskell had always found him a strange man, unappealing in spite of his courtesies, or that she was repelled by his homiletic manner of speaking. The wife of a Unitarian minister, Mrs Gaskell was far from being in sympathy with Brontë's old-fashioned style of Evangelicalism. Brontë had certainly never bargained for being branded in her book as a man given to 'Eccentrick Movements' as he described them in a letter to Mrs Gaskell, in reference to the alleged slashing of his wife's dress, the burning of the red shoes, stuffing a hearthrug up the chimney and sawing up the backs of chairs.

Nicholls also considered he had fared badly at Mrs Gaskell's hands, and the villagers of Haworth resented being pictured as a bunch of barbarians. They found an original explanation for Mrs Gaskell's lack of understanding of Haworth—what could you expect from a woman who lived in Lancashire? Lady Scott read the biography and went straight to her lawyers who threatened a libel suit and Mrs Gaskell had to print an apology in *The Times*.

It was a macabre epilogue to the Brontë saga—the old man who had outlived his family and friends sharing a home with Nicholls, who was morbidly insistent that Currer Bell should be forgotten and only Charlotte Nicholls remembered. Brontë was rarely strong enough to go outside the house now, although people visited him on parish business and he even conducted christenings there. In November 1860 Mrs Gaskell and her daughter Meta went to see him. He received them in bed, immaculately groomed. 'He is touchingly softened by illness; but still talks in his pompous way, and mingles moral remarks and somewhat stale sentiments with his conversation on ordinary subjects. Mr Nicholls seems to keep him rather *in terrorem. He* is more unpopular in the village than ever; and seems to have even a greater aversion than formerly to any stranger visiting his wife's grave . . .' wrote Mrs Gaskell.

Brontë was ill with the familiar bronchitis and dyspepsia throughout the winter of 1860–61. He was nursed by faithful Martha Brown, a young woman who was later to say that she had always been treated as one of the family and that Mr Brontë was one of the kindest men she knew. Patrick Brontë died on 7 June 1861, with Nicholls and Martha Brown at his bedside. He was eighty-four.

For some time the old churchyard at Haworth had been closed to burials but by a special dispensation from the Secretary of State the Rev. Patrick Brontë was buried with his family in the vault. Great numbers attended the funeral. The church was crowded and all the Haworth shops closed. The Vicar of Bradford read the service, eight other clergymen officiated and Nicholls was the chief mourner. Whatever had been Mrs Gaskell's impression of Patrick Brontë, Haworth and its surrounding district had known him well as a man who involved himself in their affairs and had for more than four decades worked hard on their behalf. His parishioners did not hesitate to pay him their last respects.

The Trustees of Haworth later asserted their ancient right to choose Brontë's successor and they refused point-blank to have Arthur Nicholls. Nicholls returned to Ireland, taking with him Patrick Brontë's last dog, Plato, so that the parson's companion was assured of a good home. Some time afterwards Nicholls resigned from the Church, took up farming and married again. He remained friendly with Martha Brown, who often visited the farm, and he acted as executor of her Will.

Important changes were made in Haworth. It became a rectory

in its own right, independent of the Vicar of Bradford. The parsonage was enlarged and the old church pulled down to make way for a new one. Care was taken that the old graves, including the Brontë tomb, were left undisturbed, and they were covered with a thick protective layer of concrete.

D

5

The Rev.
John Mitford
Parson and Man of Letters
1781-1859

A few early Victorian country parsons had more in common with worldly, rational eighteenth-century parsons than with the earnest members of the Evangelical movements, and such a one was certainly the Rev. John Mitford, who was as much if not more at home in London literary circles as in the splendid arboretum he planted round his parsonage at Benhall in Suffolk. He enjoyed travelling, collected classical antiquities and was a journalist and editor of note. His personal life was somewhat irregular, and it was a matter of general comment that he was not ideally suited for a career in the Church. Charles Lamb, for instance, called him 'a pleasant layman spoiled'. Very soon after his ordination Mitford was appointed to two clerical livings and he remained to the end of his days rector of Benhall and of Stratford St Andrews, Suffolk; and although his cynical remarks frequently brought him into conflict with his bishop, his conduct was never so outrageous as to suggest he should be compelled to resign the livings.

In matters of money, for example, he was completely scrupulous and he performed his duties in Suffolk every whit as competently as the general run of parsons around him. The serious charges laid rather nonchalantly, in some modern quarters, of possibly having had dealings with 'his Satanic majesty' are unfounded and based if on anything either upon a misreading of the word 'Satanist' as used in the early nineteenth century or upon a modern interpretation of the word 'wicked'.

John Mitford was born in Richmond, Surrey, on 13 August 1781, the elder son of John Mitford, who was a naval commander engaged in the China trade of the East India Company. Mitford was educated at Tonbridge Grammar School and at Oriel College, Oxford, where one of his friends was Reginald Heber, the future bishop. Both young men were rivals in university poetry competitions. After Oxford there is a gap in Mitford's life of five or six years when nothing is known, although we may reasonably infer that he travelled in Europe on money inherited from his father who had died in 1806. It was apparently during that period that he started to collect classical coins and antiquities. He returned to England at the age of twenty-seven, ready to take up any pleasant and remunerative profession which would allow full rein to his tastes and talents as a writer and classical scholar.

Accordingly in 1808 he took Holy Orders in much the same spirit as a man after the Gladstonian reforms of the 1870s might have sat the examinations for the higher civil service, in the entirely reasonable expectation that he would have enough leisure to write novels or to pursue a favourite hobby. Mitford was ordained in 1809 and became a curate at Kelsale near Saxmundham in Suffolk. All novice clergymen in similar situations looked automatically to influential friends and relations for assistance in getting a good living and Mitford was no exception. He happened to have an important though distant relative, Baron Redesdale, a judge and member of Parliament who in 1802 had been appointed Lord Chancellor of Ireland. The Rev. John Mitford was innocently proud of the Mitford connection and in a book entitled *Illustrations of Literature* published some years later he listed the four main branches of the Mitford family—first, Bertram Mitford, of Mitford Castle; second, himself in Suffolk; third, William Mitford of Pittshill, Sussex; and fourth, Lord Redesdale.

Lord Redesdale did indeed help his kinsman by having him appointed in 1810 to the crown living of Benhall, some five miles or so south of Kelsale. As this was a well-paid living, Mitford could afford to engage a curate which freed him for work on his literary endeavours. In 1815 Mitford was appointed also to Weston St Peter's, near Benhall, and in 1817 to Stratford St Andrew. Weston St Peter's and Stratford St Andrew were united in 1824. Both were crown livings, and we may see the hand of Lord Redesdale in Mitford's additional appointment.

Meanwhile, in 1811, Mitford published a collection of verse,

Agnes, the Indian Captive, and other Poems. This met with some success and Mitford was encouraged to complete a scholarly edition of the poems of Thomas Gray with notes and a memoir, and it was this second book which established his reputation as a professional critic and journalist. The rights were then purchased by another publisher who brought out a second edition in two volumes, paying Mitford the handsome sum of five hundred pounds. Once known as a Gray specialist, Mitford became the recipient of a stream of letters and details about the poet, and these permitted him to issue new editions of Gray's works, with emendations, at various intervals up to 1852, to his own literary and financial benefit.

Mitford discovered that country life had many compensations provided that he could combine it with regular visits to London. He adored his country garden and had an especial passion for trees. Because the existing vicarage at Benhall dissatisfied him he built a new one, using that opportunity to exchange and consolidate the glebe land which he used for his arboretum.[1] By the time he died he had constructed the finest arboretum in Suffolk specializing in British and European trees and shrubs.

The Rev. John Mitford was no scholarly recluse ignorant of the charms of woman, and he had an instant eye for a pretty girl. On 21 October 1814 he married Augusta Boodle, second daughter of Edward Boodle of Brook Street, Grosvenor Square. It is possible that she was related to the Boodle of Boodle's Club in St James's Street, an area which Mitford knew well as a result of attending Samuel Rogers's famous breakfast parties in St James's Place. The wedding took place at St George's, Hanover Square, and the bridal pair went to Benhall. Almost exactly nine months later, on 21 July 1815, a son, Robert Henry, was born at the vicarage and the moment that mother and babe were fit to travel Mrs Mitford took her son and left the parsonage and her husband, never to return. Presumably she went to London, for years later we find Robert Mitford in Hampstead, married to the niece of a Somerset vicar, and his mother living with them both. She outlived her husband by over twenty years.

No reasons for the break-up of the marriage were ever given and neither party spoke of it publicly. Mitford never mentioned his wife after she left him and his London friends considerately forbore to cross-examine him about her. Nor did he mention her in his Will. He mentioned his son in the Will: 'I give and bequeath to my son

Robert Henry Mitford the Picture of my father and of his first wife painted on glass in china as a mark of my affection, he having been already amply provided for in the world.'

Another mystery in Mitford's private life concerned a village girl, Eliza, whom Mitford took under his protection. For a short time he sent her (she being then about twelve years old) to stay with his friends, Mr and Mrs Jesse, and in an undated letter Mitford wrote: 'Ah, what a debt of gratitude I owe to Mrs Jesse and you, for there is no human being I regard as I do Eliza, whom I took out of the fields keeping cows, and for whom I mean to provide when I am no more.' There were those in Benhall village who declared that parson was doing more for the girl than mere compassion demanded, but the Jesses asked no questions and took her in as if she were a blood relation of their friend. It is clear from references in other letters sent to Jesse and included in *Sylvanus Redivivus*, written by Jesse's literary daughter, Mrs C. M. Houston, that Eliza lived at the rectory enjoying the status of an adopted niece or daughter of the vicar. Whatever Mitford had planned to do about her future, he either changed his mind or made sure about it in his lifetime, for there was no mention of her in his Will, dated 1853.

Possibly a clue to the story of Eliza and also to his unsuccessful marriage lay in his turbulent nature. Gossips in the literary and rather raffish social circles in which Mitford moved in London talked knowingly of 'the Mitford blood'. He once exclaimed in a deeply troubled manner to Mrs Houston: 'Will the God who made us what we are: who cursed us with evil instincts and strong passions, punish us because we were unable to resist their promptings?'

Two other Mitfords, contemporaries of his, and also well known in literary circles, had strong passions which they did not resist. One was Dr Mitford (he had changed his name from Midford), the sponging, gambling father of an adoring and successful daughter, Mary Russell Mitford; and the other was John Mitford, an ex-sailor and a cousin of the Rev. John Mitford, and almost exactly his age. The secular John Mitford was with good reason often dubbed 'rascally'. He wrote poetry and magazine pieces under the pseudonym of Alfred Burton, and Lord Redesdale tried to help him, but without much success. That John Mitford became a penniless alcoholic and died at the age of forty-nine.

Intermittently during the Rev. John Mitford's life there were rumours about indiscretions or worse which he had committed as a young man before entering the Church. His enemies seized upon these nebulous accusations, but he had many loyal friends who refused to pay attention to them, and from this distance of time it is impossible to know what substance if any there was in them. Mitford rented modest lodgings in Sloane Street where he lived part of the week when his literary engagements demanded it, leaving his curate to mind the parishes. From first to last Benhall was Mitford's real home and centre, his London rooms being no more than a convenient pied-à-terre although he retained them permanently.

He was not the kind of man to suffer fools gladly and often found Church organizational meetings remarkably tedious. Complaining once to Jesse about a visitation from a rural Dean he broke out into rueful doggerel:

> I'd give some pence from out my poke
> To be strolling with you in the park at Stoke;
> But I should like best of all to see
> The foolish virgins one-two-three
> For I'd sooner talk to those silly queens
> Than be bothered to death with rural Deans.

His London circle was wide. He knew Charles Lamb fairly well and the latter helped him with negotiations about the purchase and transportation of porcelain jars from China, a slow and complicated business. Mitford's most famous London friend was Samuel Rogers, the banker-poet-literary patron, and it was Rogers who introduced Mitford to Edward Jesse, Surveyor of Royal Parks, telling Jesse that Mitford, too, had a great affection for old trees. Rogers added: 'Poor fellow! His going into the church was a great mistake. He is no more fit to be a parson than I am to be the Angel Gabriel.'

Edward Jesse thought that Mitford was everything which Rogers had promised, and more. He was delighted by the parson's extensive learning, wit and humour, and his knowledge of trees and shrubs, and Mitford soon became a close friend of the Jesse family. Mrs Houston said that her parents liked Mitford especially for his 'kindness of heart'. She wrote: 'The fact that he came of gentle blood was evident both in his words and manner', and she quoted in support of that comment a letter from Mitford in which he refused an invitation to stay with the Jesses—'. . . And yet I like your house and home better than any others. It is quiet and gentle-manlike, two things indispensable to my comfort. I wish I were with you, far from this, for I am diabolically hipped here: [i.e. at Benhall] and to improve my temper I lost a turtle-dinner today because I had no evening dress clothes.'

Another of Mitford's letters to Jesse shows the kind of life the parson led at Benhall and also says something about his attitude towards the Church:

I was so influenza'd when your letter came that I thought of nothing but flannel stockings, warming pans and seidlitz powders. All this came of going to Church. Had I not gone to church I had not caught my cold. Had I not, on coming home, ate a spare rib of pork, my cold would not have been so bad. Now we have a fall of snow, the heaviest fall, in the space of time of its coming over, ever known. The same night it was a foot deep on the level. I came home covered with white things like feathers, looking like a Canada goose. The only comfort is I am well supplied with teal and woodcock. The snipe are over in shoals, and the Bishop of Norwich is after them.

Mitford spent much of his time inspecting stately homes all over England, sometimes in the company of Edward Jesse, and often in the company of Samuel Rogers who had the entrée into almost every famous country house. Mitford very methodically listed their best paintings, most unusual books, finest shrubs and trees, or any other interesting details, in his commonplace book.[2] He also enjoyed visiting churches and carefully noted memorials of literary or historical persons associated with the church, accumulating data, one imagines, for future periodical articles. He waxed heavily romantic over Anne Boleyn, a lady for whom he had conceived a special interest after staying with the Jesses when they were living in the Surveyor's apartments at Hampton Court Palace, and was enchanted by Hever Castle. A good part of his excitement arose from being able to inspect Anne Boleyn's bedroom—'. . . the room Anne Boleyn slept in—her bed—her chairs—her toilette—her little turret staircase. Oh, what a charming, thought-suggesting thing it was!', he confided to his commonplace book. We may be sure that the thoughts suggested were not those commonly associated with a country parson!

As a literary man the Rev. John Mitford will be remembered as the influential editor of the *Gentleman's Magazine* from January 1834 until December 1850. He wrote almost every leading article during that period in addition to most of the book reviews. Under his guidance the magazine became much more scholarly and far-ranging than before, and he began the practice of a regular 'Retrospective Review' of past English literary figures. Mitford did not limit himself to the *Gentleman's Magazine* but contributed to other periodicals and was a successful editor of many of the Aldine editions of English poets, some in collaboration with his friend, the Rev. Alexander Dyce. Dyce was another literary parson who seemed miles removed from the conventional cleric. Samuel Rogers's nephew knew both Mitford and Dyce well and gave it as his opinion that they were both 'very little of clergymen'. Dyce indeed resigned his livings to devote himself entirely to writing and to literary journalism.

When not writing his editorials and reviews for the *Gentleman's Magazine* or editing more books, Mitford indulged in his hobby of beautifying Benhall Vicarage. Little of that seeped into the consciousness of his parishioners who would have been amazed to know that in London the parsonage was frequently described as 'the tasteful residence of the accomplished Rev. John Mitford'. Indeed, until well into the twentieth century Mitford was apparently remembered in his parish only as 'the wicked old parson who haunts Mitford's Lane', the 'wickedness' being unspecified.

Compared with the sophistication of London, Suffolk was limited and depressing although Mitford usually had a very full social diary and was constantly dining with Suffolk squires. He would have enjoyed Sydney Smith's quip that heaven, to him, was eating fois gras to the sound of trumpets. Unfortunately, although the table fare and the wines were usually excellent the conversation was less so and Mitford once described his Suffolk life as a black, monotonous existence 'without even a well-dressed lady to stimulate it to a momentary appearance of satisfaction'. Periodically Mitford yielded to fits of gloom but, lacking a stable private income and with tastes above his literary earnings, he could not afford to resign his benefices, and after all there were compensations, particularly in the summer when the garden bloomed so abundantly and there was boating on the Stour and the Orwell. Above all, in the summer there was cricket, a game which Mitford regarded with the vision of an artist and the reverence of a disciple. He believed that games and pastimes were part of the social history of a nation and should be described as seriously as any other aspect of a nation's cultural background. He expanded this theme in his review of C. C. Clarke's book, *The Young Cricketer's Tutor*,[3] transforming the article into a monograph on cricket.

He traced the origins of the game to the eighteenth century, citing as his authority an early rustic song, but he also quoted a Swiss gentleman who alleged that the game came from Iceland where the inhabitants played a rough and tumble version called 'club and ball'. He described the teams of Hambledon under the patronage of the Duke of Dorset and Sir Thomas Mann—'The down of Broad Halfpenny was the arena of their glory.' He set forth the names of the players like a roll of honour. He described Tom Suetor as a batsman with 'the eye of an eagle, and a giant's paw; and when he rushed in to meet the ball, his stroke was certain, decisive and destructive. Off went the ball, as if fired from a gun.' Some of his cricketing stalwarts sounded more like Greek heroes than mortal men. There was stocky Noah Mann of Sussex who once hit a ball so firmly that he scored ten runs! There was the bowler, David Harris:

> Lord F. Beauclerk has been heard to say, that Harris's bowling was one of the grandest sights in the universe. Like the Pantheon, in Akenside's Hymn, it was 'simply and severely great'. Harris was terribly afflicted with the gout: it was at length difficult for him to stand; a great armchair was therefore always brought into the field, and after the delivery of the ball, the hero sat down in his own calm and simple grandeur, and reposed.

Mitford deprecated the modern fad of playing in white trousers, fearing that the trousers might get in the way of the ball and for that reason he advocated playing in breeches and stockings.

Parson Mitford was too impatient a man to become a fishing enthusiast although his friend Jesse had a passion for angling and wanted Mitford to share it. The parson tried to explain his point of view: '. . . I should like it extremely if my life were 450 years in extension, and if some very pretty girls would sing to me all the

time; without this it has always appeared to me rather dull.'
As the parson became increasingly knowledgeable about Thomas
Gray, so he came to admire the breadth of the poet's interests and
learning, and to aspire to a similar breadth himself. One of his
most notable 'outings', as he liked to call them, was in the company
of Dyce and Jesse to Stoke Poges. Mitford had an especial vener-
ation for Stoke because of the Gray association. He was fairly
widely known by this time as an expert on Greek and Roman
classics, was also well read in Italian, French and German literature, and appreciated good painting, exhibiting a preference for the
Italian school. His Benhall base allowed him to pursue his outdoor
hobbies of landscape gardening, ornithology and botany. Snow-
covered woods and gardens had the unexpected merit of revealing
the footprints of birds and animals, leading him to another branch
of nature study. 'Do you know the different footprints of a stoat
and a weasel?' he wrote to Jesse. 'Because I do. You see what snow
lessons I am taking. I shall be a second Gilbert White.'

He continued his double life as both country parson (who wrote
the sermons and delivered them in church but left most of the
remainder of his parish work to his curate) and hard-working
literary editor. In 1859, while walking in the street in London, he
suffered a stroke which left one leg entirely paralysed although his
mind remained fairly clear. He was in his late seventies and realized
the seriousness of his condition. Mrs Houston, having heard of his
accident, visited him at the Sloane Street lodgings, entering his
rooms for the very first time in all their years of friendship. She
wrote:

It was on the second floor, small and low-pitched, with shabby
well-worn furniture. It was sad to see in such surroundings the
man whose delight it had ever been to live among trees and
flowers. I found my old friend greatly altered, confusing me with
someone else; nevertheless, before his departure for Benhall I
made frequent pilgrimages up those narrow stairs which led to
the small comfortless room, and a sadder close to the life of a
brilliant scholar could not be well imagined.

He had never attempted to conceal his want of religion, and
when, in a confused manner, he first spoke to me on the subject,
I was startled by the terror of the unknown future which his
words disclosed.

It was obvious that Mitford could not look after himself alone in London so arrangements were made to have him taken back to Benhall. He died soon afterwards and was buried in Stratford churchyard.

His collection of coins and antiquities was auctioned at Sotheby's and fetched rather more than £1,000. His library, which was interesting because many of his books were annotated by the authors, fetched just under £3,000 and his own manuscripts went for a little more than £800. His estate in the probate was valued as 'under £5,000'. He left everything to his friend and executor, John Mitford Ling, surgeon, of Saxmundham, and then to Ling's children. If Ling had no children and predeceased Mitford, then the estate went to the other executor, Joseph Edward Bury, agent, of Diss. It was a very straightforward Will, revealing no secrets, possibly because by that time there were no secrets to reveal.

So why does his memory linger on as the 'wicked parson'? His literary works were eminently respectable. In addition to the volumes on Gray and to the books in the Aldine Poets series— Spenser, Milton, Dryden, Butler, Prior, Swift, Young, Parnell, Goldsmith and Falconer, all edited with memoirs and notes—he wrote a short life of Milton as a preface to a collected edition, and he edited the Latin poems of Vincent Bourne with memoir and notes. He selected some 'Sacred Specimens from English Poets' with a prefatory poem of his own composition which Lamb praised. He edited a two-volume edition of the correspondence of Walpole and Mason, and he also published an edition of letters exchanged between Gray and Mason. Only three years before his death, in 1856, he published an article, 'Cursory Notes in various passages in Beaumont and Fletcher as edited by the Rev. A. Dyce'. In the year of his death there appeared a collected volume of his best poetry, entitled *Miscellaneous Poems*, and when he died another book was in the press, *Passages of Scripture, illustrated by Specimens from the Works of the Old Masters of Painting.*

The Rev. John Mitford was a prime example of the scholarly parson. His lack of religious conviction in no way interfered with the overall supervision of his parish responsibilities. He belonged to the early part of the century when the country village was a microcosm of the State, containing parson, farmers and labourers, all presided over by the squire. So long as parson made sure that the 'parsoning' was actually performed, either personally or by his curates, he could, simply by being parson, reasonably rely upon the loyalty of his parishioners just as on the broader scene England itself remained on the whole comfortably loyal to the Established Church.

William Addison in *The English Country Parson* referred to Mitford as 'this mysterious man' and suggested that no parish clerk could have kept *him* in order. He hinted that Mitford might have had dealings with 'his Satanic Majesty', an idea which was mentioned in *The Country Priest in English History* by Dr A. Tindal Hart:

> The tradition of the country priest who was in league with the Devil and could cast the evil eye, has persisted into modern times. R. D. Blackmore drew such a character, in the person of Parson Chowne, who played a prominent part in his 'Maid of Sker'. John Mitford, the poet, writer, collector and landscape gardener, who was Vicar of Benhall & Rector of Stratford St Andrew in Suffolk for forty-nine years during the first half of the nineteenth century, enjoyed a similar reputation.

In that paragraph, Dr Hart linked Mitford with the Rev. John Froude of Knowstone, Devonshire, and with the Rev. C. F. Bampfyled, known as 'the Devil of Dunkerton', who was once described by a fellow cleric as 'the worst man in the West of England'.

It is an intriguing theory, and in fairness to Mitford we might delve a little more deeply to discover how much is fact and how much conjecture. A glance at the map shows that Mitford's two benefices were not contiguous but were separated by another church and parish, that of Farnham, and it is an interesting and possibly quite irrelevant fact that Farnham Church has an evil reputation. Built above a neolithic burial mound, the church is strangely deficient in a welcoming and loving atmosphere, and in the fourteenth century it was apparently a local centre for necromancy and the black arts. To this day its slightly isolated position on its tumulus sets it apart from its village, and it disseminates an oddly hostile feeling which some people find physically painful.

Those interested in ley lines claim that Farnham Church is on a ley line linking it with Benhall Church two or three miles away. Would that secular, worldly scholar, Mitford, have been aware of this during his forty odd years in the district? Could he indeed have found an extra source of income with which to finance his collecting instincts by officiating for a coven occasionally? Before leaping to any such conclusion, we should remember that he was always well paid for his literary work, and his livings were rich ones.

Examination of his unpublished recollections and of his editorials and articles in the *Gentleman's Magazine* suggests that he had no greater interest in witchcraft and the occult than many of his contempories, particularly the antiquarians among them. Indeed, he very strongly disapproved of one man in the Rogers circle— William Beckford, eccentric millionaire and writer, author of the Gothick romance *Vathek*—who was widely thought to possess more than a passing interest in occultism.[4] It is most unlikely that Mitford would have held that opinion of Beckford if both men had shared an interest in the occult.

There is another clue to Mitford's personality in a severe comment in one of the commonplace books on a Landor (whether Walter or Robert we do not know)—'Mr Landor is an *unsafe* man. I don't like him. *Unsafe* is the worst thing you can say of a man'.

He was certainly an inveterate collector of ribald anecdotes and pasted numerous press cuttings in his writer's notebooks, most of them concerning men who might become objects of an article or book. Other topics which interested him were sex and the clergy and he particularly liked stories which showed up the clergy in a mildly risqué fashion.

Potter, the son of the Archbishop, sd. to Warburton, 'Between you and me, Bishop, I think Mrs Warburton is with child.'

Mitford jotted down the answer of Dr Copplestone, Bishop of Llandaff, at a clerical meeting where discussion had turned on a certain large magnet in the room. Asked if he had seen it, the bishop pointed to a pretty girl making coffee and replied, 'That is the magnet'. Mitford pasted in one of his commonplace books a press cutting of a rape case at Dorking apparently solely because of the circumstance that a clergyman had slept soundly in the next room and heard nothing.

It is possible that in some quarters Mitford might have been called a 'Satanist' when a young man. Mainly as a result of his friendship with Samuel Rogers, Mitford had come to admire Radicals like Charles James Fox and Horne Tooke, men who had stood trial for their advanced political opinions in the early days of the century when sympathy with the French revolutionaries could be made to sound like treason or dealings with the Devil. Mitford probably now and again sounded like a man of advanced views, although the temper of his mind was altogether too cynical and sceptical to permit him to take any deep interest or part in politics. None the less, simply uttering views of a Radical or atheistic nature was enough at that time to have branded a man as a 'Satanist', much as such a person might have been called a 'Bolshevist' before the Second World War or a 'Trotskyite' or 'Maoist' today merely for behaving in a certain manner without necessarily subscribing to a definite philosophy. Could those have been his youthful indiscretions?

His commonplace books, which might give clues to his 'wickedness', are full of items which are little more than the stock-in-trade of a professional writer planning to write a book one day on Burke, Fox, Tooke, Pitt, Sheridan, Byron, Rogers and so on. Nothing in those books indicates that he was either a strongly political man or that he was interested in Satanism in the modern meaning of the word. There is a glimpse of his circle in his later years in the form of a scrap of doggerel written to cheer up Samuel Rogers when that man, nearing ninety, was ordered by the doctor to spend the winter in Brighton.

Happy the man, and happy he alone
Who passed the winter months at Brighthelmstone,
He who, secure within, can say
I've 'scaped from all my London friends away,
From Robinson the loud, and Dyce the gay,
And Henderson, who gives the best Tokay,
And Mitford, ever prosing about Gray,
And Sharpe, who rules all Europe like a Bey;
Now, my friends, do your worst, for I have lived today.

As he grew older he was increasingly apprehensive about a life to come and was frequently depressed. In one of the last commonplace books he copied the bleak couplet

This truth how certain—when this Life is o'er
Man dies to live—and lives to die no more.

It was a far cry from the recklessness of his ardent youth to the industry of his last years, toiling over his anthology of Bible texts and gazing with fond pride at his imported Cedars of Lebanon, flourishing in the vicarage garden. Myths often die hard, but perhaps at last 'wicked Parson Mitford' may be laid to rest.

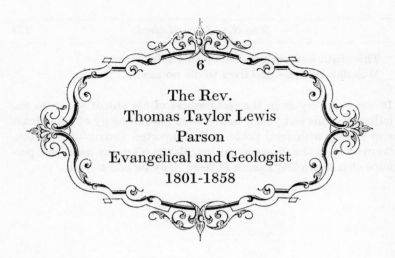

6

The Rev.
Thomas Taylor Lewis
Parson
Evangelical and Geologist
1801-1858

For some country parsons of the early nineteenth century religion
was a matter of simple faith and they lived what they professed.
God's will, inscrutable though it might sometimes be, was all-
enveloping and neither could nor should be denied. The Rev. T. T.
Lewis belonged to that generation which looked to the Bible for
revelation, and he died in the year that Darwin published his book
on evolution. Young men and women of Lewis's type were not
affected by intellectual soul-searching and the practical example
of a Christian life was more important to them than scientific or
logical argument. If Lewis's sincerity today sounds sanctimonious,
then that was the style and thinking of the Evangelicals and not a
fault of Thomas Taylor Lewis who was in every way modest,
honest and intelligent.

He was born in Ludlow where rumour has it that his father was a
successful butcher. The boy was sent to a preparatory school in
Ludlow, then to Cheam School in Surrey and finally to St John's
College, Cambridge, all obviously in preparation for moving from
the tradesman into the professional class. At Cheam Lewis became
friendly with the wealthy Penfold family. One of the boys was his
best friend, Elizabeth Penfold would become his first wife, and Mr
Penfold was to use his influence to get Lewis his first clerical
appointment. Lewis and Elizabeth Penfold fell in love when they
were both seventeen and living in Cheam. She was a serious young
woman, full of Evangelical fervour, who repressed her natural

warmth by Bible reading and prayer. It was her wish that Lewis
should enter the Church and when he went to Cambridge he studied
with the clerical profession in mind. He was a handsome young
man with a round face, clear country complexion, bright blue eyes
and light brown curly hair. The couple wrote regularly to each
other and Eliza Penfold kept a diary in which she could unburden
herself. Her father was aware of her affection for Lewis and extrac-
ted a promise that she would do nothing hasty.

Although they professed solemn religious views which suggested
that life on earth was unimportant and that they should really be
contemplating the hereafter, the couple yearned to be together in
this world. Eliza confided to her diary in 1822 how she hoped for
her father's approval to their marriage and how she worried over
Lewis's 'impatience of desire and his restlessness of uncertain
anticipation'. She longed to write to him, assuring him of her love,
but refrained because of her promise to her father.

Lewis completed his studies and proceeded to Holy Orders. He
wrote to her at length describing his ordination, and she was deeply
appreciative, both of his success and his pliancy. 'How can I
forget how near to your heart you have carried my wishes and desires,
and for me in part you gave up much of the earthly Mammon,' she
replied.

The young man was not penniless. His father had died, leaving
him £2,000, of which about £1,000 was free and clear, and an uncle
had died leaving him £4,000, of which £2,000 would be devoted to
the needs of Lewis's younger brother, Samuel. Eliza also had some
money, and could expect more from her grandparents. Accordingly,
in 1824 Lewis was emboldened to write directly to Mr Penfold
about marrying Eliza, speaking of their 'prayers of many years' to
be married. Mr Penfold made a cautious reply and spoke of the
need of a long engagement, but Lewis was grateful, and in his
response affirmed his and Eliza's love and assured Mr Penfold of
their attitude to religion:

> I can hardly think we are deceived in each other in another
> essential to true happiness, I mean Religion—not a mere enthus-
> iastic & injudicious profession of it, too often as unreasonable as
> uncharitable, but a rational conviction of apprehension of the
> truths of Christianity, cheerfully sanctioning the use though not
> abuse of this world, influencing more powerfully a grateful

heart with every motive to virtue and benevolence, and support-
it under every trial and affliction . . .[1]

Eliza shared Lewis's views and encouraged her lover with letters
exhorting the highest ideals of matrimony.

The consideration that is our most reasonable service to present
our bodies a living sacrifice holy, acceptable to God, is indeed an
awful one to many, nay to everyone, for who is there that does
not forget this great end of their being? In the giddy dance there
is not much lifting up of pure eyes towards Him who always
sees, & is too pure to behold iniquity, in feasting and revelry
there is not much lifting up of pure hands, & in the fashionable
routine of life there cannot be time for much lifting up of the
heart to the only true object of its adoration . . .

St John's College, Cambridge, produced many dedicated Anglican
ministers; the Rev. Patrick Brontë had been one such and the
Rev. Thomas Taylor Lewis was to be another. Lewis was not
interested in making a name for himself or proceeding upwards in
the Church hierarchy. He simply saw the ministry as a calling in
which he might lead a useful and happy life. Mr Penfold managed
to get him appointed curate at Aymestry in Herefordshire where,
the rector being absent, Lewis could reside in the vicarage and
behave as if he were indeed rector, the difference being that he
received only a curate's stipend of £75 a year plus surplice fees.
However, with his and Eliza's private means, it was an opportunity
to marry. He moved to Aymestry and described it glowingly to
Eliza, praising its quietness and beauty, its seclusion from the
world and the scope it offered for service to God.

At that last moment Eliza Penfold's nerve faltered. Only she
knew how much in love she was, and she trembled lest she should
deny herself married love in its physical sense because its fulfilment
might prevent her from dedicating herself to God as a true parson's
wife should. Lewis wrote her soothing letters and sent improving
biographies. Eliza tried to foresee their life together and even went
so far as to imagine how she would feel if Lewis should predecease
her. 'Let me but see my Lewis treading the steps of an Evangelist
and I shall be quite resigned to whatever God appoints.' In another
letter to him she confessed: 'Not a day passes but at its close I

find some reason for loving you better and better. Teach me dearest not to fix my attentions too much upon the passing scene tho' that scene be one of purity & love. I sadly fear I am not sufficiently grateful to our Lord & Master. I pray he will forgive me & permit me a little space of time united to you . . .'

They were married in April 1827 and were ecstatically happy. In a letter written some ten years later, when he was a widower, Lewis declared that their happiness had been too great 'for a long continuance'. When Eliza Lewis was pregnant her husband prudently decided they should go to Ludlow for the confinement, doctors being more readily available there than in Aymestry, and his mother and sister living there. Before travelling, Eliza equally prudently disposed of her personal effects to relatives and friends (her best winter shawl and silk cloak were to go to her dear mother-in-law) in a letter to be opened by Lewis in the event of her death.

The confinement was easy, a daughter, Grace Katherine, was born, and the mother was recovering with amazing speed and strength when eleven days after the birth she had 'an attack of Shivers which finally settled in her stomach and baffled all the powers of medicine'. Four days later she was dead, a victim of post-puerperal fever. Their religious faith did not fail them during that crisis. Lewis wrote to Eliza's sister: 'She died without a pain or one murmur, her looks were those of most placid resignation. I received a kiss for each of you my dear friends, received her last breath and closed her dear eyes on this world of vanity. Oh this melancholy stroke.'

The bereaved young curate certainly needed all his reserves of religious faith to see him through the following years. There had been eight years of courtship and less than two of marriage. Lewis threw himself into parish work, and took an especial interest in education. He took advantage of the government education grant made to church and chapel schools after 1833 to make sure that Aymestry had its own school, and he took great care over its classes and supervision of the teachers. He believed that pastoral work was immensely important and was soon a well-known and popular figure in the district.

A parson who constantly walks round his parish and often further afield cannot fail to notice points of interest. For some it may be scenic beauty, wild creatures, plants—for Lewis it was fossils and rock strata. That interest had been first aroused in Cambridge by the geological lectures of Professor Adam Sedgwick, famous for taking his students into the field on horseback. At Aymestry fossils appeared to lie everywhere merely for the taking. Quarry workings and railway cuttings were fruitful sources of fossils, and amateur geologists welcomed the advance of the railways because the navvies could uncover rock strata at a rate which local enthusiasts could never match. In a letter to Dr Tritton, a noted geologist, Lewis later described his methodical manner of collecting and classifying:

> I began at once very zealously to collect the fossils, which were everywhere in abundance strewed over the roads and fields, and to dispose of them in drawers, and distinguishing the row named 'Upper and lower Ludlow rocks' by the names 'grauwacke' and 'handle' (the latter being the local name); and the 'Aymestry and Wenlock limestones' by Pentamerus and coral, or nodular limestone; the former from its abounding in the Pentamerus Knightii, and the latter from its great richness in corals, and the appearance which its weakened beds assumed in this neighbourhood, even where they were considered worth working for the kilns.

Soon Lewis had a collection from most of the beds and he traced them carefully, noting the distribution of rocks in various planes and working out the geological stratification.

The hobby brought him into contact with Roderick Murchison, nearly ten years Lewis's senior, whose wide knowledge and experience in geology suggested a whole range of new ideas to Lewis. Murchison was a member of an old Highland family. He had been an officer in the Penisular War and had served with Sir John Moore at Corunna. He was bored and restless when the war ended, filling in his time with hunting while his wife urged him to find some useful occupation. The accident of sitting next to Sir Humphrey Davy at a dinner party directed Murchison into general science. He attended lectures at the Royal Institution, began performing scientific experiments in his home and gradually became involved in the newly-fashionable study of geology, which combined scientific research and travel. In 1825 he was elected a member of the Geological Society, accompanied Charles Lyell on a geological excursion to Europe in 1828, and in 1831 turned to an examination of the Herefordshire rocks following the advice of Dean Buckland.

The two men became friendly from their first meeting. Lewis took Murchison along his favourite walk, the escarpment of Yatton Hill with its splendid views, down to an old road which presented a continuous section from Lower Ludlow rock to the Old Red Sandstone. It is a moot point which man gained the more from that day. Lewis recalled it as

> . . . one of the most interesting events of my life . . . there dawned upon me the vision of the deep interest of the then comparatively unknown country, in which it was my good fortune and happiness to be dwelling, and to the true development of which I had, unknowingly, discovered the key, and made some progress.[2]

Murchison's researches during the next seven years in the Herefordshire area established his reputation as a leading geologist, and it was an open secret in the district that Lewis's earlier researches, generously and freely made available to Murchison, were of great assistance. Normally modest to an almost painful degree, Lewis nevertheless felt strongly that he should receive due public recognition for his work in geology. When Murchison sent Lewis a copy of his textbook on the Silurian system published in 1854 Lewis opened the volume eagerly, having long looked forward to the moment when he would see it in print. He examined it particularly for acknowledgements of his own assistance and it seemed to him that the notice Murchison gave to his researches was far less than he deserved. Lewis was profoundly disappointed and brooded over the apparent slight, finally deciding that he could no longer keep it to himself but must speak his mind in a letter to Murchison. Eliza Lewis—Lewis had married another Eliza in 1838—alarmed at this uncharacteristic behaviour on her husband's part, urged him to throw the letter into the fire, but Lewis persisted and sent it off.

There could be no mistake about his unhappiness. He wrote:

> . . . watching as I have the progress of the subject (i.e. the Silurian system) for the last 23 years, I cannot be ignorant of the importance of my early doings,—of the accuracy of the succession

I had observed of the rocks in the neighbourhood of Aymestry ...
and of the value of my subsequent identifications and of the richness of the illustrations I there laid before you, & the liberality
with which I continued to supply you with every thing that came
within my reach—and as you had acquiesced in the estimate
given of my labours by Dr Fitton in the *Edinburgh Review,* I
had flattered myself, as others thought, that whenever you
reproduced the Silurian System, you would record those a little
more in detail. I regret deeply that you have not done so, on
your as well as my own account; because, I feel confident, that
you have in former days, lost credit with persons who had
formed an overestimate of the assistance derived from me. You
know that I never have sought any notoriety of what I had done;
& so far from regretting the aid I gave you, it has ever been
considered by me, as one of the most fortunate events of my
life, that we met, just when we did. I can never forget the kindness I have received from you: you will believe me then that I
am very much pained to write what I have, because, if I know
you, you will be considerably affected at my disappointment ...

Murchison was indeed upset by Lewis's reaction to the book and
took pains to remedy the situation. However, it was five years
before a later, and more definitive, edition of the Silurian classic
was published, and by that time Lewis was dead. The geologist
sent Eliza Lewis a copy of the new edition, together with a heart-
felt personal note in which he acknowledged his gratitude to
Lewis and his affection for him as a friend. He drew her attention
to the Preface in which, as he said, 'I have endeavoured to do justice
to the scientific merits of your excellent and lamented husband.
Looking back as I do with lively gratification on the many happy
days we spent together long before he became attached to you—&
rejoicing in having been his warmest friend at the happy period of
his marriage, I feel assured that you will not undervalue the offering I now make.'
The Preface was indeed specific:

I cannot, however, close this Preface without reiterating the
very deep sense I entertain of the valuable assistance I received
during my earliest labours from my excellent and kind friend
the late Rev. T. T. Lewis of Aymestry, whose acquaintance with

the true order of the rocks in the environs of Ludlow, as worked out by himself was most serviceable in enabling me to establish the correct order of the Upper Silurian rocks . . .

Doubtless Eliza Lewis was gratified, but she must have reflected wryly on the irony that it came too late to assuage Lewis's hurt pride.

The book has many references to Lewis, and indeed to other country parsons, showing that the new science of geology had caught on among educated men who had the opportunity to walk about the countryside with their eyes open, and the energy and public spirit to contribute in however small a way to the main body of science. Scientific interests of various kinds were extremely popular among the clergy. The Church's boast of putting a scholar and a gentleman in every parish was in the 1840s and 1850s not so far from the mark, especially if we qualify the word 'scholar' by prefixing it with 'amateur' or 'part-time'. Lewis had many admirers among the local gentry, particularly his associates in natural history, antiquarian and geological groups, and a fellow fossil-hunter, Sir William Rouse Boughton, actually offered him the rectorship of Hopton, not far from Aymestry, where Lewis would have had the tenure which went with a rectory instead of the precarious situation of being a curate. Lewis thought about the offer and at last refused it. He wrote to his friend: 'I have a tolerable house, a very beautiful and interesting parish, in which I am pretty well known, and a more extended sphere of usefulness than I should have at Hopton, and with these I feel it is my duty to be content.'

Perhaps another reason for staying in Aymestry was the presence of Miss Elizabeth Ferguson, who lived with her father, an irascible admiral, at Yatton Court. She was an heiress in her own right and the owner of Yatton Court and of some cottages in the village. She took her responsibilities seriously as a village landlord and she felt sympathetic towards the young widower in the vicarage with his lively little daughter. Yatton Court stood in spacious grounds separated from the vicarage by a tiny stream which was spanned by a footbridge. There Lewis and Eliza Ferguson would meet of an evening. The admiral, learning at last of their friendship, exploded with rage. No daughter of his was to marry a poor curate who was no better than a jumped-up butcher's boy! To emphasize his point he ordered the servants to chop down the footbridge and he forbade Lewis to see his daughter.

But like her namesake, the first Eliza Lewis, this Eliza was a spirited and warm-hearted girl who remained steadfast to Lewis. His open and appealing nature was seen in his letters to her at this juncture:

> You know, dear love, how deeply my affections are interested; I feel as one who has never trifled with or undervalued a woman's affections . . .

His love for her was, as he said, 'as pure & full a devotion as I felt towards my first love'. The serious Evangelical tone which had characterized the younger Lewis was still very much with him.

> I do not, Eliza, think lightly of the responsibility of our relation to each other and hold it with deep gratitude to the Dispenser of all events whose hand we think we see ordering events more favourably than we could presume to pray . . .

The pair were married in 1838 and, true to his word, the admiral disinherited his daughter so far as was in his power. He married again and moved to Scotland. The Lewises began their married life in Aymestry Vicarage and when Admiral Ferguson left the district they took up residence in Yatton Court. The second Mrs Lewis encouraged her husband in his scientific hobbies and he became a corresponding friend of T. H. Huxley and of Charles Darwin and frequently attended Royal Society meetings in London.

In 1842 Lewis became vicar of Bridstow, a well deserved promotion. He continued his interest in education. Indeed, the schools at Aymestry and at Bridstow owed almost everything to his efforts and resolution. He enlarged Bridstow Vicarage and in 1848 he carried out the conveyance of land for Bridstow School, exchanging land with Guy's Hospital Governors, and financing it himself. The school was erected the following year. That done, Lewis was free to consider rebuilding the church and like so many other country parsons, he dug into his own and his wife's pockets for the work and solicited subscriptions from the neighbouring gentry.

It was not often that Lewis was in the news connected with subjects other than geology or antiquities, but an occasion arose in 1854 when a number of High Church Anglicans sought to have the traditional Ross Fair prohibited on Ascension Day. This Fair, held regularly every Thursday, had been granted to the Manor of Ross by King Stephen, and it was confirmed by Henry III who added four other fairs to the weekly one, these to be held on Ascension Day, Corpus Christi Day, St Margaret's Day and St Andrew's Day. A meeting to decide the fate of the Fair was held at the Royal Hotel in Ross, and Lewis, as a member of the Camden Society and a man well known for his knowledge of local history, addressed the meeting on the legal aspects of the matter and the history of the Fair. Discussion afterwards was heated, with supporters of the Fair insisting that to abolish the Fair smacked of Puseyism. Lewis privately would have preferred not to have a Fair on Holy Thursday, but he did not attempt to put forward his own views and ironically the meeting was swayed by the eloquence of one of Lewis's church members, Mr Wylie, who although a Presbyterian attended Lewis's church, and finally it was voted to continue to hold the Fair on Ascension Day,

Lewis had actually made his name as a local historian the previous year when he edited the *Letters of Lady Brilliana Harley* for the Camden Society. Lady Brilliana was a Roundhead who lived at Brampton Brian Castle near Bridstow during the Civil War, and she had written a number of graphic letters to her husband and to her son while the Royalists were besieging the castle. Lewis, as an Evangelical, tended to support the Puritan side, and when he found the letters, which were in the possession of Lady Frances Vernon Harcourt, he was filled with admiration for a courageous woman, as his preface to the collection showed.

The Lewises enjoyed living at Bridstow. The vicarage was an old-fashioned, square, white house with green wooden outside shutters to every window. It stood on high ground surrounded by fields, with the blue hills on the horizon and the old red sandstone Castle of Wilton on the banks of the Wye dimly seen through the elm trees. The vicarage garden was noted for fragrant roses and Cedars of Lebanon. Two ancient Lombardy poplars kept guard in front of the vicarage, a landmark for miles, and there was a graceful copper beech by the front door. The orchard was full of apple trees so old that nobody could identify them. The glebe was extensive and Lewis kept cows. The vicarage made its own butter and cheese, and brewed beer. In the winter the vicar had meat soup and dripping distributed in the village.

Eliza Lewis entered wholeheartedly into the work of a parson's wife, helping in the village and playing the harmonium in church. She and Lewis had three daughters, and of course his eldest daughter also lived with them. In the summer the family moved to Yatton Court for their holiday, travelling in style with numerous possessions and most of the vicarage servants. The children loved the spaciousness of Yatton and its grounds and Lewis had an opportunity of renewing his Aymestry associations.

He was one of the founder members of the Woolhope Naturalists' Field Club and was elected president in its second year. The club had an extensive programme of activities and the members enjoyed contributing to the general body of scientific knowledge with no thought of gain or renown beyond a possible mention in a footnote of someone else's book. Yatton Court was thrown open to the club members in the summer, where Lewis's beautifully arranged collection of stones and fossils could be examined. (After his death the collection went to the Natural History Museum in London.) Yatton Quarry was also a promising hunting ground for the naturalists.

Lewis had found a satisfying place for himself in his Herefordshire village. He did not complain that as a geologist he was known to relatively few. His work as a parson fulfilled him.

Early in 1858, at the height of his powers, both pastoral and scientific, he had a slight stroke which he made light of. He and his wife had intended to take a holiday in London, visiting museums and looking up his scientific friends, but they postponed it in view of his sudden weakness. Instead of regaining his strength in the ensuing months he became progressively weaker and more tired, and on 28 October, 1858 the Rev. T. T. Lewis died.

His death at a relatively early age shocked his many friends. The report of the Woolhope Naturalists' Field Club said that he was one of Herefordshire's 'best and most accomplished men. We may claim him one of its worthies, for although born out of the limits of the country, his life has been spent within it, and to it he was deeply attached.' An obituary appeared in the *Gentleman's Magazine* of January 1859: 'Mr Lewis was, indeed, one of those unostentatious labourers to whom science often owes much more than it acknowledges . . . Mr Lewis's name, as a scientific inquirer, will nevertheless be perpetuated in those of a certain number of the fossils of his native district which have been named after him, such as the Lingula Lewisii, the Cephalspis Lewisii, the Spirobis Lewisii, etc.' When the *Edinburgh Review* reviewed Murchison's book on the Silurian system it singled Lewis out for praise as a pioneer.

Eliza Lewis returned to live permanently at Yatton Court. The first Mrs Lewis had been buried in Aymestry and the second Mrs Lewis had a tablet to the memory of her predecessor and of their joint husband, Lewis, erected on the wall of the church behind the organ. The Lewis link with Aymestry was continued by Katherine Lewis who married a Welsh country parson, the Rev. Owen Phillips, but visited Aymestry frequently. She died in 1916 at an advanced age and her death occasioned an article in the local press which not only recalled her association with the village but also paid tribute to the life and work of her father.

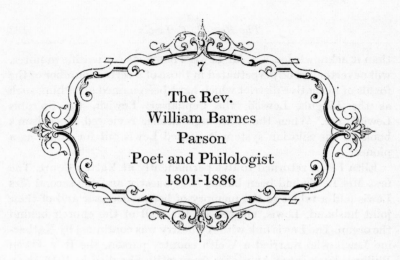

The Rev.
William Barnes
Parson
Poet and Philologist
1801-1886

When William Barnes, the Dorset poet, died in 1886 few people realized that for the last twenty-four years of his life he had been a country parson, or that as early as 1827 he had prepared himself for an eventual life in the Church. Consideration of his life and the times he lived in gives the clue to the simple piety which pervaded all his work, a piety which was installed into him very early by three people; his mother, Grace Barnes, a country girl of unusual refinement and culture; and the Rev. Thomas Henry Lane Fox and the Rev. John Henry Richman, two clergymen of wide learning with particular interests in education. Barnes amply repaid his debt to all three by the multiplicity of his activities and attainments.

He was born on a tiny farm at Rush-hay in the Vale of Blackmore on 22 February 1801, the fifth child of John and Grace Barnes, and was christened in Sturminster Newton Church on 22 March 1801.[1] Barnes folk had lived for centuries in the Vale as small yeomen farmers, but they fell on hard times after the beginning of the nineteenth century. John Barnes worked as a casual farm labourer and was glad of his Common grazing and other privileges to add to his meagre wages. Grace Barnes died when her son William was only five, but not before she had taught him to love art and beauty. He never forgot her and in many ways he might be said to have spent his life striving to be worthy of her. The orphaned Barnes children fortunately had a happy substitute home at their aunt's and uncle's farm at Pentridge, also in the

Vale, where Barnes soon outgrew his childish delicacy and raced in
the fields with his sturdy cousins. He loved the rapturous freedom
of growing up on a Dorset farm, as we can tell from his early poem,
'Rustic Childhood'—

> No city primness train'd my feet
> To strut in childhood through the street.
> But freedom let them loose to tread
> The yellow cowslip's downcast head;
> Or climb, above the twining hop
> And ivy, to the elm tree's top;
> Where southern air of blue-shy'd day
> Breath'd o'er the dairy and the may.
>   I knew you young, and love you now,
>   O shining grass, and shady bough.

He repeated the theme years later when he was writing also in
Dorset dialect:

> Wi' happy buoyish heart I vound
> The twitterin' birds a builded round
> Your high-boughed hedges, zunny woodlands.
> You gie'd me life, you gie'd me jay,
> Lwonesome woodlands, zunny woodlands,
> You gie'd me health, as in my play
> I rambled through ye, zunny woodlands.

The strong interest in folk lore and antiquities which Barnes
showed as an adult had its genesis in forbidden boyhood visits to
the cottage of Jemmy Jenkins, a male witch, who possessed over
two hundred fascinating books on magic and occultism. Barnes was
a natural artist and earned a few pennies making pen and pencil
sketches for his neighbours. He was clever with his hands and at
the age of twelve constructed a sundial. He and his friends made
all their own toys. They braided horsehair for fishing lines and
peeled withy wands for fishing rods. A stripped piece of ash became
a 'whistle-pipe' and an eel-skin provided a whip for wooden tops.
School was two miles distant at Sturminster Newton, a pleasant
town whose bridge still bears the forbidding notice that damage is
punishable by transportation. In Barnes's childhood it was the

busy capital of Blackmore Vale. Its vicar, the Rev. Thomas Henry
Lane Fox, took an especial interest in the church school, and being
wealthy—a millionaire by modern standards who spent some
£40,000 on restoring the church—he could afford his benevolent
paternalism. Barnes was a true scholar and Lane Fox infected him
with the joy of learning. By the time he left school, aged thirteen,
he had learned everything available there and he had grown to
regard books as tested and valued companions.

The boy's first paid job was copying legal documents in the office
of Lane Fox's good friend, a solicitor called Dashwood, who admired
the boy's talent for drawing and permitted him to enliven many a
conveyancing deed with Bewick-like sketches of trees and buildings.
Dashwood and Lane Fox ran the town's Evening Institute,
organizing concerts and recitals as well as lectures, and Barnes,
hungry for culture of every kind, was a regular attender.

Soon afterwards the long war came to an end with the victory of
Waterloo. There were public celebrations in Sturminster Newton
but the longed-for peace brought unexpected problems, and
Barnes's uncle was only one of the many victims of the subsequent
agricultural depression. Pentridge Farm was sold up like hundreds
up and down the Vale and close-knit families were divided, the
boys going to some big town or even away to sea, the girls going
into service. When Dashwood died Barnes decided to leave the
Vale and seek a wider fortune in a grander town; he went to
Dorchester to become an engrossing clerk to another solicitor, Mr
Coombs.

Dorchester was Sturminster writ large and Coombs proved as
indulgent towards Barnes as Dashwood had been and did not
object to Barnes earning extra money by engraving copper-plate
and woodcuts after office hours. When work was slack in the office
Barnes read Latin and Greek, hiding the books under his desk. He
shared lodgings with another young man, William Carey, and
enjoyed life in Dorchester. He liked plays especially and frequented
the Dorchester Theatre where Edmund Keen, not yet 'spotted' for
Drury Lane, had recently appeared. One day Barnes was introduced
to the Rev. John Henry Richman, vicar of Holy Trinity and St
Peter's. Richman was really a scholar who had drifted absent-
mindedly into the Church and, recognizing the quality of Barnes's
mind, he generously put his fine library at the boy's disposal, a
discerning gesture which opened up limitless opportunities for

Barnes's education. Few men illustrate better than William Barnes the infinite possibilities of self-education.

Young Barnes congratulated himself on the wisdom of his move to Dorchester and even more so on the day when he noticed a slight, elegant young girl of sixteen alight from a stage-coach. She was Julia Miles, daughter of the newly-arrived Supervisor of Excise, and Barnes knew intuitively that she was to be his future wife. He discovered her name, invited her to a concert and soon they were taking walks in the country and boating on the river.

> I turn the boat, the stream is wide
> And we are sailing with the tide
> And throwing down the oars to rest
> I sit me down by Julia's side
> And press her to my breast.

His first published poem, 'To Julia', appeared in 1820 in the *Weekly Entertainer*. Emotionally awakened by love, Barnes simply exploded into poetry and most of his letters to Julia had poems written on the reverse side of the paper. He designed woodcuts for a Dorchester guide book to get the money to publish an ambitious long poem inspired by Julia. The Miles family, however, was large and poor and the young couple were told they could be engaged, but were too young and too poor to think yet of a marriage date.

Meanwhile William Carey learned that his former schoolmaster at Mere, in Wiltshire, had left that post so Carey suggested that Barnes should go there and fill the vacant gap. As a schoolmaster Barnes ought to be able to make a living wage, enough to marry on at least. Barnes had never thought of teaching but was always ready to try something new. Julia encouraged him, rather liking the notion of being a headmaster's wife. So Barnes went to Mere, not knowing what awaited him, and needed all his starry-eyed enthusiasm for he attracted far fewer pupils than he had expected and had to open his school with ten and the hope of a further dozen the next term.

He bombarded Julia with letters and clung to her replies as his only escape from deep depression. Once she had bad news for him. Dorchester had been struck by a freak storm and the Richmans had been killed in their beds when their chimney stack crashed through the roof. In 1824 Julia's father was transferred to Nailsea and the family left Dorchester. Barnes became so discouraged that he considered closing the school and setting up in Bath as a freelance engraver. His work had been praised by Ackerman, the famous London engraver, and Barnes knew he would not be short of employment. However, just at that moment he was offered the Chantry House, near the church, as new school premises. It was a Tudor house with mullioned windows and a fine garden which won his heart. He signed the papers and kept on with his school. A pupil described him then as being of medium height, stoutly built and prematurely bald. A few years later he developed a striking resemblance to the familiar portrait of Shakespeare. He dressed rather strangely, and wore a blue flannel dressing gown for teaching. He loved that garment and even scythed the lawn in it.

It was at Mere that Barnes first decided to prepare himself for the Church. The serious impediment was his informal education and he resolved to study for university entrance in order to apply to St John's College, Cambridge, as a ten-year student. He began learning Italian, keeping his diary in that language so that he was forced to use a grammar and dictionary regularly. When he dug in the garden he noted it simply as 'Zappando'. Music was another favourite relaxation. He sang well, played the organ in church, and bullied his friends into forming a music and dancing group. He played the violin and piano well and could manage a little on the flute, which was the instrument of his good friend, Edward Fuller. Barnes and Fuller studied French together.

Barnes and Julia were married at Nailsea in 1827. In his autobiographical notes Barnes wrote, 'On a happy day—happy as the first of a most happy wedded life—I brought into it my most loveworthy and ever-beloved wife, Julia Miles.'[2] She proved not only his perfect wife but a fine school organizer, assuming duties which Barnes had previously performed, and thus freeing him for engraving, which was well paid. He spent the money on gifts to surprise her. 'At one time a silver butter knife would appear on the table, and when Julia took it up wondering, she would find engraved on the handle her own name and his entwined together.'[3]

Their first daughter, born two years later, was named Laura because Barnes was reading Petrarch at the time. In that same year he published his first book on philology. He wrote articles for the *Gentleman's Magazine* under the pen-name, 'Dilettante', and in one of those articles he asserted that the Dorset dialect was the

The Rev. T. T. Lewis

Yatton Court: a pencil drawing by Mrs Lewis

The Rev. William Barnes

true English language, all others being base corruptions. He began to experiment with poetry in the Dorset dialect, first out of interest and then from a fondness for the words and phrases which he had known since earliest childhood. The dialect poems were printed anonymously in the *Dorset County Chronicle* and were instantly successful, especially the humorous ones like 'A Bit o' Sly Courten''. There were one or two serious poems, dealing with the bald facts of Dorset poverty, like 'The Common a' took in', which touched on enclosures, and 'Two Farms in Woone'. His readers were quick to grasp the point, and when guesses were made as to the authorship of these social poems, the crusading Rev. S. G. Osborne was one of those given credit.

The serious poems, taken with two short books written later, *Humilis Domus* and *Views of Labour and Gold*, are enough to disprove E. M. Forster's criticism that Barnes ignored social problems. Indeed, some of Barnes's ideas anticipated by many years comments and opinions of John Ruskin and William Morris, although Barnes was far from being a Radical. He was a romantic conservative yearning for a pre-industrial past, a man who would have supported the 'small is beautiful' theory. He insisted that the true values of human relationships were well demonstrated in the little Dorset villages because those had remained longer than most others in England free from the contamination of the industrial revolution. His view of science was similarly unsophisticated, wedded to his love of nature and his instinctive belief in God.

Meanwhile everything was going well at Mere. The Barnes family was growing and the school prospered; and when Mrs Miles was widowed she joined the Barnes household. With two capable women helping with the school, Barnes had even more time for his inventive fancy. He wrote a school textbook on mathematics, dedicated to his neighbour, Major-General Henry Shrapnel, who was inventing a shell during his retirement. Shrapnel often lectured at the school on mathematics. Barnes spent a holiday in Wales and at once began learning the language, a step which led to changes in his views about language and the Ancient Britons. Happiness shone through his diary entries, many of them ending with the word 'Felice'.

Julia, on the other hand, complained repeatedly that her husband's genius went unrecognized. 'Mr Barnes, you are burying your talents in this poor, out of the way place.' So in 1835 they left

E

Mere and opened a school in Dorchester. Barnes hated to leave his garden. 'Gardening is one of the sweetest amusements that an unambitious man, who lives far from the din of cities, can find,' he wrote, and composed a farewell sonnet to the Chantry garden.

> No more, at breezy eve, or dewy morn,
> My gliding scythe shall shear thy mossy green:
> My busy hands shall never more adorn.
> My eyes no more may see, this peaceful scene.
>   But still, sweet spot, wherever I may be,
>   My love-led soul will wander back to thee.

He had a good muster of pupils from the first at Dorchester, and charged boarding fees ranging from twenty-two to thirty guineas a year. There was special coaching for boys wishing to enter naval and military academies. The first lesson each day was taken by the headmaster.

> From first to last I took up daily a morning hour's piece of teaching which was as good to quicken myself in learning as I thought it good for the minds of the boys. To dictate a passage on any matter of science or history, botany, mechanics or any one of the hundred other things and then to parse it and analyse every word of it and lastly to give a little lesson which the boys were to bring written notes on the following morning.

His lectures were impressive. Frederick Treves, aged seven, heard Barnes declare solemnly, 'Logic is the right use of exact reasoning,' and although he did not understand a word of it, he appropriated the entire sentence as an intellectual talisman which he used for years to great effect.[4] Barnes kept discipline by making an offending boy ashamed of his misdoing. There were no obligatory tasks and the cane was used only for bad cases of lying. Treves wrote about Barnes:

> My recollection of the poet and philologist is that of the gentlest and most kindly of men. His appearance was peculiar. He had white hair and a long white beard, and always wore knee breeches and shoes with large buckles. Out of doors he donned a curious cap and a still more curious cape, while I never saw him

without a bag over his shoulder and a stout staff. During school hours he was in the habit of pacing the room in a reverie, happily oblivious of his dull surroundings.[5]

Barnes still loved music and drama, and the Mere music teacher, Frederick Smith, followed Barnes to Dorchester where Smith and his wife opened a popular music and dancing school. Smith and Barnes, with two members of St Peter's Church orchestra, formed a group to play quartets, mainly Beethoven and Haydn. On Sunday evenings the Barnes family sang hymns round the fireside. 'Father's voice is like the big drum and mother's like the flute,' said the children.

Barnes applied to St John's College for acceptance as a ten-year student.[6] This accomplished, he could expect to gain his divinity degree in 1847 provided he spent three full terms in Cambridge during those ten years and passed the college examinations. He applied himself to every branch of study: languages (he taught himself sixty languages and dialects by the time he died), art, technology, archaeology, divinity and the classics, the last two in which he was already very well founded. His contributions—articles and woodcuts—to the *Gentleman's Magazine* were far-ranging—harmonic proportion in building, ancient battles, Roman remains in Dorchester, 'Hindoo Shasters', Phoenicians, Goths, Teutons, and of course his favourite theme that the Dorset dialect was English undefiled. Like many of his contemporaries, Barnes prided himself on finding interest and moral profit in practically every subject. No inhibitions held back those men in days when experts were not required to possess great depth of scholarship or narrow specialization.

His circle of friends was visited by death in 1838 when his friend, Mrs Edward Fuller, died of consumption, to be followed two years later by her husband, who died of the same complaint. Barnes wrote in his diary: 'This day I have lost my early, worthy, and much-loved friend,' and he composed a tender dialect poem, 'The Music o' the Dead' for Fuller, changing the name Edward to John.

When music, in a heart that's true
Do kindle up wold loves anew,
An' dim wet eyes, in feairest lights,
Do zee but inward fancy's zights;

When creepen years, wi' with'ren blights,
   'V a-took off them that wer so dear,
   How touchen 'tis if we do hear,
      The tuens o' the dead, John.

Don't tell o' zongs that be a-zung
By young chaps now, wi' sheameless tongue:
Zing me wold ditties, that would start
The maiden's years, or stir my heart
To teake in life a manly peart,—
   The wold v'ok's zongs that twolde a teale,
   An' vollow'd round their mugs o' eale,
      The music o' the dead, John.

The poem illustrated a number of characteristic Barnes features. He never aimed at a telling phrase or striking couplet. Every poem was a harmonious whole, not lending itself to brief quotation. The thought was simple and there was no embarrassment at grief over the death of a man friend publicly expressed. The rhyming scheme was complex but the words were common coin, a Wordsworthian ideal of poetry for everyone.

So successful were his dialect poems in the Dorset press that in 1844 they were published in volume form, thus reaching a wider public. He prefaced them with a long dissertation, pleading passionately for the survival and appreciation of the Dorset dialect, 'rich in humour, strong in raillery and hyperbole and altogether as fit a vehicle of rustic feeling and thought as the Doric is found in the Idylls of Theocritus.' The poems sprang, he said, from memories of Blackmore Vale and from his love of people upon whose 'sound Christian principles, kindness and harmless cheerfulness' he thought of with delight.

The poems were well received, one or two reviewers even seeing political significance in them because they spoke honestly of country workers. 'Anything which exalts a man in his own opinion as a member of an honest and honourable class ennobles him,' wrote one critic rather pompously. The Dorset gentry took Barnes up, especially Caroline Norton, the 'witty sister' of the famous 'Three Graces', who often stayed at Frampton Court, near Dorchester, where her brother, Richard Sheridan, lived.

Meanwhile great things were happening around Dorchester as the trains went thundering through to the west and Barnes, like other amateur geologists and antiquarians, watched breathlessly as the railway excavations unfolded exciting fossils and artefacts. The Dorset intelligentsia, Barnes foremost among them, established a museum and library. Three parsons, the Rev. Charles Bingham, the Rev. Osmund Fisher and the Rev. Henry Moule, helped Barnes to arrange and classify the specimens which arrived hourly. When it was rumoured that the Great Western Railway would cut through the Roman camp at Poundbury, the Dorchester museum supporters aroused local opinion and one of Barnes's friends, Charles Warne, persuaded I. K. Brunel to divert the line—an early example of outstanding success by a local pressure group.

However, all these absorbing interests of Barnes had the unfortunate result of placing heavier burdens on Julia's shoulders, so her husband applied for the vacant post of headmaster of Dorchester Grammar School, for which he was ideally suited. He was confident of being appointed, but local politics among the members of the appointments committee led to very unfair discrimination against him and he was unsuccessful. It was a public rebuff almost unique in his experience, and the measure of his unhappiness and shock was reflected in his inability to write poetry for over a year. Barnes was not a fighter, and he survived adversity only by policies of massive resignation. He was thus forced to continue with the school, and as his reputation in the region grew as poet, antiquarian, philologist and engraver as well as schoolmaster, so his pupils grew in number and he looked round for bigger premises.

The success of his dialect poems led to a demand for a collection of 'English' ones, and he put a number together. Some were totally English, while others were English variants, or translations, of Dorset originals. The latter were not very good, although the poet's great technical skill raised them well above the level of mediocrity. Many readers felt, rightly, that the translations lacked the spontaneity of the Dorset poems. It would be quite wrong none the less, to think that Barnes always thought and wrote in dialect and translated into English afterwards. His poem to Julia after her death was written in English, and the Dorset counterpart, which was an entirely new poem, was written later after the first wild edge of his grief had abated. His sermons,

although preached to dialect-speaking congregations, were always
in English.

His Micawber-like habit of waiting for something to turn up was
vindicated when Colonel Dawson Damer, father of one of his pupils
and patron of the living of Came, close to Dorchester, promised
Barnes the tiny donative living of Whitcombe, which was an ad-
junct to Came, as soon as Barnes was ordained. It carried a stipend
of only thirteen guineas a year, but it would be a start, and Barnes
could hardly wait to get his degree. In June 1847 he went to St
John's College to keep the first of his three terms; he had had to
wait until his pupils went home for the summer holidays.

At first Barnes was overwhelmed by a rich man's university but
he soon settled in and made friends. He invited people to tea. 'You
are not to laugh at my tea-party. I was not so silly as to make the
tea myself. The other man brought a tea-making thing called a
wife . . .' wrote Barnes to Julia.

Cambridge was thronged when the Queen accompanied Prince
Albert for his inauguration as Chancellor.

> I went with an impetuous wave that carried everything before
> it; and in which doctors in their red robes were pushed into
> scarecrows; and masters had their hoods torn off, and your
> unworthy admirer got his silver chain broken.

The following June he went again to Cambridge, plunging happily
into philology and studying dialects from Lapp to Manchu. In the
year when Europe smouldered with revolution, Barnes was
closeted in his ivory tower. His linguistic and social history
questions seemed answered by philology, and he summed up his
conclusions in a book on philology entitled *Anglo-Saxon Delectus*.
John Russell Smith, the publisher, bought the manuscript for five
pounds and twenty free author's copies, publishing the book for
around two shillings and sixpence. Barnes, no haggler, meekly
assented to the terms, eager to see his ideas in print. The *Athenaeum*
gave him a good notice, and in 1866 the book was reprinted. Shortly
after publication of the first edition, Barnes had his *Humilus Domus*
published, a prose counterpart to the social dialect poems. Its
subtitle spoke for itself—'Some Thoughts on the Abodes, Life, and
Social Condition of the Poor, especially in Dorset.'

The following year was his last in Cambridge; he took the exam-

inations and passed, and by 1850 had his degree. He had taken
Holy Orders earlier, in 1847, upon which the Bishop of Salisbury
had appointed him to Whitcombe. His letters to his wife during
the time he spent at Cambridge reveal very clearly his pleasure in
meeting so many 'superior minds', a stimulus for him and a change
from Dorchester, where his own was one of the 'superior minds'.
But when as an old man he reviewed that period he could find
nothing more commendable to say about it than, 'At last, in 1850,
at a more trying cost of time in residence in Cambridge than even
of money, I took my degree.'[7] The most likely explanation of these
contrasting views is that with hindsight, after his wife's death,
Barnes regretted and resented every moment which had been
spent away from her side and so his pleasant memories of Cambridge were tarnished by remorse.

His Sundays as parson at Whitcombe gave him great pleasure.
It was a tiny hamlet, hardly more than a farm and a couple of
cottages, about three miles from Dorchester. The church overlooked the farmyard, and on one occasion the ricks caught fire,
which accounted for the only occasion when the flock deserted its
shepherd, as Barnes enjoyed saying. It occurred to him that running a parish must be considerably less onerous than running a
school, and he deeply envied the rector of Came, whose snug
thatched rectory he passed twice on his journeys to and from
Whitcombe.

Barnes found larger school premises at South Street and moved
in. He had enough money to indulge himself, rare for him, by
buying two small fields at Bagber near the River Stour, his 'clotey
Stour'.[8] At last a Barnes owned land again in the Vale of Blackmore! He wrote exultantly, humorously and only half ironically:

I got two vields, an' I don't ceare
What squire mid have a bigger sheare.
My little summer-leaze do stratch
All down the hangen, to a patch
O' mead between a hedge an' rank
Ov elems, an' a river bank.'

He rented the fields out to a Vale farmer who came into Dorchester
on fair days and called at South Street with the rent. Once there
was a disagreement between landlord and tenant, arising because

the farmer had noted a line of elms along the stream and thought they would look more 'tidylike if they were pollarded, so if Mister Barnes did agree, he'd see about having it done'. Barnes gave him a quizzical glance and inquired: 'Would you let me cut off your arm, or even your thumb?' The farmer saw no analogy between men and trees and Barnes ended the matter by declaring firmly, 'God made elms, and man made pollards,' so the elms survived to grow as nature intended for a further hundred years.

That was the rosy peak of Barnes's private life. He had an adored wife, a happy family, a prospering school, a growing reputation, hobbies and interests to keep him busy for ever, and enough money to live modestly. Then his life fell apart. It became apparent that Julia's persistent tiredness was due not to overwork but to a breast cancer which the doctors said was too advanced for medical help. Her distracted husband did everything he could think of to spare her exertion and to give her pleasure. He resigned the Whitcombe living at once in order to devote his Sundays exclusively to her and he planned little excursions. That was not very easy because Barnes could not afford a carriage and had to rely on the generosity of friends to take his wife into the country.

He took Julia and the children to see the cherished places of his boyhood. He found the money to take Julia and the family to London for the Great Exhibition of 1851 and they stayed at a neat lodging house kept by a Dorchester woman. It was such fun that the money was declared well spent. They visited the British Museum, admired the stands at the Exhibition, were terrified by the rapid horse-drawn traffic of the capital and met a Dorset farmer, a giant of a man, whose comical adventures were incorporated into Barnes's rollicking dialect poem, 'John Bloom in London' —Bloom being of course a fictional name.

Doubtless Julia's strength was overtaxed by the holiday, but her days were numbered in any event, and she had happy memories to relive during the following winter. When she became too weak to go out her husband purchased painting after painting—many of them from a promising Dorset landscape artist called Thorne who was drinking himself to death—and hung them on the walls until the house in South Street glowed with country scenes. Winter finally trailed away into a cool spring and the family doggedly carried on with the school, impatiently awaiting the end of term.

Julia was growing weaker every day and was not expected to last the summer. Some months earlier Barnes had promised to preach at Frampton Church on Sunday, 20 June, and so felt obligated to go when the day came, although he hated to leave his wife. His worst fears were realized when he returned that evening; the end was only hours away and she died peacefully before noon on Midsummer's day, 1852.

Although he had known it would happen, Barnes was utterly devastated. He picked up his diary and wrote:

Oh, day of overwhelming woe! That which I greatly dreaded has come upon me. God has withdrawn from me his choicest worldly gift. Who can measure the greatness, the vastness of my loss. I am undone. Lord, have mercy upon me. My dearest Julia left me at 11.30 in the morning.

He had recommenced his habit of writing diary entries in Italian when Julia collapsed at the beginning of June, and for days after her death he simply wrote, 'Giorni d'orrore'. His daughter recounted how for ever afterwards to the day of his death he ended every entry with the word 'Giulia', 'like a sigh'.[9]

He composed a poem to stand at the head of the mourning notes which were sent out to friends. The poem was later included in a collection, altered merely by omitting the personal note of the name 'Julia'. It is significant that this most personal and heartfelt of all poems was written in standard English.

My Julia, my dearest bride,
Since thou hast left my lonely side
My life has lost its hope and zest.
The sun rolls on from east to west,
But brings no more that evening rest
Thy loving-kindness made so sweet,
And time is slow that once was fleet,
    As day by day was waning.

How can I live my lonesome days?
How can I tread my lonesome ways?
How can I take my lonesome meal?
Or how outlive the grief I feel?

Or how again look on to weal;
Or sit at rest, before the heat
Of winter fires, to miss thy feet
   When evening light is waning.

Thy voice is still I lov'd to hear,
Thy voice is lost I held so dear.
Since death unlocks thy hand from mine,
No love awaits me such as thine;
O, boon the hardest to resign!
But if we meet again at last
In heav'n, I little care how fast
   My life may now be waning.

He was depressed and apathetic in the months following his wife's death. His poetic impulse died and he turned to philology. His daughters, by this time in their twenties and late teens, encouraged visitors, and there were weekly madrigal sessions with Mr Patch, organist of St Peter's, lending his bass, and Mr Arden, the surgeon, joining with his tenor. Barnes's baritone and the girls' sopranos completed the group. His daughters persuaded him to take the boys out sketching, and Barnes purchased a box of watercolours, but it was noticeable that his paintings were as melancholy as his mood, no matter what the scene. Fate seemed determined to batter the unfortunate man. His mother-in-law, who had been a wonderful support to him, died the next winter, and Barnes was heard to murmur at her funeral, 'I sink a step lower in sadness.'

His philological studies matured in a lengthy treatise called *Philological Grammar*, a work so original and provocative that John Russell Smith would only publish it if Barnes sold the copyright outright for five pounds. Once more Barnes agreed to barbaric terms and thus in 1854 the product of years of patient reading and speculation was published. He slowly came back to life. He haunted antique shops and auctions, carting home dusty treasures which he restored according to his own recipes. He collected engravings, using his expertise, and in answer to accusations of extravagance retorted that he spent nothing on wine, tobacco or horses. Periodically he accompanied Charles Warne on visits to archaeological sites in Dorset, and took one or two holidays in the Isle of Wight. He studied church architecture, examining harmonic proportions

in colour and building, and reframed all his pictures along the same
principles.

As soon as he felt resigned to the loss of his wife he wrote a
second poem to her, in the persona of a Dorset countryman sorrow-
ing for his 'Wife a-Lost'.

> Since I noo mwore de zee your feace,
>   Up steairs or down below,
> I'll zit me in the lwonesome pleace,
>   Where flat-bough'd beech do grow:
> Below the beeches' bough, my love,
>   Where you did never come,
> An' I don't look to meet ye now,
>   As I do look at hwome.
>
> Since now bezide my dinner-bvord
>   Your voice do never sound,
> I'll eat the bit I can avword,
>   A-vield upon the ground;
> Below the darksome bough, my love,
>   Where you did never dine,
> An' I don't grieve to miss ye now,
>   As I at hwome do pine.

His dialect poems shot into popular demand at Penny Readings
as a result of the success of the Rev. Edward Nares Henning in
reading them aloud. Henning had clipped them out of the local
paper and made his own private collection. Barnes's publisher
requested a second collection, so Barnes put together what poems
he had by him and posted them to London, requesting fifteen
pounds for an edition limited to four hundred copies. The publisher
agreed, and Barnes commented ruefully that poetry was more
profitable than philology. Caroline Norton and her friend, Charles
Tenant, were delighted that the poetic worth of their Dorset
protégé was at last being recognized, and persuaded the Duchess of
Sutherland to help Barnes in London literary circles. It was considered most appropriate that Barnes, the Dorset poet, should
make his London début in the centenary year of Burns, the
Scottish poet. Accordingly Barnes began to practise reading his
poetry to audiences in preparation for the London readings. He

began at the Working Men's Institution in Dorchester, and the readings were immediately so successful that he continued them. He drew large audiences from miles around.[10]

The London visit never materialized, but Barnes did not seem to be disappointed. Perhaps he sensed that he functioned best in the womb-like security of his admiring native county, and that London might have presented awkward problems and the need for decisions. In any event, Barnes put it out of his mind and concentrated upon antiquarian studies, completing a book entitled *Britain and the Ancient Britons*, in which the Welsh language and culture played a large part. Barnes's publisher exhibited his usual doubts about the profitability of a philological book, and indeed refused to give Barnes any fee at all, beyond twenty free copies. Once more Barnes meekly agreed.

We have several glimpses of Barnes at this period through the eyes of the teenage Thomas Hardy who lived in South Street and was friendly with some of the school pupils, and especially with Barnes. Hardy developed a respect and affection for Barnes both as a father-figure and a poet. As Hardy recalled, Barnes was then robust and upright, with a bucolic complexion and an artist's darting, restless eye.

The poet's career was entering upon one of its most ironic phases, for as his reputation as poet, philologist and antiquarian spread far beyond Dorchester, so his income from schoolmastering fell. Parents refrained from sending their boys to him, concluding that with so many outside interests he must be neglecting his school. Previously his varied interests had increased the fame of his school but at this point it seemed as if his greater success made parents nervous. Soon Barnes was continually nagged by anxieties about money and unpaid bills, and had to face the sneers of tradesmen when he went out in the street. His son, William, was ready for college and Barnes was determined to make any sacrifice so that the boy could follow him to St John's College. It would certainly be a sacrifice, for quite aside from finding the money for his university expenses, Barnes would be losing an unpaid teacher when William went to Cambridge.

He looked round for regular paid work but found none. He seemed doomed to soldier on with his unprofitable school and his poorly paid public lectures, the latter covering many subjects including the agricultural depression. He evolved a highly idio-

syncratic answer to life's difficulties, the idea of 'threeness'—
'There are three divine gifts which are the elements of true happiness or wealth; the spiritual one of righteousness, the bodily one of health, and the social one of good government.' He elaborated these views in a book which was published in the same year as a very different work, Charles Darwin's *The Origin of Species*. Darwin's theory of evolution opened up new speculations some of which, agnosticism in particular, Barnes found so distressing to contemplate that he closed his eyes to science, although for twenty years he had taught various branches of science in his school, and had indeed been something of a pioneer educator in this respect. He felt comforted when Charles Tenant wrote to congratulate him on his latest book, saying he had particularly enjoyed 'the tone of Christian Philosophy which pervades your Political Economy, and I see the same delightful tone through all your Pastorals'.

However, kind words paid no bills, and each mail brought the same maddening mixture of well-meant eulogies and unpleasant dunning letters. One day Barnes exclaimed to his daughter, Laura, 'What a mockery life is. They praise me and take away my bread. They might be putting a statue to me some day when I am dead, while all I want now is leave to live.' A prophetic remark. After his death his admirers had a statue by Roscoe Mullins erected in South Street.

His highly-placed friends bestirred themselves and Lord Palmerston was persuaded to add Barnes's name to the Civil List and meantime to send thirty pounds from the Royal Bounty to help him pay immediate debts. Colonel Dawson Damer called to assure Barnes that as soon as the living of Came fell vacant it was to be his. The Barnes family already knew the parish and the rectory, for Barnes had stood in for the incumbent to enable the latter to take a holiday. On that occasion Barnes had felt it intolerable, after the rustic innocence of Came, to have to return to South Street with the classrooms empty of pupils and the school looming over his head like a cloud of trouble.

His next published book was his philological masterpiece, *TIW*, dealing with the roots of Teutonic speech and named after the god Tiw who gave his name to the Teutons. The study of word roots and stems had been engrossing Barnes for a considerable time and he had come to see social history through the medium of language development. Philology in the 1860s was not yet a respectable academic discipline, although in Oxford Max Müller was pioneering the subject with his Sanscrit studies, and Barnes was rightly flattered when some reviewers coupled his name with Müller's. Most of Barnes's readers, however, were repelled by this learned and unwieldy tome and regretted he had not written more dialect poems instead.

In 1862 the Colonel came again to give Barnes a date. In the summer he would definitely become rector of Came, and his long decade of despair and difficulty would be over. But there was to be one last turn of the screw. A pupil of Barnes came top of the annual competitive Indian Civil Service examinations, with Barnes's name alongside as his tutor, and in the very week when his last pupil left and Barnes was selling up the school he was inundated with letters from parents imploring him to coach their sons. 'When I was drowning no one offered help; now I have come to land, hands are held out to me,' remarked Barnes. He could not wait for August when he would move into Came Rectory. It was the year that Thomas Hardy, too, left Dorchester. He and Barnes remained friendly, and when Hardy returned to Dorset he lived at Max Gate, only a short walk from Came.

So in August 1862 the Dorset poet entered his domain as a country parson and remained rector of Came until his death nearly a quarter of a century later. He moved into the quaint, thatched parsonage and the tranquil pastoral life with a serene expectation which was not misplaced. Even a wonderful garden was returned to him and only his beloved Julia remained denied him. As his daughter put it, '. . . the country life he loved was his portion, and the rustic poor he sympathized with were his care'. There was time for other interests and social pursuits. His study-bedroom was on the first floor, overlooking the fruit garden, and his eagle eye surveyed the apricots and apples and asparagus plants. He had a big lawn, but scything was quite out of fashion and his children bought him a new-fangled mowing machine which he hated.

Came was a wide and scattered parish which the new rector sensibly divided into four areas for the purpose of cottage visiting. Two of his daughters were living in Italy but the other two were with him at Came and acted as his 'curates'. The daughters shared two of the areas and he took the other two, and each week they alternated. Barnes went out in all weathers without demur, and affected a highly eccentric dress, with a cassock and wide-brimmed hat, knee breeches and large ornamental buckles on his well-shod and shapely feet. In bad weather he donned a home-made poncho or else a Scotch plaid. A friend one day gave him a red Basque hat as a travel souvenir and thereafter he wore nothing but red hats. When the Basque hat disintegrated he used a red Turkish fez and, when that fell to bits, his devoted daughters made a succession of red caps. He quickly developed the artist's disregard for convention and wore exactly what he thought was sensible and convenient. He and his peculiar apparel were local bywords in Dorchester where he walked each week on market day to do his shopping and to set his watch by Dorchester's 'London time' on the town clock. Over his shoulder Barnes slung a capacious leather bag which held prayer books and sweets and dolls during his parish visits, and on Dorchester days did double duty as a shopping bag.

He quickly established his routine. After breakfast he inspected the garden, then went indoors to face the uncongenial task of answering his letters, which chore finished he could go out with a light heart for the cottage visiting which he loved best. There was no social embarrassment due to class distinction on these visits. As one of the village women told his daughter, 'There, miss, we do all o' us love the passon, that we do: he be so *plain*. Why, bless you, I don't no more mind telling o' un all my little pains and troubles than if he was my granmother.' Most afternoons Barnes worked in his study and in the evenings after supper he sat in the drawing room while his daughters sang or played to him.[11]

His postbag grew larger every year. Many letters came from strangers who had been emboldened by his strange book *TIW* to ask his opinion on the origin of a family name or their birthplaces. Barnes answered each letter to the best of his ability. Some came from Dorset people, like the one from 'an old Domestic Servant', as she signed herself. She was dusting some books which had come from a sale and happened upon his dialect poems; 'Sir, I shook hands with you in my heart, And I laughed and cried by turns. The old Home of my Youth and all my dear ones now mouldering in the grave came back to mind,' she wrote.

Some of his poems were included in anthologies and he received a seal of approval when Coventry Patmore praised him in the *North British Review* and in *Macmillan's Magazine*. Patmore and Barnes became friendly through their mutual experience as widowers, although in other respects their modes of thought were quite dissimilar. After the years of travail the mellowness of life at Came was honey to William Barnes. In addition to his clerical duties he continued the public poetry readings, going now as far afield as Hampshire and Berkshire. He had mastered the technique of public speaking and held his audiences like a polished actor. Sometimes he asked riddles. 'Tell me, my men,' he asked at a poetry reading given to the soldiers in a militia barrack room. 'Why is the Dorset militia like blue vinne'yd cheese?'[12] Blankness on every face. 'Because they'll stand fire and never run!' was the triumphant answer, to roars of laughter.

He attended the national congress of the Archaeological Institute held in Dorchester in 1865 and was the unanimous choice for its guide to the Roman and Saxon remains in the area, leading a party round Maiden Castle. He finished a history of the Anglo-Saxons in England, which John Russell Smith published at the now customary fee of twenty free copies for the author. In that book Barnes advanced the interesting theory that the ancient dykes were constructed to delimit settlements rather than serve as defences in warfare, and he insisted that the Ancient Britons had possessed a fine road system which the Romans took over and improved. That particular volume brought Barnes to the notice of Dutch scholars who began to correspond with him over the linguistic relationship between English and Fresian, and it also produced a commission from Arthur Kinglake for Barnes to write a short book on King Arthur.

The rector's circle of friends and acquaintances widened and he kept virtual open house at Came. In 1878 he published *Speechcraft*, stating his linguistic preferences boldly in the preface, or rather 'Fore-say'; '. . . the upholding of our strong old Anglo-Saxon speech, and the ready teaching of it to purely English minds by their own tongues'. Saxon words were used instead of foreign ones. Nouns became 'thing names' and adjectives were 'suchness'. The glossary gave alternative words: acoustics were 'sound-lore'; an ancester was a 'fore-elder'; a bibulous man was a 'soaksome man'; botany was 'wort-lore'; a bicycle was a 'wheel-saddle'; a photograph was a 'sun-print'; democracy became 'folk-dom'; foliate was 'leafen' and an aeronaut was an 'air-farer'. It was all difficult stuff for most people and the only journal to spare a kind word for this curious work was the *Athenaeum*. But Routledge and Kegan Paul published an edition of his poetry in the same format as a collection of Lord Tennyson's, and that pleased him. 'I win more fame than worldly gain,' he wrote very truly to his daughters in Florence.

Eminent visitors dropped in to the Rectory. Thomas Hardy was a neighbour, and he and Barnes exchanged jokes about Dorset life, each trying to outquip the other. A barrister named J. S. Udal, who had laboured for ten years on a book about Dorset folklore, met Barnes who gladly wrote a foreword for the book. There were frequent inquiries from American folklorists investigating the English origins of American folk games, and the Oxford philologist Professor Rhys congratulated Barnes on some of his conclusions with regard to the development of Celtic word forms. His daughters living with him at Came often invited house guests and the girls in Italy sent their friends over with invitations to stay, so that in his old age the rector, to his great pleasure, was surrounded by young people. He cultivated an old-fashioned flirtatiousness towards the young ladies and used to pick tiny posies to put at a guest's breakfast plate, rather as he once presented Julia with little gifts at mealtimes. He made up names for the visitors, if they were girls— 'Heartsease', or 'Gliding cypress'—and they responded by teasing him and spoiling him. Safe at last in his identity as a Dorset 'character' and protected by his ecclesiastical office, Barnes lived and worked happily. His speech, including his sermons, became almost entirely purged of foreign words and derivatives. His 'den' was lined from top to bottom with dearly loved books. His writing desk stood in the window embrasure and there he worked, often gazing out into the gardens and the fields beyond, and sometimes, as he confessed, having 'visions'. After tea he went down to join the others, sitting on the verandah facing the sunset, and dominating the conversation.

He had become a grandfather many times over. The youngest children could not reconcile their affectionate 'granny-pa' with the rector in church on Sundays 'up in a box with a white frock on, and talking so loud'. He respected their childish logic and did not disdain to adopt at least one of their words for his glossaries, 'baby-cart' instead of the current word, 'perambulator'. At Christmas the rectory, like all rectories, was a hive of activity. In addition to the usual parish charities at that season there was a special one at Came, a bequest of meat and coal left by one Hugh Millar, who had lived at Came about three hundred years before. Barnes and the girls administered this charity, as they did all the others. On

Christmas evening the sextons and choir singers from Came and Whitcombe Churches were invited with their wives and children to have supper at the rectory, and afterwards they would sing carols while the rector sat at one side, nodding proudly in time to the music.

His stamina was extraordinary even in his late seventies, as illustrated by the events of one particular Sunday in February 1881, recounted by his daughter. The day followed two weeks of atrocious weather with violent snow-storms which had stopped all trains and had forced the horse-drawn coal waggons to make their journeys across the fields instead of through the roads, which were deep in snow-drifts.

> The snow had disappeared, though the country ways were very muddy and much broken up. After his breakfast of porridge and milk, father put on his leather gaiters, and started at half-past eight for Came, to take a wedding there at nine o'clock. On his way a messenger met him and begged him to go on to Whitcombe, two miles in the opposite direction, to administer Holy Communion to a dying woman.
>
> The messenger was sent to the Rectory to tell someone to meet him at Whitcombe in an hour with the Communion plate. He married the couple at Came, and reached Whitcombe soon after ten, in time to perform the offices for the sick before the service in the church at eleven o'clock. On his return he could only take a hurried dinner, having to be at Came again before two, for a funeral service before the Evensong. So besides his walk of five or six miles to and fro, he had performed two full services, a wedding, a celebration, and a funeral service on this day!

Not bad for a man in his eightieth year!

As he grew older he turned more to philology than to poetry. Every time he finished a linguistic book he mourned like a parent whose child leaves home. 'Another work is finished to be put away or buried,' he remarked sadly after completing his *Etymological Dictionary of our Common Names of Animals*, a companion study to the immense *TIW*. Again he was prophetic. *That* book found no publisher at all, not even for the twenty free copies.

His son, William obtained his degree, was ordained and became rector of Monkton, a parish not far from Came. That was fortunate because Barnes still refused to engage a curate and William was near enough at hand to take services if the need should arise. In the summer of 1883 William took his father on a tour of Blackmore Vale, a purely nostalgic journey which the old rector loved. He needed a change, for that year had seen an unusually large number of visitors and Barnes was overtired. Thomas Hardy had brought Edmund Gosse along, and Gosse described Barnes as having 'long, thin, silky hair flowing down and mingling with a full beard and moustache almost as white as milk, a grand dome of a forehead over a long, thin, pendulous nose, not at all a handsome face, but full of intelligence, and a beauty of vigour in extreme old age'. The previous year had seen Sir Arthur Quiller-Couch at Came. He said that Barnes was like a 'Saint Mark from any number of stained glass windows' and was a man 'at once idyllic, shrewd and solid'. Both he and Gosse were struck by Barnes's air of distinction, something which Mrs Cameron had missed when she scornfully refused Tennyson's offer of Barnes as a sitter on an occasion when Barnes was visiting the Tennysons at Farringford.

The holiday in 1883 with William was the last important journey which William Barnes took. His great strength began to ebb in the autumn, although his true decline did not begin until one stormy January day in 1884. Thomas Hardy noted it precisely as January 26, for he had met Barnes in Dorchester and they had started to walk homewards together in the cold driving rain. Barnes refused to shelter at Max Gate but insisted upon pushing on to Came, where he collapsed with severe rheumatism. That ailment was no stranger to him. It was, of course, an occupational hazard for country parsons, most of whom walked everywhere and in all weathers. Barnes had long suffered from severe arthritis in his hands so that his graceful handwriting, once the delight and envy of his correspondents, had become impossible to decipher and he employed his daughters as his 'pen-hands'. Barnes was unable to leave the rectory for two months and his clerical friends established an informal rota to take his services. Early in 1885 he took his last service in Came Church and then his last one in Whitcombe Church, thus ending his ministry in the place where it had begun in 1847.

As news spread that Barnes was dying, more and more visitors arrived at the rectory, some to pay their respects and others to see him while time remained. Frank Palgrave brought his father,

Professor F. T. Palgrave, to see him and Barnes felt so honoured
that he struggled out of bed so that he could receive the Palgraves
sitting muffled up in a chair in his 'den'. The professor was greatly
impressed. 'Few in our time equal him in variety and novelty of
motive, in quality of true sweet inspiration and musical verse. None
have surpassed him in exquisite wholesomeness and unity of execu-
tion,' he wrote later for the Palgrave family journal.

It was when the Palgraves left that Barnes wrote his last poem,
'The Geate a-Vallen To'. He had always hated to hear the last
click of the garden gate as favourite guests departed, and when
special friends came he gave orders that the gate was to be left
open after they had passed through. Now in a whisper he dictated
to Laura his swansong:

> And oh! it is a touchen thing
> The loven heart must rue
> To hear behind his last farewell
> The geate a-vallen to.

Local friends dropped in and out of the rectory, bringing him
news of literary matters, of the Dorset Field Club, of the latest
moves in the possible disestablishment of the Church. They read
him the newspaper and whenever it came to news about theft or
murder the rector would murmur, 'Tut, tut', and demand something more agreeable. He had always been too gentle and diffident
a soul to look squarely at the brutalities of life. He was delighted
when the Dorchester printer gave him a first copy of his *Glossary of
the Dorset Language*, the culmination of many obsessed years. It
had begun as the appendix to his first collection of dialect poems
and it had been added to ever since. Barnes knew that it was an
important piece of work and that it would be well received, but
he also knew he was too old to see this for himself. 'Ah; just as
I am going out of the world things begin to mend,' he told
Laura.

He clung on to life through that Christmas and most of 1886.
The Bishop of Salisbury visited him, with his wife. The North-
Western Literary Society of Sioux City, Iowa, elected him an
honorary member. Barnes wrote an article opposing the currently
fashionable theory that the Ancient Britons were the lost tribes of
Israel. There was a new influx of visitors in the summer of 1886

and Gosse wrote to Coventry Patmore, 'It is curious that he is dying as picturesquely as he lived.' But even Barnes's vitality sank with the autumn leaves and his peaceful end came on 11 October 1886, so gently that Laura, dozing off in a chair by her father's bedside, was not aware of the moment of death.

His funeral was appropriately simple. A bright elm coffin on a little hand carriage was trundled from the Rectory to Came Church, and as Thomas Hardy set off by the path from his house across the fields he caught the glint of the sun on the coffin:

Thus a farewell to me he signalled on his grave-way
As with a wave of his hand.

Professor Palgrave gave an account of the burial for the Palgrave family record, describing the coffin with its white wreaths and crosses, and then the cloud of blue and violet flowers as the village children flung their bunches down when the coffin was lowered into the grave. 'No poet,' concluded Palgrave, 'was more true, more sweet, more human and spiritual at once than William Barnes.'

His contemporaries compared Barnes with Chaucer, but the Dorset poet was a Chaucer sans satire. He turned his face consistently from violence and politics.[13] Yet he was not a sundial poet recording only sunny hours; grief and poverty had their places in his verse as they did in life, but he was above all else a pastoral poet, drawing characters from life, even if he had a weakness for the most brilliantly coloured characters. His early dialect poems certainly came easily from his heart and mind. As he said, 'I wrote them so to say as if I could not help it. The writing of them was not work, but like the playing of music—the refreshment of the mind from care or irksomeness.'

Barnes's daughter and biographer rightly calls her father 'Poet and Philologist', for philology was his true passion and the dialect poems represented the artistic side of the linguistic scholar. Coventry Patmore praised Barnes for 'the faultless expression of elementary feelings and perceptions', adding that he idealized the realities of life by deliberately omitting coarse and sordid matters, but he was never sentimental. A reader looking for social content in the poetry of William Barnes will find covert expression of it. When he described social issues like land enclosures he was shrewd and humorous, but he made people think of the consequences of these agricultural changes by the way he concentrated with immense simplicity upon external images. Thomas Hardy, who may be prejudiced because of his long friendship with Barnes, but who could be relied upon to give an impartial criticism, said that Barnes was a 'lyric writer of a high order of genius'.

His popular audiences, especially the Dorset ones, demanded the humorous poems, but Barnes preferred poems like 'Woak Hill', an intricate piece modelled upon a complicated Persian metrical form called the Pearl because it contained a hidden series of rhymes in the second word of the last line of each verse, strung like pearls on a necklace. Another of his favourite pieces was 'Green', composed according to another Persian metre, called the ghazal. Barnes loved to experiment with words and metrical patterns ranging from Italian metres to Welsh bardic patterns and Anglo-Saxon alliteration. His readers and listeners may have thought their poet homely, but his was supremely the art which conceals art.

In 1883 Gerard Manley Hopkins had begun to read Barnes's poetry and was impressed by its skilful use of word adornment and by the elaborate rhyming schemes which gave such careful shape to his message that 'Nature and true art are faithful'. Hopkins continued to admire Barnes when most literary critics underestimated him, and Hopkins's own poetry, with the sprung rhythms which had a revolutionary effect on modern poetry, owed a considerable debt to William Barnes's poetry. Both men had found it necessary to invent critical terms to describe what they were each trying to achieve in poetry. Barnes wanted to revitalize language. He followed Homer in searching for the one exact epithet for his descriptions, and he believed that poetry, fastidiously written, was the highest order of language. He indicated pronunciation and stress by phonetic signs in his poems, and once said that if children were taught phonetics in school they would be relieved of much of the burden of English spelling.

Thomas Hardy mentioned Crabbe in connection with Barnes, and indeed both men were similar in being both regional poets and country parsons, but Crabbe went much further than Barnes in questioning the justice of life. To quote Geoffrey Grigson, Barnes 'was narrowed by Dorset; yet Dorset, for all its indifference, kept him safe . . .'.[14] William Barnes was almost too perfectly the Victorian gifted amateur, but in his poetry, in his school and in his rectory he was meticulously professional. Had life treated him differently, he might have become a famous engraver, an educational pioneer or a national poet, but in the final analysis, nothing could have been happier for him than that last anchorage in a country rectory.

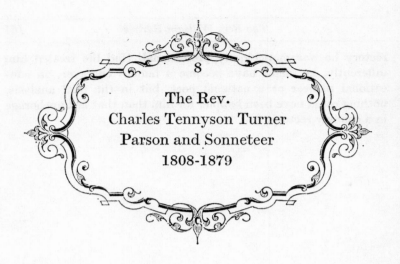

The Rev.
Charles Tennyson Turner
Parson and Sonneteer
1808-1879

Ask anyone who the poet Tennyson was and the answer is bound to be 'the Poet Laureate', yet there were three Tennyson brothers who wrote poetry; Frederick, Charles and Alfred, although only the last-named made it his avocation. Their father, the Rev. Dr George Tennyson, was a reluctant vicar of two Lincolnshire hamlets, Somersby and Bag Enderby, whose combined populations barely topped the two hundred mark. He had been propelled into the vicarage by his forceful father, a successful solicitor who married into the Lincolnshire gentry, purchased an imposing country estate and retired. The one-time lawyer unashamedly reserved his affection, pride and ultimately his fortune for his younger son, Charles, who entered Parliament and finally became a junior government minister. Such deliberate favouritism was not unnaturally a cause of distress and resentment to the elder son, George, and surely contributed to his frequent attacks of depression which he tried to remedy by heavy drinking. Apart from that weakness, the Rev. Dr George Tennyson had much to commend him. He was tall and handsome, well read, and with a leaning towards poetry. He had an attractive speaking voice which could be either impressively stern on the magistrate's bench or seductively appealing in the county drawing-room.

He married Elizabeth Fytche, a local beauty of good family, whose tender Christian faith contrasted strongly with her husband's prosaic views on religion. As the children arrived—she was relentlessly pregnant for fifteen years—a rift arose between the parents over the matter of the children's upbringing. The rector was sharp and often downright hard on the children, with the unfortunate result that his wife spoiled them all by way of making amends for their father's severity. Twelve children were born to the couple, of whom Charles Tennyson, born in 1808, was the third, and Alfred, born in 1809, was the fourth. These two boys, so close in age, remained close companions all their lives.

Although prejudiced in favour of his younger son, old Mr Tennyson was not completely deaf to his elder son's pleas for financial help, and he obtained a better living for the Rev. George Tennyson at Grimsby, a few miles away from Somersby. With his improved stipend, the rector was able to engage a curate at £120 a year and still afford to live in some style with servants, a carriage and pair, and a regular supply of excellent claret from London. The rector sent his sons to the village school and augmented that education by drilling them at home in the classics so that in due course they could pass the entrance test for Louth Grammar School, whose headmaster, the Rev. Dr Waite, was a cousin of Mrs Tennyson.

Louth was not geographically speaking far from their home but in atmosphere it was worlds away and the headmaster was authoritarian to a degree, believing discipline to be essential for the continued academic excellence of his school. The Tennyson boys found it a miserable change from their free, family-centred rectory life where they had been able to wander at will over the Lincolnshire fens, fishing, reading or scribbling poems and stories to their heart's content. Charles and Alfred were clever, as was their elder brother, Frederick, and they all did well at school.

At the age of nineteen Charles fell in love with a governess, which occurrence alarmed his parents and made them decide to send Charles and Alfred to join their brother Frederick at Cambridge. The two younger brothers entered Trinity College in 1827, a pair of country lads so shy that on the evening of their first dinner in the college hall they panicked and returned supperless to their lodgings rather than face strangers. They settled down, however, and within a year were part of a circle of brilliant students. Frederick had already made a reputation as a young man determined to go his own way no matter what the dons might say or think. All three Tennysons wrote poetry, dressed oddly and refused to bother about their future. Their father and grandfather were united in one thing at least; they despaired of the three young men. Charles and Alfred each published a volume of poetry in 1830. Charles's book was entitled *Sonnets and Fugitive Pieces* and Alfred's was *Poems, Chiefly Lyrical*. Charles's poems were attractive and conventional, and gained a kind word from Coleridge. Alfred's poems were different. They were varied in content, atmosphere, word coining and metre and took the fancy of the university although they left most of the London critics cold.

In sad contrast to his sons, who in a quirky fashion were making a name for themselves, the Rev. Dr George Tennyson was going through one of his worst periods. He had even gone abroad in the forlorn hope that he could overcome his drinking problem, but he resumed drinking soon after his return. In 1831 he caught what the doctors called 'low typhus' which was followed by a stroke from which he died on 16 March 1831. With the breadwinner removed, Mrs Tennyson turned to her father-in-law for help. Only the three older Tennyson boys were of an age to work, the others being at school, and their grandfather decreed that the three eldest should take Holy Orders.

Frederick acquiesced quite blithely. Charles had decided to be ordained in any case because his uncle, the Rev. Samuel Turner, parson and squire of Caister and Grasby, in Lincolnshire, had already named Charles as heir to the estate and to the livings. Alfred, however, refused to take Holy Orders. His life was poetry and he was not afraid of being poor.

Charles Tennyson was ordained in 1833 and through his grandfather's patronage obtained the curacy of Tealby to enable him to support himself until his uncle died. On the face of it, a curacy was a sensible step but Charles felt unhappy. He was lonely in his new life, depression and chronic neuralgia debilitated him, and the change of work and the responsibilities he had to assume at Tealby drained him of energy instead of providing a stimulus as his family had hoped. Charles was not the only Tennyson to suffer badly from nervous and emotional tension. Most of the family were subject to it in some degree or another. Alfred was morbidly sensitive. A younger brother, Edward, went mad and had to live under confinement until his death in 1890. Charles consulted a doctor for his neuralgia but the remedy was worse than the disease for the doctor prescribed opium to dull the pain. Within a short time the patient had become addicted. When Frederick visited his brother at

Tealby he returned with the gloomy report that Charles was 'making no use either of body or soul'.[1]

The curate seemed as strange in his dress as he was disordered in his thoughts. His cousins, children of his successful and wordly Uncle Charles, described him then as 'going about in a rabbit skin and looking like the dogs' meat man'. Moreover, his drug habit scandalized the neighbourhood and his unsympathetic grandfather grumbled incessantly about Charles's 'hubble-bubble method' of carrying out his parish duties, a phrase which had an inescapable association with Oriental smoking habits and possibly even with drugs. The year 1833 was a tragic one altogether for the Tennysons, darkened not only by anxiety about Charles but by profound sorrow at the death of Arthur Hallam, close friend of Alfred and fiancé of Emily Tennyson.

Fortunately things began to improve for Charles after his uncle died in 1835 and he inherited the livings. He added 'Turner' to his name, honouring his late uncle's wishes, and moved into the big house at Caister which he found too far from Grasby for his liking. Old Mr Tennyson also died in 1835 leaving the bulk of his lands and fortune, as expected, to his younger son, Charles. From that time onwards the gap between the two branches of the family widened, particularly after Charles Tennyson M.P. assumed the additional name of 'd'Eyncourt' by special licence from the king. Alfred Tennyson was left a small property at Grasby which Charles managed for him until it was sold. Charles himself received nothing because he had already been provided for by his uncle.

By a supreme effort Charles freed himself of the opium habit and became engaged to Louisa Sellwood, a charming, spirited girl, daughter of a local solicitor. It seemed an excellent match and the Sellwood and Tennyson families became very friendly. The wedding took place in May 1836, with Louisa's sister, Emily, acting as bridesmaid, and Alfred as Charles's best man. Alfred Tennyson wrote a sonnet about the wedding.

> Love lighted down between them full of glee
> And over his left shoulder laughed at thee,
> 'O happy bridesmaid, make a happy bride.'

The poem ended with the poet musing:

> And thought, 'My life is sick of single sleep;
> O happy bridesmaid, make a happy bride.'

The wedding brought Alfred and Emily together, as weddings often do, and two years later they became engaged. The happy development of their relationship contrasted sadly with the course of married life for Charles and Louisa. The responsibility of being a parson, which was heavier than being a mere curate, together with the responsibility of being a husband weighed upon Charles so heavily that his old swings of mood returned and he resorted to opium again to see him through his blackest days. No marriage could hope to survive such strains, and after battling for two or three years to free him from his addiction, Louisa Turner took refuge in a nervous breakdown and left her husband. The Sellwoods became disenchanted with the whole Tennyson family, and since by their bourgeois standards Alfred Tennyson was not making much of his life, they lost patience and, in 1848, ordered Emily to break off her engagement.

The following year Louisa was so much better that she and Charles resumed married life. Her long breakdown, for which he took the blame, gave him the strength of mind to free himself permanently from the opium habit and thereafter the Turners were a model married couple, living excessively quietly in Grasby. Meanwhile Alfred Tennyson was becoming better known in London as a poet. His poem 'The Princess' had a splendid critical and popular reception; he was granted a Civil List pension and he began work on the series of Arthurian poems. Charles visited his brother in London, reporting to the Sellwoods on his return to Lincolnshire with the advice that they should withdraw their opposition to the marriage of Emily and Alfred. Their disapproval had indeed been based chiefly upon religious grounds, and now that Alfred's recent poems indicated that he was in fact religious at heart, all obstacles were removed, and in June 1850, a few weeks prior to the publication of 'In Memoriam', Alfred and Emily were married. The acclaim with which 'In Memoriam' was greeted, coupled with the timely death of Wordsworth, made Alfred the front runner for the vacant post of Poet Laureate and it was indeed offered to him.

Of the three Tennyson poets, then, it was the youngest who had remained truest to his muse. Frederick, an ordained minister but hardly a parson, was living in Italy and writing occasional verse, and Charles was a country parson first and a poet second. The rector of Grasby limited himself to the sonnet form and wrote over 340 sonnets.

His poetry reflected his personality and his daily life in the quiet Lincolnshire village. It was a gentle existence except for one unpleasant experience in 1850 when his agent swindled him. Charles shrank from going to law to recover the money but his friends persuaded him to take legal proceedings as the amount involved was too large to let go by default, and in the end most of it was recovered, to be expended on the church and the schoolhouse. The redbrick school, situated immediately opposite the church across a narrow lane, was rebuilt in 1855.

Grasby Church is thirteenth century Gothic built of Kirton and Normanby stone, with a western tower topped by an imposing spire. It clings to the low but steep hillside and commands a wonderful sweep of the Lincolnshire fens. Charles Turner rebuilt the north aisle in 1850 and the remainder of the church in 1869. The clock tower which had four bells, one of which dated from 1500, was given two more bells by Charles in 1869 as memorials to Louisa's father and to his mother. The rector also built a new vicarage in Grasby, preferring to live in the village instead of five miles away at Caister, and he received a grant of £1,200 towards the building.

The men and women of Grasby were on the whole rough diamonds, existing on low agricultural wages, and Charles and Louisa, who had no children of their own, adopted the parish as their family. It became their pleasure as well as their charge to spend their time and money trying to improve the lot of their parishioners. The vicarage and its garden were open to everyone on village festivals and the rector recorded the simple annals of his parish year in verse rather as other parsons noted such incidents in their diaries. After the summer school feast he wrote:

The Feast is o'er—the music and the stir—
The sound of bat and ball, the mimic gun;
The lawn grows darker, and the setting sun
Has stolen the flash from off the gossamer,
And drawn the midges westward; youth's glad cry—
The smaller children's fun-exacting claims,
Their merry raids across the graver games,
Their ever-crossing paths of restless joy,
Have ceased—

When smallpox raged through the village he and his wife, his faithful unpaid 'curate', went cottage visiting to do what they could. Charles wrote a sonnet entitled 'Alice Wade versus Small-pox'.

> Thy golden hair is left—its silky mesh
> The spoiler shall not mar, whate'er he takes;
> Nor that still brilliant eye, that sleeps and wakes,
> Among the flowing sores . . .

He employed the sonnet form almost exclusively finding, as no doubt many parsons did, that the fourteen line model was peculiarly apt for the brief thoughts and fancies which struck him during the day. A busy parson must expect to have his day broken up into uneven and often unexpected lengths and, like a doctor or social worker, to be constantly on call. Not for him the luxury of sustained hours of concentrated reflection demanded by epic poetry. Within his chosen limitation Charles used whichever rhyme scheme seemed appropriate, an independence of choice which provoked the critical charge that many of his sonnets were 'very incorrect in form'. However, as his friend James Spedding, a professional civil servant who was also a well respected critic, hastened to stress, a poet had the right to feel free to follow whatever metrical arrangement seemed best. Brightness and freshness were the hallmarks of all Charles's sonnets, declared Spedding, and the remark is as true today as it was then.

The rector was a modest man who took pleasure in modest things. Birds, insects and animals were as much God's creatures as men and women. 'A Brilliant Day' was made more brilliant by watching a bee at work:

> The bee looks blithe and gay, and as she plies
> Her task, and moves and sidles round the cup
> Of this spring flower, to drink its honey up,
> Her glassy wings, like oars that dip and rise,
> Gleam momently. . . .

He watched the seasons pass, regretting the onset of winter which was always a harsh time in Lincolnshire when the blustering winds howled across the flat plains below the village. In 'The First Week in October' he described the first signs:

While, ever and anon, the ashen keys
Dropt down beside the tarnish'd hollyhocks,
The scarlet crane's-bill, and the faded stocks,—
Flung from the shuffling leafage by the breeze.
How wistfully I mark'd the year's decay,
Forecasting all the dreary wind and rain.

The Turners looked odder than ever when they did their winter rounds, Mrs Turner in her clogs and the rector in a huge coaching cape.

They were unsparing in their charities to individuals in need, and in a valiant attempt to counteract village drunkenness Charles purchased the village inn and installed a reliable man as innkeeper. It had been abundantly clear from his first months at Grasby that witchcraft was common and that Christianity held relatively little meaning for the local people, but the kindness and Christian example of the Turners gradually helped to change the religious atmosphere. The loyalty to religion, such as it was, was really a personal tribute to the rector.

Canon Rawnsley paid them a visit in the 1870s. He was taken to church for morning prayers and was surprised to find a congregation of only three, his hosts and himself, the curate reading the prayers. When the trio returned to the vicarage for breakfast there were lengthy prayers for the servants before the meal could be eaten, good for the soul but fatal for the stomach, as the Canon silently reflected when the cold cooked food was brought in. The spartan simplicity of the Turners' lives could be seen in the austere furnishings of their house. All surplus income was reserved for village needs.

The rector and his wife took holidays, however, sometimes in North Wales, sometimes in Scotland, and frequently on the Isle of Wight where they stayed at Farringford with Alfred and Emily Tennyson. Charles and Alfred were still personally close and the fact that their wives were sisters tightened the bond, although their lives were so different that they did not meet much more than once a year. The Turners greatly enjoyed the weeks on the island where they met interesting and congenial people. 'How grieved was I those social walks to lose, Those friendly hands!' wrote Charles Turner. Mrs Cameron greatly impressed him and inspired a sonnet. In 1867 the Turners visited Jersey where Charles's

delight in the tiny incident of noticing a tree reflected in miniature
on his silver watch case led him to pray:

> God of small things and great! do Thou ensure
> Thy gift of sight, till all my days are told,
> Bless all its bliss, and keep its pleasures pure!

That was an especially private prayer because at one dreadful
moment he had feared the permanent loss of his sight. There was
a blind man living in Grasby and Charles had imagined all too
keenly what a life of blindness would entail. Mercifully the threat
was only temporary and as his health improved, so did his sight.
Then he felt ashamed of his natural fears.

As he went round the district the rector saw the changes in
farming techniques as the new machines made their appearance on
the farms. They were certainly impressive.

> Flush with the pond the lurid furnace burn'd
> At eve, while smoke and vapour filled the yard;
> The gloomy winter sky was dimly starr'd.
> The fly-wheel with a mellow murmur turn'd;
> While, ever rising on its mystic stair
> In the dim light, from secret chambers borne,
> Climb'd and fell over, in the murky air.

But Charles Turner reserved his softest spot for the old world of
his boyhood which was rapidly vanishing with the march of
science.

> I love this unshorn hedgerow, in this farming age:
> The thatch and house-leek, where old Alice lives
> With her old herbal, trusting every page . . .

His attitude to his poetic muse, and indeed a clue to his personality, could be seen in the motto he had chosen for his 1830
collection—'The sonnet's humble plot of ground'—and he remained
a tiller of the humble plot. Occasionally some episode from the
world outside Lincolnshire thrust itself forward. After reading in
the paper that the organ in the great church at Strasbourg had
been bombed in the Franco-Prussian War, he wrote:

The Rev. Francis Kilvert

Kilvert's vicarage at Bredwardine

The Rev. Sydney Godolphin Osborne

O thunderbolt of war! what did'st thou there?
Methinks it suited with thy function more
To burst the war-drum, or explode the store,
Or spurn their eagles into drift, than bear
Down on this ark of praise with hostile force . . .

It was noticeable that whenever he wrote about war and politics
his vocabulary became formal and classical but that when he
celebrated the country life he knew and loved, his style was altogether simpler. When occasion demanded he was capable of
sardonic irony:

He was a little heir of shame—his birth
Announced by peevish voices, and his death
Welcomed by all; he staid not long on earth
Nor vex'd them long with his fast-fleeting breath . . .

That was the comment of a man who had love and compassion for
all.

He scornfully repudiated the suggestion that any churches which
were half empty week after week should, because of that fact, be
turned into museums, and employed unusual sarcasm to make his
point:

Apes, mummies, minerals are scatter'd o'er
The nave; new wines and patents meet our eyes;
Young prigs and gnostic maidens pace the floor;
The altar's self is mask'd with butterflies!

He was however not totally opposed to technology which he
regarded as the key to England's greatness—a greatness he did not
doubt any more than the Poet Laureate did.

Full long ere Europe knew the iron road,
The 'Railway' thunder'd on our English soil;
There was a trembling in the sea-girt isle,
Where 'Hercules' or mighty 'Samson' trod.
Heavy and swift . . .

He approved of railways because they were liberators, making
people mobile, taking them to visit distant relatives and showing

F

them new places. They were an exciting force and workers in the
Lincolnshire fields would pause from their labours to look up and
wave when the train rushed by.

The rector was opposed to hunting and had no sympathy for the
squire who lived for the sport.

> To-day will be the first meet of the hounds;
> The wind blows south, and, in the early dark,
> The squire sits gazing o'er his dusky park,
> While, in his ears, the horn already sounds;
> Yon furzy levels harbour all his hopes,
> No other field of glory ranks with them . . .

Charles Turner's favourite horse was no hunter but dear old Maggie
with a white star on her forehead, grazing with 'mild, progressive
motion' in the rectory meadow.

For such a gentle person, Charles Turner took a stern unbending
view of books like the *Life of Jesus* by Strauss ('a book of pleasant
phrase, but narrow span of thought') and the notorious *Essays
and Reviews*:

> O, ye winds!
> Blow them far off from all unstable minds,
> And the foolish grasping hands of youth!

was his cry.

> Ye dews of heaven! be pleased to rot them where they fall
> Lest loitering boys their fancies should abuse,
> And they get harm by chance, that cannot choose . . .

Nor did he waste any time with the new 'Higher Criticism' of the
gospels, which in his view merely substituted 'a dreamy, hollow,
unsubstantial creed' for a sound Christian faith. He was afraid that
those tendencies merely devitalized the true celebrations of
Christian festivals throughout the year and even placed some
clergymen in an invidious position. Like his brother, Alfred, he had
no sympathy for the High Church clergyman, the 'priest-philo-
sopher', ignorant of the ideas and needs of 'poor Hodge', the country
labourer:

What does the white-robed hireling, simpering thus
At his poor neighbour's spiritual desire?
Of all that honest faith incredulous
The tainted vestal mocks the holy fire!

Although a number of his sonnets dealt with classical and historical subjects, Charles Turner seemed most at ease when paying tribute to the minutiae of daily life. Who else would write a comforting sonnet to a rocking horse which the children had outgrown?

And thou must be content with casual look
From those, who sought thee once with earnest will,
And gallop'd thee with all their might and skill.

In 'The Process of Composition' he described how he set about writing a sonnet, a description confirmed by his family. Some half formulated thought would drift into his mind, there to incubate until it grew and became precise. That was half the battle, but still only half. He had then to arrange those ideas into 'a well-balanced scheme of words and numbers, a consistent aim'. If he felt pleased with this half-written poem he would continue to work on it during the rest of the day and expect to have it completed by evening. Many poems of this nature sprang from watching birds and animals during his parish walks. He had a particular fondness for birds, an emotion which had an unusual quality because it sprang from atonement after killing a swallow when a boy. In later life this heedless act preyed on his mind and the memory never faded. Indeed, he deliberately kept it alive—'Since then, methinks, I have a gentler heart.' Any wounded bird he saw was identified with the one whose life he had taken all those years ago.

He asks me why they swept him from his peers,
When wheeling gaily in his wondrous course;
And now he comes, with trembling wings, to plead
For some brief record of his cruel fate . . .

He rescued nightingale's eggs from a nest when the mother had been killed, and set them to hatch in a thrush's warm nest. He fed all the birds which came hopping over the rectory lawn in winter,

as well as the squirrels and hares. When their beloved pet canary
died the Turners sent it away to be stuffed and on its return put it
back in the cage! The rector's bald head was a magnet for flies and
he tried not to hurt them.

> But still beware! thou art on dangerous ground:
> An angry sonnet, or a hasty hand,
> May slander thee, or crush thee . . .

He mused over the scarecrow, deserted after harvest:

> Thy posture, hat, and coat, are human still;
> Could'st thou but push a hand from out thy sleeve!
> Or smile on me! but ah! thy face is nil.

> As some poor clerk survives his ruin'd firm
> And, in a napless hat, without employ,
> Stands, in the autumn of his life, alone.

Years of exposure to wind and rain brought on rheumatism, and
he was also afflicted with gout, which latter complaint often cropped
up in his poetic apologies to birds for having spoken harshly to
them. Blame the gout, not him, he told them. Towards the late
1870s his family and friends noted with concern that he seemed
weaker with each successive year although his conversation
retained all its charm and humour, reinforced by a strong Lincolnshire accent. As the rector's physical health deteriorated, so unhappily did his wife's state of mind. She reverted to the first days
of their marriage and became obsessed with the mistaken idea that
she had failed her husband because of her nervous breakdown. She
sat for hours, sunk in melancholia, while her loving and distracted
husband tried to comfort her; Emily Tennyson wrote daily in an
attempt to convince her that her marriage to Charles Turner was
the best thing that had ever happened to him, and that it had been
Louisa's love and patience, coupled with his love for her, which
had enabled him to break the opium addiction, a release from
bondage few addicts achieve. 'This darkness will pass, as God is
just and loving, it will pass,' wrote Emily Tennyson earnestly.

With both Turners so ill, their doctor ordered a complete rest
and change of scene, and so early in 1879 they went to Bath. It was

however too late: Charles Turner died in April, and his grief-stricken wife in May. Alfred and Emily Tennyson mourned a two-fold loss.

The Turners were buried in Bath, but a memorial tablet to their life and work in the village was affixed to the wall of Grasby Church. Alfred Tennyson arranged for a collected edition of his brother's sonnets to be published, edited by James Spedding, and he contributed a brother's heart-felt poetic preface:

Midnight—in no midsummer tune
   The breakers lash the shores:
The cuckoo of a joyless June
   Is calling out of doors:

And thou has vanish'd from thine own
   To that which looks like rest,
True brother, only to be known
   By those who love thee best.

9

The Rev.
Francis Kilvert
Parson and Impressionist
1840-1879

One day in 1937 William Plomer received out of the blue twenty-two diary notebooks sent to him by the nephew of the dead diarist. They had been written by the Rev. Francis Kilvert, a Victorian country clergyman, and although they spanned only ten years with several gaps and contained few famous names, yet they described life and manners in the Anglo-Welsh border country and in parts of Wiltshire in such faithful and loving detail that a whole vanished age came sharply into focus. Plomer was naturally excited and began editing the million-and-a-quarter words into manageable proportions, publishing the first instalment in 1938.

That was the fateful year of Munich, when ominous Nazi war clouds hung over eastern Europe, and *Kilvert's Diary, Vol. I*, which happened to include his most lyrical and fascinating extracts, was escapism of the purest kind, providing a nostalgic glimpse into what another Shropshire lad called 'the land of lost content'. Success for the Diary was instant, and Plomer immediately applied himself to the rest of the material until he had edited three volumes, totalling about 400,000 words; Volumes II and III appeared in 1939 and 1940 respectively. The outbreak of war in 1939 only whetted the appetite for Kilvert. Much of the Diary's appeal lay in the contrast between the stable values of Kilvert's society and the shifting ones of a war-torn world. Kilvert's poetic prose was an added attraction because the tensions of war had brought a sharpened demand for poetry. He had an artist's vision of landscape, and composed Impressionist word paintings. He fretted for hours to find the word 'dazzle' to describe the play of light on poplar leaves and the word takes us right into the Impressionist world. He was, after all, writing the Diary at a time when the Impressionists were holding their first exhibitions in Paris, and the Pre-Raphaelites were painting in London.

Furthermore, Kilvert had a direct view of life and celebrated universal emotions, so that a Kilvert community seemed a pastoral Arcadia blessed with those qualities of life which the British in 1940 were quite literally fighting to preserve. His own personality, too, was unusually attractive. He was a tolerant young man, responsive to decency and sincerity in others no matter what their creed or social station. In a word, he was a natural democrat, the antithesis of the conformist Nazi or Fascist, and what Rupert Brooke's poetry meant to the generation of the First World War, *Kilvert's Diary* meant to the generation of the Second World War.

Now we are seeing a resurgence of interest in Kilvert. He is in danger of becoming a cult figure, for reasons which are not hard to understand. The beauty of his well-loved countryside accentuates the ugliness of our cities, and his complex network of village relationships, so different from urban anonymity, generated feelings of warmth and satisfaction which are rarer today in our industrialized society. There is a fascination, too, in the very complexity of Kilvert's personality, a complexity heightened by the gaps in the Diary which we are fairly certain can be ascribed to Mrs Kilvert after her husband's death. There was, quite simply, nothing in life or on earth which did not interest Francis Kilvert: he was tender, comic, exultant, indignant, sentimental, optimistic and pessimistic by turns—aggressive, egotistic and cold, never. His sensitivity was almost feminine, and Dr A. L. Rowse's comment that Vol. I of the Diary reminded him of Dorothy Wordsworth's *Journal* would have flattered Kilvert because he had a particular affection for her work.

Perhaps we can best try to understand the Rev. Francis Kilvert by placing him in the context of his family, who were Shropshire folk, several of whom became Anglican ministers. A great-uncle, the Rev. Robert Kilvert, entered the Anglican church and became a Prebendary of Worcester Cathedral. His branch of the family lived around Worcester. The diarist's branch was descended from Robert Kilvert's younger brother, Francis, who went to Bath and became a coach-builder. His business never recovered from the Napoleonic war and he suffered a nervous breakdown.

> As his weakness increased, delusions came on of the most touching and painful kind; self-accusations utterly unfounded, and a dread of taking food lest he should be eating the last morsel we had to live upon.[1]

The coach-builder died relatively young leaving a penniless widow to bring up seven sons and a daughter. The eldest son, also named Francis,[2] was serious and clever; he went to Oxford, became a parson and was soon the financial support of the family. His younger brother, Robert,[3] followed his brother to Oxford and went to Oriel College in 1822, becoming a student of John Keble and a contemporary of John Henry Newman. A third brother, Edward,[4] also went to Oxford. Curiously enough, not one of these three Kilverts made any mark on the university, although Newman said of Robert Kilvert, 'He left a fragrant memory behind him at Oriel', and for his part, Robert Kilvert never forgot the melody of Newman's delivery of sermons.

Robert Kilvert lived very quietly in Oxford, partly from poverty and partly from shyness. Each afternoon he went for a long walk. He was a nervous young man who went to pieces at examination time, and he was convinced that his poor results were a result of being unable to afford a private tutor to coach him during the last crucial months. '. . . before it was over I was quite worn out, sick in head and at heart, and broke down sadly towards the last. The consequence was that instead of being in the First Class, I was in the Third, both in Classics and Mathematics, to my great disappointment and mortification.' It is interesting to read this account because his son, the diarist, was to duplicate those experiences when he went to Wadham College in 1859. He made very few friends and he performed far below his best in examinations, leaving Oxford with a disappointing Fourth Class degree.

Meanwhile, Robert Kilvert followed the example of his admired brother by taking Holy Orders. Even without the example of the Rev. Francis Kilvert to point the way, it is difficult to see what other profession would have been open to a poor, serious and intelligent young man with an Oxford degree. The Rev. Francis Kilvert had become curate of Claverton, near his favourite city of Bath.

He loved Bath so much that he steadfastly refused all offers of preferment because they would have removed him from Somerset. He had made a romantic marriage with a young lady of minor French nobility, Adelaide Sophia de Chièvre, who had escaped in a row boat from revolutionary France. He combined schoolmastering with parsoning, purchased an imposing mansion called Claverton Lodge and, until his death in 1863, ran a boarding school for boys preparing for university entrance.

His brother Robert was appointed rector of Hardenhuish in Wiltshire, near Chippenham, which was also close to Bath. There the six Kilvert children were born, the diarist, born in 1840, being the second child and first son. In order to increase his income, the Rev. Robert Kilvert took in boys preparing for common entrance, and had an extension built on to the rectory so that he could take twelve pupils and a resident tutor to help him. The most famous of the Kilvert pupils was Augustus Hare, who attended the school from 1843 to 1846 before going on to Harrow. He painted a scarifying picture of the Rev. Robert Kilvert in his autobiography, claiming that the rector, a tall man with 'red hair encircling a high bald forehead', used to lash the boys' hands with his ruler until they went in abject terror of him. However, before we accept this account at face value we should examine the relationship between the Kilverts and the Hares, and between Hare and his mother.

Robert Kilvert had met Mrs Hare when he was acting as temporary curate for her brother-in-law at Alton Barnes, and when she became unexpectedly widowed he wrote her consoling letters. She accordingly decided to send her son to his school because it was kept, in her son's words, by 'a good man' rather than 'a good master'. Young Augustus Hare was morbidly attached to his mother and lived in fear in case she should die once she was out of his sight, so any separation would have been torture for him. In addition, his first months at Hardenhuish School were made wretched by the ending of an emotional friendship he had formed for another boy. In his autobiography, Hare's only kind remembrances are for the Kilvert women, Mrs Kilvert and her sister, Miss Sarah Coleman, who taught in the school on the afternoons when the Rev. Robert Kilvert did his pastoral visiting. In spite of this account, Augustus Hare remained on friendly terms for many years with his former headmaster, as is evidenced by a letter he wrote to him in 1870 which probably gives a truer picture of the school than the one in his autobiography.

> I remember Mrs Matthews so well and going to tea there, for consolation, the first day I was left with you. It all seems very long ago, but so vivid still, the garden with its laurel hedges and the large elm tree, the dusty hot little courtyard, the romantic adventures of climbing down by stealth into the vault under the church, persuading May the cook to give us hot little cakes of bread out of the window when she was baking. Asking the French master with Walter Arnold, 'Who won the battle of Waterloo?' and being well punished for it too. . . .'[5]

The diarist's sister, Emily, had only happy memories of the school, with games in the garden, a succession of tutors and special foods for the delicate boys. Thersie, the diarist's older sister, used to help the boys make pop-guns out of elder wood and watch-springs. Frank Kilvert was very proud of a cross-bow he had been given.

He was educated first at his father's school and then at his uncle's school at Claverton Lodge. The Rev. Francis Kilvert senior became almost as important a figure in Frank Kilvert's life as he had been in the Rev. Robert Kilvert's life, and the lack of personal ambition which is so marked a feature of the diarist certainly closely resembled his uncle's attitude towards worldly promotion. Not that the latter was undistinguished. The *Dictionary of National Biography* lists Francis Kilvert of Claverton Lodge as an antiquary. Even without the educational links, ties were strong between the two households. To quote Emily again: 'In the Winter we sometimes went to stay at Claverton Lodge, on Bathwick Hill, Bath, where Papa's eldest brother, the Revd. Francis Kilvert, lived. How we loved and revered him; and in what awe we stood of our Aunt Sophia, his wife, who wore a black wig.' The Rev. Francis Kilvert also wrote literary and historical monographs, some rather mediocre poetry, and was a leading light in Bath literary circles. His nephew could feel justifiably proud of him and look up to him as a man to be emulated.

Frank Kilvert acquired a conventional literary taste, doubtless formed when his father read the literary classics aloud to the family in the evenings, starting with Scott and Dickens and proceeding to Shakespeare. Both Kilvert's parents had bad eyesight, passing on this weakness to him, and his father wore a monocle. The children grew up with animals. There was Trim, the Welsh cob, and Barebones, a sorrel pony. Among the dogs there was Dragon, half mastiff and half lurcher; Dash, a spaniel of course; and a black and tan terrier called Billy. Among the many rectory cats were two magnificent white Persians with mismatched eyes, very grandly called Murad and Johrad.

We have no account of Frank Kilvert's life at Oxford although by a curious coincidence his father was writing his recollections of Oxford at the time when his son had begun the extensive Diary. Neither Kilvert told the other of his writing. We have to infer what we can about Frank Kilvert's life at the university from hints in the Diary. Thus, on a return visit to Wadham years later, he wrote that the gardens were the same, with the copper beech and the three glorious limes, poplars towering like steeples, and the golden rain of the laburnum with the blue flower clusters of the wisteria. This is a typical Kilvert vignette, lyrical and even sensual, but it is Nature unpopulated. He makes no association in that passage with life, ideas, attitudes or young men. Francis Kilvert had been too shy at Oxford to risk swimming in the midstream of turbulent intellectual debate and he found his pleasures in solitary communion with Nature. He read history and jurisprudence and graduated in 1862. His church views were as moderate and conventional as his literary ones, and when he attended a service in St Barnabas's Church, Oxford, in 1876 he described it disapprovingly as 'pure Mariolatory'.

In his introduction to the first volume of the Diary, William Plomer said that Kilvert knew Lewis Carroll at Oxford and that both men had a strong liking for little girls—what might be termed a 'Lolita complex'. It is true that both men were at Oxford at the same time, but there is no proof that they knew each other there or subsequently, and the difference in their ages, careers, special subjects and accomplishments make it unlikely that they would have even met socially. Charles Lutwidge Dodgson, later better known as Lewis Carroll, had after all matriculated at Christ Church, Oxford, in 1850 when Frank Kilvert was ten years old. Since then, Dodgson had done well academically, ending as an Oxford don and an author of mathematical books. By the later 1850s, when Kilvert went to Wadham, Dodgson was already contributing to comic papers and knew many of the leading writers and painters of the day. He began keeping a diary in 1854 but the years 1859 to 1862, when Kilvert was at Oxford, are unfortunately missing. However, since neither he nor Kilvert appears to have alluded to the other in those years for which we have their respective diaries, it seems safe to assume that they did not in fact know each other.

Certainly Frank Kilvert liked girls of all ages and wrote about them at great length, and presumably thought about them at even greater length. He had a particular penchant for nubile brunettes. As a curate he often called at cottages at the children's bath time and loved to watch the mothers bath and dry their little daughters. He enjoyed village festivals when the young schoolgirls sailed upwards on their swings so that their skirts billowed skywards above their plump thighs. A snatched kiss, or the pressure of a hand on a girl's palm, sent him into flurries of excitement and there are many examples in the Diary. It must, however, be kept in mind that in *Kilvert's Diary* we have necessarily been given an edited account, and the needs of publication and sales would have forced Plomer to omit many repetitive and routine items dealing with a curate's professional duties. What emerged, then, was a tuppence coloured Kilvert, often in either his most sociable or most introspective mood. He was ingenuous even in his most intimate moments, showing a pre-Freudian honesty which allowed him to recount his hopes and fantasies without shame or embarrassment. Had this not been the case, he would surely not have wished the Diary to be preserved and read by others after his death; and we know he did wish this because of explicit references in the Diary. As Kate O'Brien said, placing him among other British diarists, he sailed through life 'simply by the grace of God and the luck of the innocent' and innocence has often proved a sure protection.

Ordained deacon in 1863 and priest in 1864, the Rev. Frank Kilvert went to Langley Burrell, where his father was rector following Hardenhuish. The Wiltshire village of Langley Burrell was presided over by an obstinate and autocratic squire, Mr Ashe, a relation by marriage of Mrs Kilvert's, which family connection did not inhibit the squire from dominating his parson as he did his village. Kilvert, serving as his father's curate, resented the squire's behaviour but the Rev. Robert Kilvert was too poor and too diffident to take an aggressive line with a man upon whom so many village and church charities depended. To make matters worse, the squire was an ordained clergyman which he considered gave him the right to have the last word on church affairs. Kilvert remained as curate at Langley Burrell long enough to get an appointment of his own, as curate to the Rev. Richard Lister Venables of Clyro in Radnorshire near Hay. It was a lucky appointment for Kilvert since his rector, a wealthy, cultivated man treated him like an adopted nephew and introduced him to the local gentry. Kilvert became a welcome visitor to the kind of houses he would never have visited in the more snobbish Wiltshire, although he was still only a humble curate. Indeed, a very old lady from one of the great houses, when asked after the publication of the Diary if she could remember Kilvert, replied with some surprise that of course she could not. Who would remember a curate?

Clyro had escaped the changes of industrial villages and had never been fashionable, so it still functioned as a close community with comparatively little social friction. Most parish suffering, especially if medical or mental, was alleviated as a matter of course by the parson. The whole district around Hay boasted at that time a group of well-to-do, literary-inclined and socially responsible Anglican clergymen who by their mere presence brought about a minor Anglican revival in that area. It made a particularly pleasant social milieu for the new curate. Pressures and frustrations which had Joseph Arch organizing the farm workers in other parts of the country were almost unknown round Clyro. Social pleasures were predictable. There was archery and croquet in the summer months, the first sport allowing young ladies to strike exhibitionist poses and the second sport allowing competitiveness to raise its fiendish head. There was also, of course, hunting, shooting and fishing; monster picnics; dances and balls; and village concerts and Penny Readings. Parson and squire, as befitted their social positions and privileges, had additional responsibilities centred around the church and school; these mainly involved prizegivings, summer parties, Christmas carols and Easter festivities.

Mr Venables was a J.P. as well as a clergyman and Chairman of Radnorshire Quarter Sessions for many years. He sat on many local committees and in all performed many of the duties which today would fall to the lot of a county councillor. He was pleased with Kilvert, who was a careful assistant and kept the church well organized. 'In Advent, evensong with sermon (generally by a guest clergyman) was held on Friday evenings and was popular. Holy Communion was celebrated on Christmas Day, and on New Year's Day there was sung evensong with sermon. Ash Wednesday was observed with Commination and sermon, and there was a weekly service at 11 a.m. every Wednesday in Lent.'[6] Good Friday itself, as Kilvert noticed when he arrived, was 'a holiday and mere day of pleasure'.

One of the finest pieces of descriptive writing in the Diary deals with the decoration of the churchyard graves on Easter Eve, 1870. That morning Kilvert awoke at 4.30 when the moon was still casting strong shadows on one side of the church as the rising sun bathed it in a warm glow on the other. After admiring the scene he rose at five o'clock and spent two hours before breakfast composing a sermon. He had several tasks to do throughout the day but he kept returning to the churchyard to help with the decoration. People were constantly coming and going, decking the graves until moonrise, and latecomers went about their business quietly, listening to the choir which was practising inside the church. Kilvert was the last to leave. 'As I walked down the Churchyard alone the decked graves had a strange effect in the moonlight and looked as if the people had lain down to sleep for the night out of doors, ready dressed to rise early on Easter morning.'[7] Easter Day saw him up early again so that he could pick primroses for a grave which he had noticed to be neglected. He was delighted to hear the cuckoo. 'It is very well to hear the cuckoo for the first time on Easter Sunday morning.'

Harvest Festivals were also celebrated at Clyro, differing from the Easter ones in that the church and not the graveyard was decorated. In 1870 the church bloomed splendidly with ferns, convolvulus, hop vine, red barberries, dahlias and coleus, stringed ivy pulled down from the trees, and of course wheat, barley and oats, with plums, apples and pears lying on a field of moss.

Even without the affection shown him by Mr and Mrs Venables, Kilvert would have loved Clyro. The contrast between the English and Welsh cultures excited him, and the dark Welsh life, with its hints of passion and secrecy, called on profound emotions within him. He longed to identify completely with the Welsh, and convinced himself that Welsh blood must run in his veins, which was completely untrue. He was fascinated by Radnorshire customs and superstitions and took copious notes about them, intending to use them for articles to be submitted to archaeological periodicals. Many years after his death a niece used them for an article she wrote in the *Occult Review*. Another parson, the Rev. R. S. Thomas, was dismayed by the harsher aspects of the lives of the border hill farmers and wrote about 'muck and blood, spittle and phlegm' but Kilvert was enough of a romantic to regard the rough-hewn peasant as an integral part of his austerely beautiful landscape. Kilvert found the Celtic life a salutory antidote to the calmer life of an Anglican clergyman with its unavoidable little hypocrisies from time to time. It was essential to his inner well-being to take long solitary walks, and he greatly resented sharing the hill country with tourists or even natural history clubs—'most vulgar, ill-bred, offensive and loathsome'.

He had been curate at Clyro for over four years when he began the Diary as we know it, and he gave no explanation of why he started such a full account of his life. It was, of course, the rule rather than the exception for clergymen to keep diaries, and Kilvert always had a small pocket notebook on him in which he jotted down incidents, descriptions, reflections and phrases. The Rev. D. N. Lockwood has propounded the interesting theory that Kilvert began to keep a fuller diary after reading a popular American book which had just come out in England, called *Stepping Heavenward* by Mrs Prentiss. It was a readable account in diary form of a young woman's spiritual pilgrimage, almost rationalist in tone, and free from sentimental moralizing but with plenty of strong feeling. Kilvert certainly admired the book for he purchased many copies to give away as presents.

It may be, however, that the genesis of the Diary was more humdrum, and arose simply from a Christmas present, or maybe even just the realization that he was in his thirtieth year and still unmarried. The Diary would be a gift for a future bride.

What is absolutely certain is that once he had started on 1 January 1870 to transfer his day's jottings into the Diary, polishing his rough drafts into literary pieces of anything from 200 to 1200 words, writing became essential to his emotional balance. He had the Kilvert flair for words and he enjoyed the intellectual exercise. The Diary took the place of a friend and he felt a sense of release as he relived the activities of his day. He possessed to an unusual degree 'the power of stealing hearts', as he called it, and as an attractive young curate he was obviously in an exposed position.

He spread his affections over a number of individuals and the
Diary was his sole confidant. It is certainly a fair assumption that
had he married in 1870 he would have left us a very different kind
of Diary. Over the nine years' span there is a change of tone as the
Diary charts the progression of the magnetic, carefree young man[8]
into the sober parson at last whose susceptible heart had been
broken more than once.

The published Diary begins on 18 January, 1870 when Kilvert
was in Mitcham, near London, on holiday and staying with family
friends. He took his host's sons on outings, bought presents at the
Crystal Palace for his friends in Clyro and admired the Murillo
painting of *The Good Shepherd* at the Royal Academy. He stopped
at Langley Burrell on the way back to Clyro, took a few services to
relieve his father and slipped back easily into family habits. In the
evenings the Rev. Robert Kilvert read *Les Misérables* aloud to the
family while Kilvert sat making a bird net to protect the morello
cherry tree in the rectory garden. Then it was off to Wales, where
the early February weather was so cold that Kilvert's beard,
moustache and whiskers froze solid to his mackintosh when he
went 'villaging', in spite of his wearing two waistcoats, two coats
and a muffler. He officiated at a christening when the unheated
church was so cold that pieces of ice floated in the font.

He was not sentimental about the conditions in which many of
his flock lived but did not consider it his place to change society or
to persuade others to do so. He alleviated distress where he could
by the time-hallowed acts of clerical charity like giving out sheets,
blankets and tickets for coal.

Grand handsome Mrs Evans nursing her baby in the dark
ruinous old hovel, a brave patient woman and practically
religious. The children at tea. Black-eyed, black-haired Mary
in her blue check pinafore growing so like her mother. Gave Mrs
Evans an order for 2 pairs of sheets. Slithering down the steep
rocky lane full of a torrent of ice. How this poisonous E. wind
strains and weakens the eyes.[9]

Kilvert's eyes frequently troubled him, sometimes so much that
he could not decipher his handwritten sermons. He also suffered
from bad headaches which he often attributed to over-indulgence
in wine—'I drank too much port after dinner at Cae Mawr last

night and a splitting headache all day in revenge. Eyes better but not much. Everything in a daze and dazzle . . .' The symptoms sound more like migraine than a hangover, with icy east winds bringing on sinus pains.

He was no prude and enjoyed a mildly improper story. 'Mrs Pearson was telling us about a child's conception of the meaning of "committing adultery".' He shared the human weakness of enjoyment of scandal in high places. 'Reading the Mordaunt Warwickshire Scandal Case. Horrible disclosures of the depravity of the best London society.' Clyro and Hay drawing-rooms resounded happily to that scandal for many days. It was a highly publicized case which was referred to in many other diaries besides Kilvert's.

Cottage visiting, 'villaging' as he called it, gave him particular satisfaction. He would set off in the morning, his lunch in one pocket and notebook and opera glasses in the other, to combine a long walk over the hills with his visits. If nobody was at home, he would leave a flower or leaf in the door latch as a message that he had called. He frequently saw buildings in terms of their human associations. 'Poor Maria Lake, what would she say to see her cottage now? But her place knows her no more though the wind blown larch still bows over the roof as if mourning for her.'

His particular vision, both ocular and poetic, rewarded him with striking comparisons. 'The Clyro women stride about the village like storks.'[12] He collected words and phrases: 'Jinny says "unhackle" for undress and "to squeeze your ears against your head and say nothing" means to be discreetly silent.' His notes were really a writer's or artist's shorthand. He looked forward indulgently to nights of superstition like May Eve. 'I ought to have put some birch and wittan over the door to keep out the "old witch". But I was too lazy to go out and get it. Let us hope the old witch will not come in during the night. The young witches are welcome.' And lacking the young witches, he had to make do with young children and with sentimental encounters which could withstand the scrutiny of bright afternoon sunshine, as when he called at the Newchurch school to find the parson and curate absent and the school under the supervision of the parson's daughter— 'pretty Emmeline . . . with an austere look on her severely beautiful face'. He flustered her little sisters by looking at their arithmetic books. 'Janet was doing simple division and said she had done five sums, whereupon I kissed her and she was nothing loath. Moreover

I offered to give her a kiss for every sum, at which she laughed . . .
Shall I confess that I travelled ten miles today over the hills for a
kiss, to kiss that child's sweet face. Ten miles for a kiss.' Three days
later he was back at Newchurch to find a very different scene, for
Janet and her little sister, Matilda, were helping their father to
castrate the lambs. Kilvert had an 'initial turn of disgust' partly
because they were infants and partly because they were daughters
of a clergyman. Still, 'I made allowance for them and considered
in how rough a way the poor children have been brought up . . .'.

He loved travelling by train and enjoyed the sights outside the
train and the situations inside. Consider his journey to Chippenham:

> The carriage was nearly full. In the Box tunnel as there was no
> lamp, the people began to strike foul brimstone matches and
> hand them to each other all down the carriage. All the time we
> were in the tunnel these lighted matches were travelling from
> hand to hand in the darkness. Each match lasted the length of
> the carriage and the red ember was thrown out of the opposite
> window, by which time another lighted match was seen travel-
> ling down the carriage. The carriage was chock full of brimstone
> fumes, the windows both nearly shut, and by the time we got out
> of the tunnel I was almost suffocated. Then a gentleman tore a
> lady's pocket handkerchief in two, seized one fragment, blew his
> nose with it, and put the rag in his pocket. She then seized his
> hat from his head, while another lady said that the dogs of
> Wooton Basset were more sociable than the people.[11]

Like all country clergymen, Kilvert took classes in the school,
rightly considering this an important part of parish work. He
worried when school board inspectors paid their periodical visits,
but rejoiced the year that the school beauty, eight-year-old Gipsy
Lizzie, was put in his class. He mooned interminably over her.
'Oh, child, child, if you did but know your own power.
Oh, Gipsy, if you only grow up as good as you are fair. Oh, that
you might grow up good. May All God's angels guard you, sweet,'
he wrote rhapsodically. It was impossible to feel as rapturous,
however, over young Eleanor Williams, who as a result of two
months' Bible study with him could do no better than tell him that
on Palm Sunday Jesus Christ went up to Heaven on an ass.

His romantic daydreams extended to every attractive girl he

met. Whenever he was introduced to a socially acceptable young
lady he longed to kiss her hand 'even at the imminent risk that it
would instantly administer a stinging slap on the face of its admirer'.
He went to Cornwall for a holiday and could hardly bear to take
the train home: 'the cold heavy dull pain of the rest of the long
nine hours' journey as we flew through all the length of the Three
Western Shires . . .'.

As a rule he paid scant attention to world affairs, Clyro being
world wide enough, but he made an exception for the Franco-
Prussian War and, like most of his friends, considered that
Napoleon III was a war-monger who deserved what had come to
him. Kilvert was always attracted to vital people, and soldiers, by
profession, were vital; one of his particular friends in Clyro was
John Morgan, a veteran from the Peninsular War. Mr Venables
had managed to get a war pension of 9*d.* a day for Morgan. But
when Kilvert spoke to the old soldier about the war he was surprised to find that Morgan was bored by it, and when pressed
acknowledged that he preferred the French to the Prussians. He
well recalled the kindness towards him of the French peasants in
the war, and how the French and English troops had fraternized
on piquet duty when their officers were not around.

Because everything interested him, Kilvert was a rather un-
selective recorder. He gave as careful an account of an evening
lecture about Napoleon on St Helena given in Hay School by an
S.P.C.G. lecturer as he did to his visit to the half-built monastery
established by the self-styled Father Ignatius, son of Kilvert's
friends, the Lynes, and one of the oddest and most remarkable men
in Victorian Church circles. Kilvert was intrigued by the movement
to return to monasticism, but he was far from converted and after
meeting a young novice he commented, 'I hope he is reserved for a
better fate.' Kilvert's taste in books was similarly undiscriminating
and he liked novels with strong moral lessons. He prided himself on
being modern, however, and sent postcards to his family as soon as
they appeared. 'They are capital things, simple, useful and handy.'

He never shirked visiting the sick. His entry for 7 October 1870
was vivid and compassionate.

Poor Edward is very ill. What a scene it was, the one small
room up in the roof of the hovel, almost dark, in which I could
not stand upright, the shattered window, almost empty of glass,

the squalid bed, the close horrid smell, the continual crying and wailing of the children below, the pattering of the rain on the tiles close overhead, the ceaseless moaning of the sick man with his face bound about with a napkin. 'Lord have mercy. Lord have mercy upon me,' he moaned.

I was almost exhausted crouching down at the little dirty window to catch the light of the gloomy rainy afternoon.[12]

He went faithfully each week to the old man, sadly recording the deterioration in the old man and in his cottage. 'Imperial Caesar dead and turning to clay would have done better, and could not have done worse.'

But it was mortality with an urbane and satiric flavour which was the theme of his account of the visit to Worcester to attend the funeral of Maria Kilvert of the Worcester branch of the family. He gave a masterly description of the Worcester servants who thought themselves too grand to wait upon the impoverished Langley Burrell Kilverts, and accordingly hired a charwoman to take them meals on trays in their bedrooms, and of the ceremonious burial itself.

Human nature was continually surprising him. There was the time when Mrs Jones suspected a neighbour of stealing her washing which she had left out all night to dry on the churchyard hedge. To find the culprit she and her husband opened a Bible at random to produce a name; they toasted a live frog inside a ball of clay; and they fashioned a clay figure which they pricked all over. 'It is almost incredible,' commented the curate.

His solitary walks sometimes repaid him with moments of almost religious ecstasy. The following passage was inspired by a March sunset after a wild, stormy day:

The last cloud and mist rolled away over the mountain tops and the mountains stood up in the clear blue heaven a long rampart line of dazzling glittering snow so as no fuller on earth can white them. I stood rooted to the ground, struck with amazement and overwhelmed at the extraordinary splendour of this marvellous spectacle. I never saw anything to equal it I think, even among the high Alps. One's first involuntary thought in the presence of these magnificent sights is to lift up the heart to God and humbly thank Him for having made the earth so beautiful. An intense glory of primrose light streamed from the west deepening into rose and crimson. There was not a flake of snow anywhere but on the mountains and they stood up, the great white range rising high into the blue sky, while all the rest of the world at their feet lay ruddy rosy brown. The sudden contrast was tremendous, electrifying. I could have cried with the excitement of the overwhelming spectacle. I wanted someone to admire the sight with me. A man came whistling along the road riding upon a cart horse. I would have stopped him and drawn his attention to the mountains but I thought he would consider me mad. He did not seem to be the least struck by or to be taking the smallest notice of the great sight. But it seemed to me as if one might never see such a sight again.[13]

No religious ecstasy gripped him when he read accounts of the Paris Communards. '. . . the beastly cowardly Paris mob. Those Parisians are the scum of the earth, and Paris is the crater of the volcano, France, and a bottomless pit of revolution and anarchy.' Doubtless he had been aroused by the fate of the Archbishop of Paris, but these were very strong words for Kilvert and we must hope that his reading matter for that day, a life of Bishop Cotton, did much to soothe him. Country graveyards usually had a calming effect, and he preferred the simple prayers on the old Catholic tombs to the stern exhortations of eighteenth-century Puritans who, he thought, 'seem to have tried to make the idea and place and associations of death and burial as gloomy, hideous and repulsive as possible, and they have most signally succeeded'.

His private visits were full of interest. In April 1871 he was invited to the home of Miss Hutchinson, niece-in-law of William Wordsworth and a god-daughter of Dorothy Wordsworth. As he had long admired Dorothy Wordsworth he was excited by this encounter with a member of the family, and he obviously took Miss Hutchinson's fancy for she sent him 'a relic very precious to me, a little poem of her aunt Dorothy Wordsworth in her own handwriting'.

In sharp contrast to that happy occasion was a duty call at the house of Hetty Gore, when that lady begged Kilvert to intervene with the schoolmaster on behalf of her epileptic daughter, Hannah. That unfortunate child had been beaten by the schoolmaster for being slow at her lessons, and the mother showed Kilvert the scars. As he examined them he also noticed the blemishes left on her body when she fell into the fire some years earlier. He promised to do his best, and that evening wrote up the visit as factually and methodically as a social case-worker. Beating of children, including girls, was fairly common practice. It was a well established method of punishing persistent lying, and in one instance the mother asked Kilvert if he would object to helping her administer a beating. Although he was not in fact called upon to assist, the Diary does not show any surprise or indignation at the request, and the curate would probably have helped if called upon.

With the spring came the fishing season, and his friend, Morell, whisked Kilvert off to Cabalva to watch the men netting salmon in the river. Kilvert was deeply interested and reminded forcefully of the cartoon of the Draught of Fishes. The great Hiring Fair took place every May at Hay and all the Clyro villagers went there; it was a happy occasion for them although Kilvert did not care for it, and always avoided it. The gentry went to Clyro Court for rook shooting on the fair day, and Kilvert was invited as a guest, but shooting never appealed to him. 'It may not be cruel, but I don't think I could ever be a sportsman.' He preferred going about his pastoral work, especially if he had the bonus of meeting interesting characters in the course of it.

There was, for example, the vicar of Glascwm who was a parson of the old school with white hair and a merry twinkle in his eye. He had been a mighty walker when young, and had once covered sixty miles in a single day, a feat which commanded Kilvert's respect. The vicar gave the young man bread-and-butter and Herefordshire cider before taking him over to the church with the jest, 'I am bishop here. Come and see the Cathedral.' He told Kilvert that the church had owned three sound bells brought from Llandewi Brefi by enchanted bisons. Glascwm villagers were apparently an intolerant group, for when the bells were rung for a wedding, before the old vicar's time, one bell sounded too quiet for their liking and they took an axe to it and hacked it to pieces.

Another interesting character whom Kilvert made it his business to meet was the eccentric vicar of Llanbedr Painscastle, the Rev. John Price, B.A. Cantab., who lived like a hermit in a shambling filthy hovel. He was famous for miles around as a holy man in the medieval mould, and the rascally element in his parish took shameful advantage of him. Kilvert was impressed by the 'Solitary's' innate courtesy but appalled by the poverty and squalor which surrounded him. It seemed pathetic that he should have filled his lonely hours by inventing shorthand systems. Mindful of the laws of hospitality, the Rev. John Price washed out three glasses which he filled 'with some black mixture which he called I suppose port and bade us drink'. Kilvert was baffled by the man but noticed that the local people greeted him with respect and noted in his Diary that in earlier centuries he might have qualified as a saint.

On May Eve, 1874, Kilvert enjoyed another 'happy and memorable day' when he was taken by the Rev. Henry Moule, the elderly vicar of Fordington and old friend and neighbour of the Rev. William Barnes, to visit the man whom Kilvert called 'the great idyllic Poet of England'. Kilvert was greatly taken with William Barnes. 'He is a very remarkable and a very remarkable-looking man, half hermit, half enchanter.' Moule and Kilvert persuaded Barnes to read aloud his famous comic poem about John Bloom in London and all three were in gales of laughter, but in discussion later they all agreed that their preference was for the more pathetic poems. Barnes told the young man that there 'was not a line which was not inspired by love & kindly sympathy with the things and people described', a sentiment which Kilvert was sure was utterly true. The meeting with Barnes was a red letter day in Kilvert's literary life. He wrote poems himself, chiefly in pastoral vein, and appreciated the genius of the Dorset parson.

Clyro was a well-run parish. Mr Venables was very much occupied with local affairs in the county and frequently his parish work was confined to taking the services on Sunday. The pastoral responsibility and much of the school supervision fell to Kilvert, but even so he was often able to take days off and frequently paid brief visits to his many friends and relatives not too far away. Not unexpectedly, he took a professional interest in churches, parsons and services outside Clyro, and commented critically upon them in his Diary. During a holiday in Devonshire he had occasion to go to a church where the methods displeased him. 'Mr Carn, late Fourteenth Light Dragoons and Curate of Horsham took the service.' He 'wore a green stole and gabbled the prayers. . . . No sermon. Imitation Mass, the clergyman going about the chancel, to and fro like a puppet on wires in a play.'

Kilvert was so irritated by what he had seen in the church that

on returning with his friends he had to down quantities of home-
made cider to regain his equanimity, and he was moved to quote
some lines from Barnes:

And when in Dorset you're a-roaming
Or have business at a farm,
Won't you see your ale a-foaming
or your cider, down to warm.

but to his disappointment his friends did not know of Barnes's
poetry.

He often returned to Langley Burrell to see the family and to
give his father a few days' rest while he took the duties. The
Kilverts were a loyal and united family and Frank Kilvert enjoyed
being an uncle to his nephews and nieces. He could be sure of a
welcome in Langley Burrell from the parishioners. On one visit in
1871 he was almost suffocated by the kisses of seven-year-old
Carrie Britton. When he wrote up the entry, reliving every detail,
he ended, 'I am exhausted with emotion.' Even in an age when
surrogate uncles were permitted almost unbridled licence in kissing
little girls, such surfeit of emotion was unusual and Kilvert was
undoubtedly ripe for marriage and his continued bachelordom was
not his deliberate choice.

On Friday, 8 September 1871, he made a lengthy entry which
began, 'Perhaps this may be a memorable day in my life.' It was
an entirely correct assumption for it was on that day he fell in love
with young Daisy Thomas, home for good from boarding school.
Thereafter a chain of events was set in motion which would lead
Kilvert within a year to bid goodbye to Clyro and its beloved
surroundings. In September, however, he was still full of hope and
with marriage in mind began for the first time in his life to take
stock of his future prospects. He wrote to his father for information
about any possible inheritance and by return post had his answer.
The Rev. Robert Kilvert could not afford to retire so that Kilvert
could take over the Langley Burrell living, but in due course
Kilvert might look to inherit about £2,700. That was less encouraging than he had hoped, and he was gloomily aware that it would
hardly impress Daisy's father, but Kilvert was buoyed up by his
new-found love and determined to make a career for himself. 'I
believe that this is one of the matches that are made in Heaven.

All is hers now. It is all for her, life, talent, prospects, all. . . '.[14] Mr Thomas, however, did not share those views. After allowing the curate to think that eventually there might be an engagement he abruptly made it clear that marriage was out of the question, and furthermore that Kilvert must not let Daisy suspect that he loved her. Mr Thomas appears to have been an extremely possessive father to all his five daughters (Daisy was the youngest), and none of them married. Kilvert meanwhile was stunned by this latest development and he plummeted into the depths of despair. He felt he could not endure to continue living and working in an area where he would be bound to come in contact with the Thomases.

His father arrived to take him for a brisk week of walking and fishing, and tried to cheer him up. October saw the two clergymen making a pilgrimage to St David's Cathedral, walking first to the shore to admire the fine seascapes. Kilvert was so entranced that he left his notebook on the beach and had to run back to retrieve it. 'I found it happily for it was full of people's names and notes and private matters.' It was raining, but the Kilverts made light of that, wet weather being an occupational hazard of parsons in the pre-motor car days. They walked back to the town, talking about Chaucer, and met the venerable Canon Thomas who escorted them round the cathedral. Kilvert approved of the shrine of St David. 'The tomb is simple and humble like the spirit of the man who sleeps below.' Father and son gazed quizzically at the dilapidated tomb of the Earl of Richmond, father of Henry VII. They poked their umbrellas reflectively through holes in the tomb, stirring the royal dust which Kilvert decided felt 'much like common earth'. Still in pensive mood, Kilvert mounted the Bishop's Throne and his father climbed into the pulpit while the aged Canon droned on about the difficulties Gilbert Scott had faced when he restored the building.

The day did a good deal to restore Kilvert's spirits and he liked the look of the town and the inhabitants. 'The fishwives were moving about the streets, crying their fish, dressed in their peculiar picturesque national costume, the tall conical hat and scarlet dress over a blue short petticoat, or a blue dress over a scarlet petticoat.'

But the Daisy Thomas affair had bitten very deeply and he could rouse himself to none of his former verve, although he shared in the national rejoicing when the Prince of Wales recovered from illness, and felt remorseful over the many criticisms he had made in

the past about the prince's playboy mode of life. He even broke
into loyal verse. He tried to submerge his personal unhappiness
in work and was even more assiduous than usual in his parish
visiting.

> Mrs. Parker was better today. The poor little black dwarf Emily
> was at home from school with a bad cold. Her mother told me
> how some of the village children laughed at Emily and called
> her 'dwarf'. Poor child. I called her to me and she came and
> nestled to my side as I caressed and kissed her and bade her not
> to mind. It is a beautiful noble spirit caged in a poor deformed
> stunted body.[15]

He made up his mind to leave Clyro, to the distress of the
Venables, who had been told of his hopes of marriage to Daisy
Thomas and did all they could to encourage him. Mr Venables
offered to retire from Clyro and to use his influence with the bishop
to see that Kilvert was offered the living, which might make him a
more desirable suitor in Mr Thomas's eyes. Kilvert refused. Like
his father, he was diffident when it was a matter of pushing himself
forward and he could not bear to face Mr Thomas in the light of
the latter's adamant posture. He confessed to Mrs Venables that
he would always consider himself in honour bound to Daisy, even
if she never knew of his love. He wrote in his Diary: 'Love makes
us very humble. Here am I at the feet of this child. I wonder who
will one day long hence read and smile over these records of hopes
and fears and thoughts and desires, when the fire has gone out
and the ashes grown cold.'

Everyone in his personal circle tried to help him through the
crisis. Mr Venables changed his plans, postponed leaving Clyro
and offered Kilvert an increased salary as an inducement to stay,
but to no avail. The Rev. Robert Kilvert arrived for one last week
of Welsh fishing with his son. Kilvert was clearly going through a
minor nervous breakdown, and was in a strange, feverish, hysterical
mood. He met two travelling Irish singers on a train and for one
mad moment thought of throwing everything up to follow the
younger one, but of course it was a momentary fantasy and the
girls left the train and he completed his journey. 'Goodbye, sweet
Irish Mary.'

As news of his departure spread throughout Clyro he had to

face the countless expressions of regret. He had visited regularly at least ninety out of the 130 families in Clyro, and twenty-four out of the thirty-four families in the associated hamlet of Bettws, a remarkably high record considering that not every family belonged to the Anglican church. He had taught in the school, joined in the Penny Readings, given lectures and helped operate the Penny Bank and the Clothing Club, as well as taken services in the church. 'If gold would keep you with us, we would gather a weight of gold,' declared Sophy Ferris at the Old Forest farmhouse. The schoolchildren stayed away from the Fair to save their pennies and sixpences and buy him a gold pencil case as a farewell present, and he was so taken aback when they gave it to him that he could hardly find the words to say thank you. None the less, he left Clyro at the end of August and in true Victorian literary style wrote in the Diary, 'A chapter of life closed and a leaf in the Book of Life turned over.'

Langley Burrell was not as attractive a parish as Clyro although he had a special niche there as son of the parson and former curate. The children seemed rougher and ruder, and he became aware of more snobbish elements among the gentry and a callous attitude towards the farm labourers which had either been absent in Clyro or had passed unnoticed by him. He tried to persuade himself he had done the only thing possible and that there would be gain for his father, at least, who was growing deaf and needed assistance now and again.

It was however hard to settle down at Langley Burrell knowing that it was permanent. His early weeks were miserable and his nights were tormented by disquietening dreams and nightmares. A month after leaving Clyro he noted, 'The dream of Grace Darling' —and from the use of 'the' instead of 'a' we must assume that this was a recurrent dream. Grace Darling, the lighthouse keeper's daughter, was a popular national heroine who would have appealed to his passionate and chivalrous nature.

Two weeks after the Grace Darling dream he endured a complicated nightmare so vivid and horrible that he recorded it in detail. It was a dream within a dream. He thought he was back in Clyro where Mr Venables was administering poison to him, and sleeping under the effects of that poison Kilvert had an inner dream in which Mr Venables was attacking him in Hardenhuish Church (a significant place since the church was sanctuary and Hardenhuish

was Kilvert's birthplace and scene of his secure and happy childhood). He awakened safe from that inner dream, to be still at Clyro
and in a murderous mood towards Mr Venables, whom he attacked
and killed with an axe. After the murder he went into Clyro
'villaging' but the cottage visits were an ordeal because he could
tell from the expressions on the faces of the people he met that
they all suspected him of murder, and for his part he was grimly
conscious that he would be caught and would swing for it at the
next Assizes.

Ironically, it was the very morning after that horrendous dream
that he received a letter from Mr Venables with the news that on
his recommendation Kilvert would soon be offered the living of
Disserth, and Mr Venables thought that Kilvert should accept it.
The young man, however, was too discouraged to feel capable of
taking sole charge of a parish and, after much heart-searching, he
took the line of least resistance, applied to be his father's curate
again, and so remained in Langley Burrell, uneasily aware that
life was slipping by and he was thirty-three years old.

He became increasingly irritated by Squire Ashe's interference
in parish matters. Take, for instance, the controversy over church
music. 'Troubles are looming upon us about the singing in the
church. George Jeffries' voice is breaking down, after 40 years
during which he led the singing. No one can take his place, and the
Squire has resolutely set his face against having an instrument in
Church.' It seemed an untenable position, because churches up
and down the country were being fitted with harmoniums and
organs. As the quarrel over the music continued Kilvert grew
increasingly despondent and wished to go to some place 'where
people were not so unreasonable and hard to please'. Finally the
vicarage stood firm against the squire, whose womenfolk basely
deserted him over this issue, the matter was resolved, and a
harmonium was installed; the first time that music was played
when the squire was in church he actually remained silent.

Then there was the flare-up at the school when the squire went
inside and told the schoolmistress she had to keep the doors and
windows open no matter what the weather. 'This is my school and
I will have my word attended to. If you don't do as I tell you, Miss
Bland, instead of being your friend I'll be your enemy,' he threatened, about which Kilvert commented: 'What a speech for an
elderly clergyman.' In fairness to the squire, we should remember

that he had built the school on his land, and doubtless paid the teacher's wages, and might therefore be forgiven for having a proprietorial attitude.

A visit to a beautiful country scene was always a pleasure which renewed his spirit, and Kilvert waxed lyrical about a pastoral scene in Bowood Park. Then he added:

> Why do I keep this voluminous journal? I can hardly tell. Partly because life seems to me such a curious and wonderful thing that it almost seems a pity that even such a humble and un- eventful life as mine should pass altogether away without some such record as this, and partly too because I think the record may amuse and interest some who come after me.[16]

On his thirty-fifth birthday he took stock of his past year and found it disappointing. He hoped to be able to do better in the year ahead. He was pleased with his birthday presents, especially his mother's gift, which was Dorothy Wordsworth's *Journal* of a holiday in Scotland. On Sunday 31 January 1875 he wrote in the Diary that Charles Kingsley's death had been commemorated in the churches: '"His body is buried in peace, but his name liveth for ever more." We could ill spare him.'

He had some news of Clyro, which was rather sad news because under its new vicar (Mr Venables having indeed retired to live at Llysdinam, not far away), the village was at sixes and sevens. It is rather curious that no thought appears to have crossed Kilvert's mind that had he accepted the responsibility of being Mr Venables's successor, the village would have been happier. He visited the Venables and stayed a few days with them in their new home, and walked over some of his old haunts round Clyro. His reactions were entirely subjective. Ten years earlier he had wandered there as through an enchanted land; now everything was entirely different.

He returned home and found satisfaction in assisting his father at Langley Burrell, while his sisters tried to take him out of himself by arranging parties and excursions. He took a holiday in the Isle of Wight. His Oxford friend, Anthony Mayhew, then a Fellow of Wadham College, stayed at the vicarage and Kilvert let him read the Diary. 'He has been much entertained by some of my old journals which I gave him to read, more especially by the accounts of my interviews with the three remarkable men, the Solitary of Llanbedr Painscastle, Father Ignatius and William Barnes the Dorsetshire poet.' Kilvert paid a visit to Stonehenge. 'As I entered the charmed circle of the sombre Stones I instinctively uncovered my head. It was like entering a great Cathedral Church. A great silent service was going on and the Stones inaudibly whispered to each other the grand secret.'[17]

Of sentimental encounters there was really only one worth remembering, and that was with a reserved and very religious-minded girl whom he called 'Kathleen Mavourneen'. He believed he was not good enough for her, and looked forward to her letters as spiritual encouragement. Their friendship was carried on across distances and never looked like becoming a blazing fire. In September 1875 Kilvert met a girl who blotted Kathleen Mavourneen from his mind. She was Ettie Meredith Brown, a handsome, dynamic girl, poised and fashionable, who possessed the dark gipsy looks which Kilvert had always admired, with an 'exquisite figure' and cheeks which had the 'dusky bloom and flush of a ripe pomegranate'.

We can deduce from the Diary that during the next six months Kilvert and Ettie met, talked and exchanged gifts to demonstrate their growing affection for each other. The exact details are lost, because there is a gap of six months in the Diary—one of the gaps almost certainly made by Kilvert's widow. We know, however, that Ettie made a sermon case for him, and that he copied his poems into a leather-covered manuscript book with her name stamped on the cover. The girl's parents discovered the relationship and must have felt their daughter was worthy of a more eligible suitor than an unambitious curate in his mid-thirties; they broke up the friendship and sent the girl away on a long trip to forget him. Kilvert tried to comfort himself by writing poems to her, and by reliving 'the Bournemouth memories of last December . . . and these wild sad sweet trysts in the snow and under the pine trees, among the sand hills on the East Cliffe and in Boscombe Chine'.

She had returned to England by the following Easter and he sent her his poems together with a long letter, but her response was sad and puzzling: two unhappy little verses which began 'When shall we meet again?' The answer was going to be 'Never', as he found out a few days later when he received a long farewell letter from the girl, and a friendly but extremely firm letter from her mother saying that the friendship must definitely end.

Poor Kilvert. Once again he had to try to console himself with the belief that they would all 'meet in heaven', but his entries are rather calmer than in his Daisy Thomas period, as if he had never really thought he would be successful. Once again his friends did all they could to help him. Anthony Mayhew took him to Paris, and there they met Miss Elizabeth Rowland, an Oxfordshire lady given to good works whom Kilvert had met previously. She was not the kind of person to inspire a torrent of emotion, being cast more in the pattern of Kathleen Mavourneen, but she was kind and pleasant, and Kilvert must have found his thoughts turning to her more and more. She was six years younger than he, but a mature woman by Victorian standards.

In any case he decided that he had to branch out on his own as a parson, and move on from the curate stage. Mr Venables appears to have pulled some more ecclesiastical strings and Kilvert was offered the living of St Harmon's—another Welsh parish—with an income of around £160 a year, which was only a little more than the increased salary which Mr Venables had offered him to remain at Clyro. Kilvert stayed with the Venables while he inspected St Harmon's and looked up some of his old Clyro friends. Little Gipsy Lizzie was almost grown up, and just as lovely as before, and he gave her a kiss for old time's sake. Another beautiful child, Florence Hill, was still living there, and so was the Peninsular War veteran, John Morgan, still hale at ninety years of age. 'I knew your step in a moment,' said Mrs Morgan, and the old soldier was glad to see him and said he had missed 'his shepherd', as he called Kilvert.

In sharp contrast to Clyro, the parish and church of St Harmon's were appallingly neglected. 'A bare cold squalid interior and high ugly square boxes for seats, a three-decker pulpit, and desk, no stove, a flimsy altar rail, a ragged faded altar cloth, a singing gallery with a broken organ, a dark little box for a vestry and a roof in bad repair, admitting rain.' Nevertheless the people in the village were kind and hospitable and he decided that if it were formally offered to him he would accept. His mind thus at rest, he spent a pleasant week at Oxford, staying with Mayhew in Bradmore Road. He had not been to Oxford for two years, and he experienced the familiar thrill of pride as the train steamed into the station and he saw the gleaming spires. 'There is nothing like Oxford.' He dined at High Table with the Fellows of Wadham—'an object of my undergraduate ambition realized at length'. Almost as soon as he returned to Langley Burrell he had the letter offering him St Harmon's, and although he felt a twinge of anxiety about leaving his father, he wrote to accept it. He told himself that preferment had come utterly unsought by him and not of his making. It was the 'beckoning, guiding and leading of His Hand' which showed him that God meant him to leave Langley Burrell. Before settling in at St Harmon's, however, he took a short holiday, staying with his sister, Emmie, and her family in London. On his way home he visited Canterbury Cathedral.

The following six months, covering his first experiences at St Harmon's, is missing from the Diary. It was during this period that he paid court to Elizabeth Rowland and it is most likely that the lady whom the villagers recollected visiting him at the vicarage was Miss Rowland. Kilvert applied himself conscientiously to his parish work and was well thought of, not only by his Anglican flock but by the Dissenters in the district who considered he was a friendly and tolerant gentleman. His reputation as a fine walker quickly grew, not least with the shoemaker who repaired his boots. He had hardly got a firm hand on the reins at St Harmon's when he was offered the living of Bredwardine. There was a very handsome vicarage at Bredwardine with gardens which sloped down to the River Wye, and a fair amount of glebe land, let to a tenant. Since he had marriage in mind, and must have had reason to believe that he would be fortunate in his courtship, the advantages of Bredwardine over St Harmon's were considerable, and he took the new appointment.

His 'villaging' at Bredwardine brought him quickly in contact with his new parishioners, and although there were some interesting and entertaining characters, none were quite as lively and appealing as his friends in the Clyro of ten years earlier. He enjoyed his visits to old Prissy Price, seventy-seven years of age, who looked after her idiot step-daughter, Mary, who was fifty-five. Prissy pleased him by recounting old beliefs and customs, and said that she knew a man who said he had seen the oxen kneel at 12 o'clock on old Christmas Eve. Kilvert was curious about the stories he was told concerning the Holy Thorn said to blossom at the little farmhouse of Dolfach on the hill at midnight on Old Christmas Eve.

He was given a spray gathered from the tree at the correct hour and was interested to see that the buds were not fully out but ready to open when put in soft water. The parent tree, he learned, was a hawthorn which bloomed again in May.

It was an exacting task being vicar of Bredwardine for he was also responsible for Brobury Church. Kilvert's sister, Dora, acted as his housekeeper at the vicarage, and his father and mother visited them. His father helped out with some of the services. The Diary was full of everyday details of a country parson's life; teaching in the school, arranging for the tithe audit and tithe dinner; attending a district clerical meeting; a clerical luncheon with discussion on church business; and return home. One day there was a minor worry about how to light the church as the mice appeared to have eaten the church candles; one of the women offered her own as replacements. Old Kitty Preece explained to Kilvert that the robins were nesting in the church and it was they which pulled the candles out of their sockets and threw them on the ground, so that the mice could carry them away and eat them. Kilvert was touched by the idea of robins in the church and quoted in the Diary, 'Yea, the robin hath found her an house, even Thy altars, O Lord of Hosts.'

Kilvert's health remained poor and he was prone to winter coughs. His father exchanged duties with him so that he could recuperate at Langley Burrell which was more sheltered than Bredwardine. His mother fussed over him and called in the doctor who said that Kilvert's cough was due to congestion of the lungs, or 'tightness of the chest', as Kilvert called it. The Rev. Robert Kilvert was also ailing, and he was seventy-five years old, which made his son wonder how long would 'Sweet Daffodil Parsonage' remain home to them all? Kilvert strolled in the sheltered sun at the side of that vicarage. 'After how many illnesses such as this have I taken my first convalescent walk on the sunny terrace and always at this time of year. . . . But some day will come the last illness from which there will be no convalescence and after which there will be no going out to enjoy the sweet sights and sounds of the earthly spring.' Nor was he cheered by a letter from Longmans the publishers returning his poems with a rejection letter.

The work at Bredwardine was more taxing than he had antici-pated, and the chill and rainy weather gave him continual colds. About a year after going to Bredwardine he was unexpectedly

G

offered the chaplaincy of the Anglican Church at Cannes in the south of France and considered it, although not very seriously, in spite of the advice of Mr Giles, his doctor, who urged, 'Go by all means. It is the very place. It may prolong your life by some years.' Kilvert, of course, had an ingrained reluctance to make any new moves, and he obeyed his instincts which told him to remain where he knew he could cope successfully with the work.

He enjoyed listening to Prissy Price's reminiscences of the days of George IV, as once he had enjoyed listening to the memories of the Peninsular War veteran. He heard that Ettie Brown had sailed to India to marry her fiancé and told himself he was pleased for her sake. He had enough to occupy him with helping the village get over the disastrous autumn floods. Through Mr Venables's introduction, Kilvert took on a pupil, a good-looking blonde boy of thirteen whom the villagers liked at once because of his gentlemanly manners but whom Kilvert privately considered to be abysmally ignorant. The floods were followed by weather so cold that even the river froze, and death succeeded death in the village.

That year, 1879, was his last as a bachelor. His future wife, Elizabeth Rowland, was in every way ideally suited to be the wife of a serious country parson. Her father had trained as a doctor but had given it up for the life of a country gentleman. The Rowlands were an old Oxfordshire family with a Latin motto which could be translated as 'Piety strengthens families'. Elizabeth Rowland taught in the village Sunday school and helped with village communal activities. She was a keen gardener, fed the birds in winter and took the dogs out for long walks. She had a soft voice and was companionable.

She and Kilvert were married from the Rowland home at Wooton in Oxfordshire on 20 August 1879. The villagers had erected arches of flowers and evergreens to welcome the bridal pair, but nature was against them and heavy rain drenched the decorations. The Kilverts took no notice and let nothing spoil their wedding day. They went to Scotland for the honeymoon and returned to Bredwardine a month later. The Bredwardine villagers were determined to show their respect and affection, and they too had decked the cottages and vicarage with floral arches, evergreens and banners of welcome. Once again the weather was atrocious, as was noted by the reporter from the *Hereford Times* who was sent to cover the homecoming.

The newly married couple travelled by train and then took the carriage for the rest of the journey. When the carriage crossed the river a band of sturdy labourers from Bredwardine met them, unharnessed the horses and drew the carriage by ropes to the vicarage door, where the rest of the parish awaited them with presents and a gold-printed address of welcome and congratulations. The cottagers had clubbed together to buy two massive silver gravy spoons, and the farmers gave their own present of silver forks and spoons. A tea had been organized in the vicarage front garden for the women and children and any 'sober-minded men, such as chose to partake of it'. Kilvert had not expected a welcome of that kind and was deeply touched. When he was given the gravy spoons he had to collect himself before he could return thanks, the gifts coming as he said 'from slender incomes and pockets not very deep'. There was a round of applause, the rest of the individual gifts were presented and when the Kilverts were free to go into the vicarage on their own they felt that in spite of the rain their first day together in Bredwardine had been an auspicious one.

Next day, Sunday, Kilvert took the services at both Brobury and Bredwardine as usual, but in the evening he felt ill and was unable to manage the services the following week. His father came to take the Bredwardine service for him and his old friend, the Rev. Andrew Pope, took the Brobury service. Kilvert made light of his indisposition and told Pope he fully expected to be out and about within a few days. But he felt worse on the following Tuesday and Mr Giles, who had been in attendance on him, was alarmed by this and sent for a second doctor. It was, unhappily, too late. Peritonitis set in and within twenty minutes of the arrival at the vicarage of the second doctor the Rev. Francis Kilvert was dead.

He was aged thirty-eight and had been married five weeks.

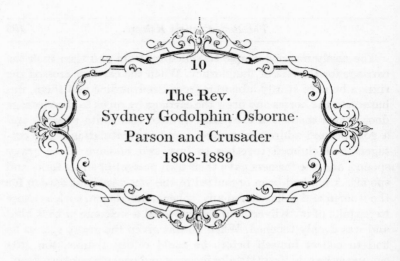

10

The Rev.
Sydney Godolphin Osborne
Parson and Crusader
1808-1889

Almost forgotten today, the Rev. Sydney Godolphin Osborne was for nearly half a century one of the most provocative clergymen in the country, with a reputation founded on a series of tart and often witty letters to *The Times*. Signed with the initials 'S.G.O.', they appeared with great regularity in that newspaper whose proprietor, Mr Walter, was a friend and admirer of the writer and allowed his letters the kind of prominent space normally reserved for leading articles. No country parson burning for a national pulpit could ask for more.

Osborne was the third son of the first Lord Godolphin and he was proud of his aristocratic forbears. The founder of the Osborne family was one Edward Osborne, a sixteenth-century apprentice who had saved his master's daughter from drowning, married her and become in 1585 Lord Mayor of London. The best known Godolphin was Queen Anne's minister, and the successful Churchills were also distantly related to the Osbornes. Born at Stapleford in Cambridgeshire on 5 February 1808, Osborne became a pupil of Rugby School in its early unreformed days. Dr Arnold, its celebrated headmaster, did not take command of the school until 1828, by which time Osborne had already left to go to Brasenose College, Oxford, where he graduated B.A. in 1830.

At Oxford he did a little study, but not much, and enjoyed most kinds of outdoor sports, especially riding. His friends called him 'Galloping Osborne' and he prided himself on knowing the finer points of horseflesh. He did not bother himself about a career. His pugnacious temperament might have marked him out for the Army had his father wished to purchase him a commission. More probably, if the snobbish attitudes of his class had not precluded it, he would have been attracted to medicine. In the event, it was all decided for him. His father took him out shooting one day, paused while taking aim and remarked that everything was settled. He was to take Holy Orders. Osborne was notably unenthusiastic but did not demur. When all was said and done, the Church was as gentlemanly a profession as any other and many a squireen had done that public service stint as a country parson before entering upon his inheritance and taking up the less demanding life of a country gentleman.

Within two years Osborne was ordained and appointed rector of Stoke Poges in Buckinghamshire, the village made famous by Gray's 'Elegy'. In 1834 he married Emily Grenfell, daughter of Pascoe Grenfell of Taplow Court, also in Buckinghamshire, a happy marriage which produced two sons and two daughters. By marrying into the rising Grenfell clan Osborne would later on become related to the Rev. Charles Kingsley, another country parson, and to James Anthony Froude, the writer and historian, as well as to bankers and Members of Parliament.

He spent nine fairly uneventful years at Stoke Poges. Buckinghamshire was a prosperous agricultural county, and as he had not gone into the Church as a missionary he went about his pastoral duties in straightforward fashion and enjoyed the domestic pleasures of his family and the usual pursuits of a man of his class. Things changed however in 1841 when Lord Portman nominated him to the living of Durweston in Dorset, almost next door to Lord Portman's home at Bryanston House. Osborne remained rector of Durweston until he retired in 1875.

Dorset was a county notorious for the low wages of its agricultural workers, and its grinding poverty could not be ignored. As Osborne tramped round the parish noting the reality of the lives of his flock, he realized he would be unable to rest until he had publicized those conditions and brought about improvements.

His first step was the obvious one of writing to the local press, which aroused the ire of his M.P., Mr G. Bankes, but achieved little else; so in 1844 Osborne directed his invective further afield by writing to *The Times*. That letter so enraged Bankes that he raised the matter in the House of Commons, claiming that Osborne had

committed a breach of privilege by writing to a national paper and
mentioning him, Bankes, by name. The House did not support its
member and the matter was dropped, to Osborne's glee. By now he
was in a ferment. He had become aware of a whole number of
issues and was determined to speak his piece on every one. As a
man of good family he was accustomed to being taken seriously,
and it did not trouble him if half the landowners and all the rich
farmers in Dorset spluttered and grew red with fury when they
heard his name.

At about this time, too, he acquired a respectful young protégé,
the Rev. Charles Kingsley, who was planning to marry Mrs
Osborne's sister, and through Osborne's influence with Lord
Portman Kingsley was made curate of the neighbouring parish of
Pimperne which, like Durweston, was in Lord Portman's gift. It
was agreed that when the rector of Pimperne died Kingsley would
be offered the living, should he want it. Meanwhile Kingsley lodged
with the Osbornes and walked into Pimperne every day. In the
evenings he listened to Osborne, who enjoyed expatiating in front
of a captive audience. Kingsley had lately been impressed by the
views of the socially-committed Christian, the Rev. F. D. Maurice,
and he also admired the moral philosophy of Samuel Taylor Coleridge. He and Osborne reinforced each other's opinions and Kingsley had nothing but praise for the older man, although some years
afterwards Kingsley observed drily that Osborne really only
worked hard for those campaigns which he had initiated himself.

Osborne believed that one of his most important functions as a
man and as a parson was to assemble such a weight of evidence
about social conditions that legislation would have to be passed or,
at the very least, that some official inquiry would have to be set in
motion which would lead to legislation. The first time this happened
was in a rather unexpected way.

Bankes had been incensed by one of Osborne's letters to *The
Times* in which Osborne alleged that Bankes had misrepresented the
average wages of Dorset labourers when he said they were eleven
shillings a week, because Osborne knew from personal experience
that the rich landlords were mostly paying nine shillings a week
while the well-to-do farmers—'yeomen farmers' as Osborne called
them—paid between seven and eight shillings a week. In addition
to that, the operation of the Poor Law Amendment Act for the

past ten years, and the existing high price of corn (it was two years before the protectionist Corn Laws were repealed), had given rise to a situation in which, as Osborne put it, 'such is the general condition of the labourers that we are obliged to assist many out of the rates who are in full work on full pay, we have to keep all who fall sick, with scarce an exception, and to bury all who die at the expense of the rate-payers.'

He went on to explain that agricultural housing was in a disgraceful state because so many of the gentry and the yeomen farmers were tearing down workers' cottages to make way for fancy parks round their new mansions, and were either not replacing the cottages at all or else erecting cheap hovels which the workers were compelled to rent.

> The man of wealth and pride
> Takes up a space that many poor supplied . . .

wrote Osborne, and as a member of the privileged class himself he was prepared to share in the blame.

Bankes sneered at Osborne as a 'popularity-hunting parson', repeating a phrase which was coined either by Lord Melbourne or, more probably, by Sir James Graham, who was home secretary in Peel's second ministry. That jibe was to haunt Osborne for the rest of his days, and to rankle, for he was essentially a sensitive man, a fact he concealed beneath an exterior of indifference which occasionally bordered on the morose. At that particular time, however, Osborne retorted that his popularity was rooted in the very class which dared not applaud him openly and which certainly did not read *The Times*. In any case, the rector held it to be an honourable ambition to 'be known as an untiring advocate of a class who, until lately, have had their sad conditions treated with neglect'.

Bankes continued his vendetta against Osborne by making a complaint about him to his bishop, but since Osborne was a hard-working parish priest who rarely left the village, and as he and his wife were well-liked for their charitable work, it proved quite impossible to remove him. Nor was the bishop able to accommodate the Dorset M.P. by arranging some promotion for Osborne which would conveniently take him out of the diocese. Lord Portman, too, had frequently had differences of opinion with Osborne, but he was also helpless and unable either to dismiss Osborne or to prevent his writing a succession of impressive lay sermons for *The Times*.

Around this time (1844), Osborne joined with Lord Ashley, the future Lord Shaftesbury, in resuscitating a labourers' friend society which had been founded in 1830 by the Bishop of Bath and Wells but had subsequently become moribund. The new society was renamed 'The Society for Improving the Condition of the Labouring Classes' and its main interests were in agriculture, housing and the provision of allotments. A number of country parsons divided up their glebe land into allotments or small-holdings as a means of providing extra income for the parishioners, and Osborne did the same. Strangely enough, in view of the fact that both men shared similar views and were doughty campaigners, Shaftesbury and Osborne were never friends. Shaftesbury some-times resented Osborne's knack of getting credit for causes which Shaftesbury felt were really his personal preserves. Nor did he, as an Evangelical, ever associate with the Broad Church movement to which Osborne might be said to belong, if indeed he could be categorized.

Mainly as a result of Osborne's letters, *The Times* in 1846 appointed a barrister named Lovesey to report on the conditions of the Dorset poor. Tempers in that county reached boiling point, and in August a number of aggrieved rich farmers from the Ryme area, on the borders of Dorset and Somerset, collectively signed an abusive open letter to Osborne which was published in the county press. The parson needed no further invitation to bound into the lists and start an investigation of Ryme. He enlisted the support of its squire, parson, schoolmaster and the best-paid labourers to help collect evidence.

Ryme was a hamlet with a population of 200, covering less than a thousand acres, and was unusual in that it was almost entirely owned by the Duchy of Cornwall and therefore a royal responsibil-ity. That fact made the parish newsworthy and Osborne remorse-lessly rammed home the unedifying details which he uncovered. Able-bodied married labourers in Ryme were earning seven shillings a week; single men and lads looked to a wage of from two shillings and sixpence to six shillings a week. At harvest and haytime, a period of about two months in all, wages rose to ten shillings a week plus a gallon of cider a day, but to earn that much the men had to work from 5 a.m. until 7 p.m. Barley was mowed at a wage rate of one shilling and sixpence per acre. Osborne complained that the wages were cut-throat and that even the cider was the farm's poorest quality. Cottage rents at a shilling a week left little money for clothing and food.

However, that was not the worst of it, declared Osborne. The men were paid almost entirely on the iniquitous truck system (outlawed in Lancashire, as he commented) so that the Ryme labourers were compelled to buy wheat exclusively from their employer, who charged fifty-six shillings a quarter for the best wheat and forty shillings for the worst, the latter being nothing more than grist. Second tailings, worth about four shillings a bushel on the open market, were sold to the labourers at six. A family needed about a bushel of wheat a week for food, so that when that was bought and the rent paid there was no money left, and the wives and children had to work as casual help, to be paid off in butter and skim milk cheese.

When it came to the meat sold to the labourers on this system the stories became truly horrifying. Sick sheep and cows were slaughtered at the point of death—'afore they are *cold* dead', was how it was described to Osborne—and sold to the labourers for tuppence ha'penny and fourpence a pound. "Tis the only meat we ever sees.' A very few farmers, to their credit, refused to sell such diseased meat to their workers and fed it to their dogs and pigs.

With wages of that order a labourer was thrifty indeed if he could save two pounds in a year. His family were forced to rely on the charities emanating from the parsonage, the village clothing clubs run by the parson and his family, and their free vouchers for coal, blankets and meat soups. It did not surprise Osborne that the labourers filched the farmer's corn, while as for drunkenness, 'the whole system of payment in cider encourages it'. The neighbouring village of Yetminster seemed even worse than Ryme and was, thundered Osborne, 'the cesspool of everything in which anything human can be recognized'.

He insisted that the Church ought to be taking a bolder stand on social issues, for it had a duty to 'preach the plain truth boldly, that God will not have the poor oppressed in body or in soul'. It is interesting to note that Osborne never spared himself in these campaigns. 'I expect no length of years, I care little how much of them I expend in this cause', he wrote in 1845. He was, in fact, in his eighty-second year when he died.

The Irish famine of 1845 attracted his attention, especially after the government made a grant to help with the distress and the Anglican Church took up regular collections for the Irish poor. Osborne complied willingly in his church but asked pertinently on behalf of his Dorset parishioners, 'When is our turn to come?' In a new letter to *The Times* he pointed out that the potato filled the gap for the Dorset labourers as it did for Irish ones in times of scarcity and a potato blight hit them also. He paid several visits to Ireland and his impressions and reflections were published in book form in 1850 under the title *Gleanings from the West of Ireland*.

A natural Tory by birth, Osborne had however supported Peel in that statesman's repeal of the Corn Laws, and when Lord John Russell became prime minister following the Tory débâcle after the repeal, Osborne addressed Russell through the medium of *The Times* to tell him that with the Tories in such disarray the Whigs had a wonderful chance to do some good. Did the new government realize that it spent less on educating the poor than was spent annually by the country on horse-racing and keeping the London Opera House open? Those two sums together could have financed every provincial hospital in the kingdom. He asked Russell to make sure that reforms were carried out, including a change in the Poor Law, for it was no longer safe 'to leave to the press the daily work of proving that while gaols profess and attempt the reformation of the criminal, workhouses imprison to contaminate the destitute'.

That particular letter annoyed Bankes so much that he declared that English landlords were no better off than Irish ones—the latter were shot at from behind stone walls and the former from behind the columns of a newspaper; to which Osborne retorted drily, again through *The Times*, that the two forms of assassination were hardly comparable. He and Bankes were soon locked in another slanging match in the course of which Bankes published a collection of his favourite anti-Osborne comments, a pamphlet which drew from the parson the characteristic observation that it was 'vulgar, false and pompous. But that is natural to the writer.' Osborne likened Bankes to Grimaldi, strutting across a stage in full plumage like a canary, and as for young Disraeli, who had also opposed repeal of the Corn Laws, Osborne called him an adder. Such epithets added to the liveliness of the public debate, although today no doubt one or other of the protagonists would have been sued for libel.

It was England which claimed Osborne's full attention again in 1848 when the Chartists, encouraged by the overthrow of the French régime earlier in the year, organized a gigantic petition to Parliament demanding an extension of the franchise to the working class. Men of property took fright, expecting nationwide riots and looting. At that critical moment Osborne's relative, Kingsley, together with F. D. Maurice and two Christian laymen, J. M. Ludlow and Thomas Hughes (both barristers), formed the spearhead of a group of liberal Christians whose aim was to educate the professional middle class into some kind of understanding and sympathy for the Chartists; while at the same time they hoped to educate the largely atheistic Chartists into an understanding of Christianity. By this means the group aimed to bring about a gradual amelioration of social injustices without upsetting the existing social order. These Christian Socialists, as Maurice called them, published a new journal *Politics for the People*, to which Osborne contributed under the pen-name of Sam Gonze.

His first Country Letter was written in the first person as a country labourer from the aptly-named parish of Scantypane, and it made the complaint that Squire made more fuss of his pigs and stock, and fed and housed them better, than he did his labourers. It was a well accepted point which *Punch* had often illustrated in cartoons and which Kingsley was making the central point of his country life serial *Yeast* for *Fraser*'s magazine. Osborne wrote:

> They expect us to do the work of meat fed men, on wages which won't find meat. Then, Sir, they are all against crowding the Stock, and say they can't thrive amidst bad smells; why, bless you, they crowds us in our cottages, till we scarce have room to turn; and as for smell—eight or ten for ever sleeping in one room, who have most of them been at hard work all day, the land undrained above us, and the ditches full of the stuff we can throw nowhere else—why, if smell hurts a pig or a sheep—the squire has not a ram or a boar which could live a week in health where most of us live; *they never think of bringing gentlefolks round to see how they lodge us*; they don't care to see that *we* are kept in good air, and in well-drained dwellings.[1]

Osborne did not think much of the six points of the Chartists. In another article in *Politics for the People* which he entitled 'A

Country's Opinion of the Six Points of the Charter', he said that annual parliaments would simply keep the parliamentary pot forever boiling, and as for paying members of parliament, why pay them to do something which they were already 'scrambling to do for nothing?' He concluded that all the Charters in the world would not make a bad master good—or a harsh landlord kind. And in this Countryman's words we find Osborne's personal faith:

> Let us have power to earn fair wages wherever we can get work; let us have decent dwellings wherever we are forced to live; give us power to worship our God on the day he appoints; let us have a chance of rearing our young ones in their duty to Him in Heaven, and to the rulers on earth; and no Chartists will ever drive us to disturb the country by asking for changes which would pull the rich down and make the poor still poorer.[2]

Osborne had now won a national reputation as an unpaid contributor to *The Times*. His letters were always controversial, if not by their content then by their provocative and even vitriolic form. His strong sense of his own social position and personal identity ensured that he had no inhibitions about using the most ferocious language. His early interest in medicine became intensified as a result of his observation of the generally unsanitary conditions throughout the country and the periodical epidemics of typhus and cholera. His heart would sink when he did his cottage rounds during a cholera visitation, and in 1853 he described the disease sardonically as 'the great scavenger of our race'. 'The cholera is cleaning out our human cesspools, removing sewage— mortal and immortal', he noted grimly.[3]

He began a series of careful experiments in the rectory on the causes of cholera, and finally decided that germs were responsible. In 1854 he described in print how he had trapped organic material in the effluvia of a cesspool by dropping a metal pipe into it to act as an air shaft and then examining the air under the microscope. He found 'countless masses of animated, active bodies' and felt sure that some were a new genus which could also be found where vegetable and animal matter decayed. As a good Christian he was convinced that all those bodies had their allotted place in the balance of nature and were nature's cleansing agents. In his usual bluff manner he wrote that 'if the public could be brought to *see* that which floats in what they *smell* from sewers and cesspools, they would be more careful in the removal of filth in such a way as to, as far as may be, limit the escape of its life-crowded atmosphere'. In thus hinting at a germ theory Osborne was far ahead of his time, for the theory did not gain general credence until T. H. Huxley came out in favour of it after 1870.

Early in the course of the Crimean War Osborne visited the battlefield at his own expense to examine the medical facilities available, and he went on to the hospital which Florence Nightingale had set up at Scutari. Her friend and government supporter, Sidney Herbert, became one of Osborne's good friends as a result of the Crimean visit. The parson was not content merely to observe conditions, but dressed the wounds of the sick and dying with great skill and tenderness. His combined role of priest and medical man made his deathbed ministrations especially solemn and consoling.

He was deeply shaken by all that he had witnessed in the Crimea, and on returning to England he wrote up and published his experiences in a pamphlet entitled *Scutari and its hospitals*; more importantly he spoke at public meetings all round the country appealing for funds for the hospital service and to help the wounded. That public work earned him the grateful thanks of the government, a sign of approval which led Mr Walter to look even more favourably upon Osborne's letters to *The Times*. From that date onwards Osborne was best known as 'S.G.O.', the initials which signed his letters, and his loyal Dorset admirers interpreted this as 'Sincere, Good and Outspoken'.

During the 1860s S.G.O. was often asked his opinion of trade unions, bodies which were coming to be much in the public eye and in great need of legal protection. His usual reply was that because the 1860s was a time when all kinds of groups with special interests were attempting to bring pressure upon the government, it was natural to find trade unions doing the same thing. Nor did he know of any law, human or divine, which forbade strikes, although he did approve of the existing legislation which forbade union members combining in order to compel other workers to join in a strike.

Like other Christian Socialists, he was convinced that education was the key to social unity. Through education workers would learn to think and to reason for themselves and cease to be victims of ranters and demagogues. As they received more of the benefits of education, so they would feel more self-respect and would in turn demand and receive respect from others. In 1864 he aired his views on education in two long letters to *The Times* in which he told the middle classes to pay more attention to the early years of their children's training and to the standards of private boarding schools. Too many people, he said, resembled the farmer's wife from Strawberry Farm who summed up her educational targets with the words, 'I like to see the girls home with good manners, the boys well muttoned.' S.G.O. was fond of children and insisted on the importance of a child's early formative years. He anticipated Dr Spock when he said, 'I hold it to be true, and to be a truth deserving all attention, that a child is born to love; it has to learn to fear.' He advised simple toys which let the imagination run free, like building bricks, and he argued that toys ought not to be given to individual children—which encouraged a love of personal possessions—but should be given to a 'nursery commonwealth' and enjoyed by all the children. He also warned middle-class parents about their habit of sending children out of the drawing room for fear that they would hear unsuitable adult gossip, because in most instances, said S.G.O., the children were only banished to the company of servants whose conversation was often equally if not more unsuitable.

He enjoyed firing off his grapeshot on behalf of sanitation, women's rights, free trade, emigration and other subjects closely linked with country life. He ran full tilt at obstacles and naturally made enemies on the way, although he never quite undestood why that should have been so. In his own village he was the complete parish rector, a tall, serious-looking man with a full beard. He was paternalistic and plain-spoken, delivering his sermons without notes in straightforward language which his parishioners could understand. Most of his sermons were practical homilies derived from his knowledge of the realities of Dorset working life and its daily problems. Like a number of parsons, especially in Dorset, S.G.O. thought that emigration was one practical solution to agricultural poverty. Australia was the favourite country and S.G.O. dug into his pocket to pay the passages of some of the Dorset people. He favoured schemes for associated emigration where families and groups went out as entities and the relation-ships of village communities were thus preserved.

S.G.O. and his wife were kindly, hospitable people who lived in an unpretentious manner and kept open house for those who shared their social and political opinions. S.G.O. disliked formal dinner parties and the Osbornes seldom gave or attended them. Local gentry did not often visit him because so many of them tended to disagree with him. In his younger days, S.G.O. would go out with the hunt perhaps one day a week in the season, for he dearly loved riding, but it would be a gross exaggeration to call him a 'hunting parson' at any stage of his career. He did not have to finance the church renovations, since these had been taken care of by Lord Portman in the 1840s, but he did rebuild Durweston Rectory, and village tradition has it that the house was almost completed before anyone realized they had forgotten to make provision for a front door.

S.G.O. became a staunch supporter of the famous slogan for country workers, 'Three acres and a cow'. Largely thanks to his untiring efforts over a long period of time, sanitation in Dorset was greatly improved. The Dorset labourers certainly appreciated all he did for them even if the 'yeomen farmers' remained hostile. There is a famous story that one day in the streets of Blandford he was stopped by a Durweston 'yeoman farmer' who exclaimed, 'If it were not for "the cloth" I'd take you by the nose and lead you down the street!'—to which S.G.O. responded like an old war horse with the warning, 'Don't worry about "the cloth", just you try it!' The farmer stumped away and S.G.O.'s admirers were sure that had he tried to make good his threat that farmer would have rued the day.

His early interest in Ireland became attenuated over the years. Staunchly Tory in that regard at least, he was a strong Unionist who disapproved of Gladstone and Home Rule ideas. Ireland, declared S.G.O., was in the 1880s and 1890s a nation 'made drunk by oratory and kept drunk by newspapers'.

Like many a strict Christian in Victorian times, S.G.O. was fascinated by crime and the seamy side of life, and prison reform became another of his pet causes. His intense interest in criminal investigation was in his own words 'almost depraved'. A century later he would have been an addict of detective stories. Like the Savoyards, he believed that punishment should fit the crime, and he had little faith in the existing penal system as a means of reforming the criminal. He was a stern opponent of capital punishment and in the vanguard of the campaign against it. The last letter he

ever wrote to *The Times*, a month or so before his death, dealt with
the Jack the Ripper murders which had been taking place in
Whitechapel.

He was above all a restless and practical man. He disliked
particularly the High Church party with its ritualism and he regarded the claim of some priests to special authority as being both
impudent and illfounded, an attitude which brought him into
conflict with several of his professional colleagues, not least Bishop
Wilberforce, for whom S.G.O. had a long-standing distaste which
was heartily reciprocated. But the parson reserved his deepest
contempt for those who uttered holy words without showing the
example of a good life to support them.

His fame brought him a heavy postbag from strangers who
were bold or desperate enough to hope that he could solve their
personal tragedies, and he answered all of them to the best of his
ability. Often the burden of human suffering exposed in those
letters depressed him so greatly that he would lapse into long fits
of silence which continued for days on end, to the amazement of
strangers who only knew of his reputation as a lively conversation-
alist and were repelled by this gloomy stranger.

After 1860 he hardly ever left Durweston, and day followed day
in placid routine: parish work in the morning, followed by answering
letters, and then reading or writing about the public issues which
were then occupying his time. He kept in touch with affairs outside
the parish through correspondence, and members of parliament
and even ministers of state often wrote to him for advice or information. Apart from his family, his friends tended to be the men
with whom he had campaigned, like Sidney Herbert, Mr Walter,
Lord Northbrook and Lord Rivers.

The titles of his pamphlets showed his strong practical streak:
The Beer-Shop Evil, 1852; *The Nature of an Oath, as taken in a
Court of Justice familiarly explained in a short Catechism. With a
few words of advice to a person about to give evidence, etc.*, 1840; *The
Savings Bank*, 1835; *A word or two about the new Poor Law*, 1835;
Letters on the education of young children, 1865; *The respective duties
of Landlords, Tenants and Labourers*, 1861. The pamphlet about
Scutari and its hospitals was in a different class in that it was widely
read, but his other papers, while earnest, were so full of facts
presented in a fluent but uneven style that they never achieved
popularity, useful though they were. He knew he was not a gifted

writer or even a well educated man. 'I have not the slightest pretence to be called "learned",' he said. His letters were a different matter. They always struck home for they had an attractive vigour and originality, and were clearly the work of a sincere man determined to get improvements made. Osborne possessed enormous energy, and had he been in the least ambitious he could not have failed to make an enduring name for himself in some field of social endeavour. When his elder brother acceded to the title of Duke of Leeds, S.G.O. was given the courtesy rank of a duke's son and became Lord S. G. Osborne, but to those who knew him he was unforgettably S.G.O., a title which had been most honourably earned.

In 1875 he retired and, his wife having died, he went to Lewes in Sussex where he lived very quietly until his death in 1889. That event brought forth a number of respectful obituaries, and a little later a two-volume collection of his letters was published complete with a prefatory memoir. Since then, however, S.G.O. has sunk into almost total obscurity, an undeserved fate for such a lively man, whose views during his lifetime generated intense emotion and whose investigations in many instances had a decisive effect on the progress of social legislation. His published work, including the letters, alone entitles him to our respect as a social force in the mid-Victorian period.

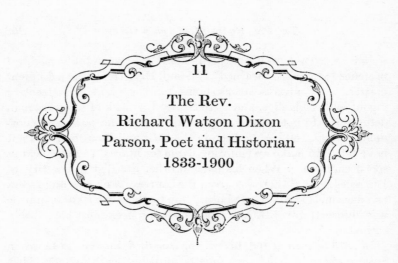

The Rev.
Richard Watson Dixon
Parson, Poet and Historian
1833-1900

The *Dictionary of National Biography* lists Richard Watson Dixon as historian, poet and divine, in that order. He was a historian by virtue of his work on *The History of the Church of England from the Abolition of the Roman Jurisprudence* in five massive volumes. He was a poet who spanned the period from Dante Gabriel Rossetti to Gerard Manley Hopkins, and his poetry infused beauty and drama into the dry bones of his church history. He was a divine, since he took Holy Orders and became an Anglican minister, although for a short time he tried his hand at schoolmastering.

Dixon was born on 5 May 1833 at Islington, London. His father, James Dixon, was a leading preacher of the Methodist Church and his maternal grandfather, Richard Watson, was a famous Wesleyan minister. His mother was James Dixon's third wife, and much younger than her celebrated husband. She bore him six children and was a kind step-mother to his daughters by earlier marriages. Methodist families were often large, and size was frequently an advantage because the rule that Methodist ministers were not allowed to remain permanently in one place but must move on every three years or so made it almost impossible for their children to make permanent friendships until they became adult. A family which could find satisfying companionship among its own members was fortunate.

Most of Dixon's childhood was spent in the industrial towns of northern England during years of intense industrial and political agitation. When he was four years old his mother impressed upon him the importance of voting Tory on the occasion of the 1837 general election. She made her son a Tory, but the injustices and deprivations which he saw as a child left him scarred for life. He approved of the efforts of writers like Carlyle and Kingsley to make such issues public, but he shrank from actively supporting political campaigns and preferred the personal philanthropy advocated by Charlotte Yonge in her novels. Dixon was not a strong boy; he was often ill, and his physical delicacy added to his natural shyness and introspection.

The Dixon family was both professionally and truly pious, and Dixon's filial biography of his father spoke of him as living on 'a vast height of holiness'. James Dixon had a melancholy and taciturn nature in spite of his national fame as a preacher, and his children stood somewhat in awe of him although they never questioned his affection for them.

As a result of the family's peregrinations and his own poor health, young Dixon did not go regularly to school until he was fourteen, when he joined the King Edward's School in Birmingham, whose distinguished headmaster, James Prince Lee, was a former teacher at Rugby School and a disciple of Dr Arnold. Although Dixon was preternaturally well grounded in religious literature and had read more English books than any other boy at the school, his ignorance of Latin, Greek and arithmetic placed him in the bottom class among pupils much younger than himself. His essays were bad and his handwriting was worse, and he was constantly summoned to the headmaster's study for a caning in punishment for unsatisfactory exercises. Those experiences marked him, and in an autobiographical short story, 'The Rivals', he stated that his natural timidity and his late schooling gave him the habit of comparing himself with others, invariably to his disadvantage. To avoid trouble he became over-anxious to please and grew adept at assuming protective colouration. Overshadowed by a powerful father, misunderstood at school, it was inevitable that he should possess more than his fair share of 'impressibility', as he termed his timidity. Poetry was an emotional release, both reading and composing it, and by the time he was ready to leave school for university his friends were all convinced he was a national poet in the making. 'In Memoriam' had just come out and Dixon and his circle were great admirers of Tennyson. Dixon thought that the poet had opened a fresh window and taught him to look at things with 'a sort of transcendental feeling'. Rather more unusually, Dixon admired the poetry of John Keats, a poet who was entirely out of favour. Poetry and idealism were linked in Dixon's mind and he and his friends wanted to devote themselves to work which would improve mankind.

His leaving school certainly became him better than his arrival, and the last few weeks were sweetened by winning a prize for prose and a prize for poetry. The poem was a 262-line historical epic decked out with overcolourful embroidery:

> . . . and the golden haze
> Of sunset was upon the daedal maze
> Of nature,—deepening the orange gleams,
> Glossing smooth olive leaves, empurpling stream,
> Gilding brown tree-stocks, glowing through the grapes,
> And dancing on the corn-tops . . .

In 1852 he went to Pembroke College, Oxford, only to be swiftly disillusioned by university life. Lectures were a farce, and the intellectual thought he had anticipated was poor in quality. His school friend, Edward Burne-Jones, joined him and introduced William Morris to Dixon, and the three of them, with others, talked of their idealistic hopes and discussed forming some celibate Brotherhood dedicated to social work in the London slums. That Brotherhood was too amorphous to materialize at the time, although later on some of its members called themselves the Pre-Raphaelite Brotherhood. By then however the notion of celibacy had been dropped, and there was no plan for social work in the slums. Burne-Jones described Dixon at college as 'another fine fellow, a most interesting man, as ladies would say—dark-haired and pale-faced . . . He is a poet also. I should be sorry to dash the romance of his character, but truth compels me to say he is an inveterate smoker.'[1]

Another Birmingham friend, Cormell Price, arrived in Oxford. Dixon was in the midst of a group of very articulate young men who talked endlessly about painting, art, poetry, architecture and society. William Morris amazed them by writing 'The Willow and the Red Cliff', which Dixon thought a fine poem. They listened to John Ruskin who brought Dante Gabriel Rossetti to their notice and the group adopted Rossetti as their hero. A number of the group saw their future in the Anglican Church. In 1855 they launched a literary magazine whose purpose was to invigorate society as a whole by its high moral tone. It survived for one year, during which period it gave support to the views of Carlyle and Ruskin and vowed loyalty to Rossetti. Dixon had discovered a minor talent for painting and he renounced poetry and went to London to study art. He lodged with Morris and Burne-Jones in Red Lion Square near the Working Men's College, where Ruskin taught in the evenings, and in which both Morris and Burne-Jones took an interest because of Ruskin. Dixon may even have taken some lessons from Rossetti. Certainly he was one of the band which painted the famous murals of 'Morte d'Arthur' for the Oxford Union Debating Room.

Dixon was busy and happy. His art experiences in London had the salutary effect of showing him that poetry, not painting, was his métier, and in a letter to his friend, Edwin Hatch, he suggested that it was 'insanely unjust' that they should waste themselves by writing for magazines to make a living when for fifty pounds a year they could live in the Lake District and write poetry. Dixon was always completely realistic about money. His father was poor, and Dixon had two brothers waiting for some money so that they could emigrate to Australia. There would be no money left to give Dixon a private income. Hatch also came from a poor background, and these two young men were forced, as much by financial considerations as anything else, to return to Oxford and study for Holy Orders.

Did Dixon make the right decision? A more determined painter or poet, or even a more self-determined man, might have decided differently. Yet Dixon's entire background pointed towards the Church. He was also sensitive to suffering, and had in youth been greatly troubled with apocalyptic visions. For his Oxford prize historical essay he had chosen the theme of life in the tenth century when men and women went in dread of the millennium. Rather unsound as to history, it had been powerful in poetic imagination.

In any event, having made his decision Dixon abided by it. He was ordained and became a curate in the slums of Lambeth, where all the curates were overworked and underpaid, so he had plenty of scope for self-sacrifice.

There was one splash of brightness in the drab Lambeth grind

when William Morris asked him to perform the marriage ceremony
between himself and Jane Burden. Dixon was delighted to oblige,
but became so flustered that his tongue slipped and he called them
'William and Mary'—to the joy of the company, who had been
anticipating that very mistake. Dixon laughed with them. He had
a keen sense of the ludicrous.

In 1861 Dixon went to another London working-class district,
Newington Butts, again as curate. He stayed there long enough to
marry a widow twelve years his senior, who had three daughters,
and he published a collection of poems entitled *Christ's Company
and Other Poems*. His marriage was happy enough. He needed a
wife who was a companion and mother figure, and he got on excel-
lently with his little step-daughters. The poems were less successful
than his marriage, partly because he included everything and did
not make a judicious selection. The reviews were unfavourable,
and he was completely discouraged. He retired from the literary
and painting scene and took refuge in his newly acquired family.
Parish visiting in all weathers brought on chronic bronchitis, and
Dixon decided to try schoolmastering as a profession, since it had
the advantage of being carried on under cover.

He resigned his curacy at the end of 1861 and for a very short
time taught at Highgate School where Gerard Manley Hopkins
was one of his students. Ill-health forced an early resignation and
he went north to Carlisle, where he took up a job in the High
School. He remained there for several years, an ineffectual teacher
whom the boys treated badly. He tried to maintain his self-
esteem by continuing with his poetry, and even published some
pieces, the best of which were word pictures as carefully detailed
as a Pre-Raphaelite painting. He discarded the metrical experiments of his earlier poems in favour of verse which owed much to
Keats and to Cowper. He became depressed, exhibiting a deep-
seated melancholy like his father's. He felt regret for his youth
which had vanished before its golden promise had had a chance to
blossom. He became reluctant to publish his work and risk public
criticism. He wrote bleakly to his friend, Hatch, 'As for me my
history is comprised in the following sentence: School will re-open
tomorrow Aug. 14.' He was thirty-three, but his wife's seniority,
and his step-daughters on their way to young womanhood, must
have made him feel prematurely middle-aged. He stuck to teaching
for two more years and then, in 1868, he returned to the Church as

a profession, being appointed a minor canon and honorary librarian of Carlisle Cathedral.

He discovered that his return to the Church sharpened the conflict between poetry and religion. Poetry was high romance, but Dixon's life was meaningless without the demands of duty; the creative act of writing poetry was physically so exhausting that when his clerical work tired him out, or his spirits sank, his poetic impulse also ebbed. None the less it was distinctly enjoyable to be working again with books around him, and Dixon began tentative research on the sixteenth-century English Church, having in view the writing of an encyclopedia article. In the meantime he was offered a literary commission of a very different nature. His father died in 1871, and the Methodist movement asked Dixon to write the official biography. Dixon was glad to agree and the book, published in 1874, was a typical Victorian biography of the public life of a public man. The Methodists were delighted with it and praise, so rare in the canon's life, was indeed welcome.

But Dixon still missed the fun and companionship of his Oxford youth. Of course, even marooned in Carlisle he could read about the exploits of the now famous Pre-Raphaelite Brotherhood, and there were letters now and again. Once indeed he had an unexpected encounter with Burne-Jones and William Morris at Naworth Castle. And then, out of the blue, came a letter from Rossetti: 'Is it a compliment or the contrary to tell a man whom one has known for 18 years that one had no idea till now of his possessing first rate powers?' The letter ended, 'Many thanks (though tardy ones) my dear Dixon, for so much good work.' Rossetti had found the volume of Dixon's poems, which he had long possessed and never read, and this time he had opened the book and read it. He told Dixon the poems were subtle and varied. He liked 'Orpheus' best of all but also enjoyed the odes 'To Summer' and 'On Departing Youth'. Dixon replied instantly. 'I would rather have had that letter than all the laudations of all the periodicals in existence.' As a brief postscript, Dixon added the information that he had just been presented to the small country living of Hayton, near Naworth; and at the end of that year, 1875, the Dixons indeed moved into the vicarage and the poet began a new chapter as a country parson. How many years ago it seemed that he and Hatch had considered living in the Lake District and writing poetry!

Now he was actually there, still writing poetry, but how different the circumstances.

Hayton was a few miles east of Carlisle in a beautiful setting with the Scottish hills to the north and the Lakeland mountains on the south-west horizon. Dixon took a scholar's interest in the numerous local antiquities, which included Hadrian's Wall, and he acted as custodian when the villagers had it in mind to plunder them as a source of free building stones for additional farm out-houses. Dixon was a scholar, too, in the pulpit; his parishioners often sat uncomprehendingly as he preached at length on some recondite theme, but they valued his conscientious pastoral ministry and liked him as a man, sympathizing with his painful stoop, his hesitant step and his persistent cough. He was the best listener in the village and always had time to stop and hear some-body's troubles. Sometimes he seemed almost too good a listener, saying so little himself, but that was the product of a lifetime's diffidence. A sophisticated companion with an ear for nuances might detect in his conversation a certain wry irony, which was his protective shell. Few guessed how he yearned for the warmth and intellectual companionship of his old Oxford friends.

He kept himself mentally alert by working on his Church history, by now greatly expanded from the original concept of a magazine article. He was to labour on this history for a quarter of a century. It had been commenced as an answer to J. A. Froude's view of the Reformation and the ensuing legislation, and it was expanded to become a straightforward chronological account. He concluded that 'a reformation was needed in many things; but it was carried out on the whole by bad instruments and attended by great calamities'. Secluded in a country village, Dixon was not close to academic libraries, a factor which added greatly to the difficulties of writing his book. He summed up these problems as 'want of books leading to constant corrections and insertions of newly found matter, remote situation, many interruptions!'

In 1876 his wife died. She was only fifty-eight and although we know little about her there is every reason to believe she had been a good and loving wife to her delicate, melancholy husband. His step-daughters, who were always fond of him, remained at home, looking after him, managing the vicarage and helping with the parish work. They were in every way daughters of the manse and a great comfort to him.

Dixon wrote one short poem which Dr Sambrook believes is a veiled lament for Mrs Dixon: 'O Ubi? Nusquam'.

She comes not: in the summer night
The trembling river runneth bright.
O look again, fond heart of love,
On darkling earth, on heaven above.

Behold, the poplar trees divide
The long-drawn space where sunset died:
There still is the redly ebbing light
Dying beneath the hand of night.

The cloud-bars now with solemn pain
Upclose, and all is wrapped in rain:
Ah no, that sky holds not her form:
It is the altar of the storm.

With the exception of that poem, Dixon's literary work during this period was limited, if that is the correct word, to a long and ambitious poem entitled 'Mano'. It was a philosophical and historical epic poem which, written, revised, published and revised again, occupied him for many years.

He preferred to work in the parish without a curate, shrinking from having to direct or criticize someone else, but as soon as his Bishop realized the exceptional quality of the vicar of Hayton he loaded Dixon with extra-parochial church duties of one kind and another until the burden of these responsibilities together with those of the parish became too much, and from 1879 he did employ a curate. Sometimes the curate was the kind of man with whom Dixon had nothing whatever in common, and the vicar had to be fatalistic about it. As a rule the vicarage household retired early at night except for Dixon himself. He would shut himself up in his study to smoke, reflect, work at his history or at his poetry, or—if a guest were staying—to talk until very late.

He had the consolation of a new friendship with Gerard Manley Hopkins, a young poet who had admired Dixon's poetry for a long time, to such an extent, indeed, that just before becoming a Jesuit priest Hopkins had made his favourite selection of Dixon's poems and copied them into a book to keep permanently by him. Hopkins wrote to Dixon in the hope that it would comfort the older poet to realize how deeply one person at any rate appreciated his poems. Hopkin's letter shook Dixon 'to the very centre', and the two men began a lengthy and valuable correspondence. Hopkins spoke about Dixon to his friend, Robert Bridges, and discussed Dixon's poems with Coventry Patmore. Patmore was so interested in Hopkins's account of the parson poet that he wrote away for 'Mano', which had been published in its first version.

Such lively encouragement gave Dixon a new burst of creative energy. Through the medium of letters he was talking to friends and poets as he had done in the glorious days of the Brotherhood. He sent newly written poems to Hopkins for criticism. Dixon had a particular warmth for Hopkins because not only did he admire the younger man's poetry, but he was in a position to understand very well the clash between the poetic and the religious vocation, and he sympathized with Hopkins's decision to put his religious vocation first—although he urged Hopkins to agree to the publication of his poetry.

In 1880 Robert Bridges stayed at Hayton Vicarage. Dixon met him at the station—'a tallish, elderly figure, its litheness lost in a slight, scholarly stoop which gave to the shoulders an appearance of heaviness, wearing unimpeachable black cloth negligently, and a low-crowned clerical hat banded with twisted silk'. Dixon walked abstractedly along the platform, his face dark and solemn, but the mouth full and tender unhidden by his beard. His eyes, under their heavy black brows, were clear and friendly and his voice was surprisingly deep. Bridges greatly enjoyed his visit. In the daytime the two men would walk in the country or play spritely and un-orthodox lawn-tennis in the vicarage garden. At night Dixon would take out his poems and the two men would sit over the fire, talking poetry until the small hours, the vicar puffing away on his pipe.

At about this time Dixon was surprised, but pleased, to be asked by Hall Caine to contribute some sonnets to an anthology. Rossetti had told Hall Caine that Dixon, although his poems had been almost totally forgotten, should be represented in a modern collection. Three poems were accordingly chosen.

One of the main difficulties in the way of popular appreciation of Dixon's poetry was his habit of employing very individual rhyme schemes. Critics felt more at ease with conventional rhymes and metres, and experimental poets, no matter how scholarly their background, always ran the risk of being criticized on grounds of incompetence.

Simultaneously with his poetry and his parish work, Dixon continued with the Church history, the second volume of which had now been published, but to his great disappointment without arousing much interest. The impression he was making on the academic and poetic worlds was sadly out of keeping with the thought and effort put into his works. He was again overtaken by depression, feeling himself to be a lonely widower without any intellectual companionship in the village. Month after month passed during which he met nobody except his parishioners, whose conversation was limited, his step-daughters, or perhaps a fellow clergyman on some church business. The correspondence with Hopkins and with Bridges was valuable to him both as a poet and as a human being.

In 1882 he had the good fortune to make a second happy marriage. The new Mrs Dixon was the former Matilda Routledge, eldest daughter of George Routledge, the publisher of Dixon's Church history. Routledge was a Cumbrian man and an unusual person. He believed it was his mission to educate as well as to entertain the reading public, and he was especially pleased when he had the opportunity of publishing scholarly but readable histories. He liked to travel his own books in the north country so that he could keep in touch with booksellers and with the book-buying public. Canon Dixon was exactly the kind of author whom Routledge liked to have on his list and he welcomed his daughter's choice of husband.

Matilda Dixon was younger than her husband but she was in her forties and there would be no children. She was a companionable step-mother to Dixon's three step-daughters, who had by this time been joined by a niece of Dixon's first wife. The household was a very feminine one, full of soothing women who made life as easy as possible for the vicar, and Mrs Dixon was a capable manager and a good hostess. She was an asset to Dixon in more ways than one, and as his time became increasingly occupied, she helped organize his life so that he did not overtax his strength.

In 1883 he was appointed to the more important and better paid living of Warkworth, not far north of Newcastle, in Northumberland. It was a large, beautiful village dominated by the great

castle owned by the Percies. Harry Hotspur had lived in the castle
and attended Warkworth Church. Indeed, a church had stood on
the same site since the eighth century, and there was an ancient
chapel hewn out of the cliffs above the River Coquet—the famous
Warkworth Hermitage.

Dixon had moved across the Pennines, but he was still a country
parson and his new Bishop, like the former one, was not slow to
appreciate his usefulness. In 1884 he was made rural dean of Aln-
wick; from 1886 to 1892 he was proctor for the archdeaconry of
Lindisfarne, and from 1891 he was examining chaplain to the
Bishop of Newcastle. His church duties were as onerous as they
had been in Hayton, and had to be performed before he could turn
to his literary pursuits.

Rossetti died in 1882 and Dixon wrote a memorial article on his
former hero. He worked on a revised 'Mano' for a second edition,
and he continued with the Church history, visiting London several
times a year to research his material. Often he asked Robert
Bridges to help by looking up special points in the Public Record
Office and in the British Museum Library.

The new version of 'Mano' came out in 1891 and could not be
ignored. It showed Dixon's Pre-Raphaelite affiliations by its
medieval setting, but it departed from the usual Pre-Raphaelite
atmosphere because of its uncompromising authenticity, which was
strikingly different from the usual contrived medieval scenes of
popular Victorian romances. In addition 'Mano' contained an
unmistakable element of doubt and fatalism which was typical of
medieval man but alien to the Victorian reading public. Critics
were as unsure of 'Mano' as they had been of Dixon's sonnets.

The younger readers had no such doubts, taking 'Mano' as
further proof that the Anglican Church ought to wake up to the
vicar's literary worth and find some niche for him which would not
be as tiring as a country parish. The Church, alas, remained deaf.
Dixon's public admirers were not influential. Algernon Swinburne,
to be sure, liked 'Mano' so much that he suggested Dixon for Poet
Laureate, but was Swinburne joking? Hopkins had become a
Jesuit priest, and who was Robert Bridges that the Church should
take notice of him? So Dixon was left in his parsonage and expected
to get on with things as best he could.

For the first three years at Warkworth he managed without a
curate—a man as gentle and unassuming as Dixon would frequently

think that curates were more trouble than they were worth—and he travelled in all weathers to the cottages of his scattered parish, holding cottage services at the more outlying places. There was the consolation that Warkworth was more accessible than Hayton had been to visitors from the south. His spacious vicarage overlooked the River Coquet where it widened into an estuary to the North Sea. Its Norman church had once been sacked by a Scottish king. The historic village, with its stone houses, was certainly picturesque. Dixon went meekly about his duties, and continued quietly with the poetry and Church history. In that latter undertaking he was not unique. Not more than twenty miles to the north another country parson, the Rev. Mandell Creighton, was working on a Church history and Dixon was pleased to find so congenial a neighbour.

Dixon's poems began to reach a new and select public as a result of Bridges' tireless propaganda, and a new edition of his poetry was printed on Henry Daniel's private press. In one of those poems Dixon spoke of the born poet who, aware of the conflicting claims of poetry and religion, 'yielded to the strict law of duty'. His was a divided nature, one half 'Long struggling with a world that is amiss' and the other longing for poetry, 'The sweetness which did never cloy.' He was in the public eye. He wrote articles for the *English Historical Review* and for the newly started *Dictionary of National Biography*. He edited a *Bible Birthday Book* for Routledge, and a new book of poems for the Daniel Press. That was published in 1887 and brought comparisons with Blake.

He became mournfully aware of increasing age both in himself and in the friends of his youth:

> Thou goest more and more
> To the silent things; thy hair is hoar
> Emptier thy wearing face; like to the shore
> Far-ruined, and the desolate billow white
> That recedes and leaves it waif-wrinkled, gap-rocked, weak . . .

Nature, his source for so many poems, now mocked the human condition.

> With laughter thou dost greet
> The human sigh and groan
> That mourns the thing that's gone . . .

In 1889 he lost two close friends, first Edwin Hatch and then Gerard Manley Hopkins. He buried his grief in work, and when his fourth volume of Church history received good notices he hoped, unavailingly, to be rewarded with some academic church position which would relieve him of parish work. Disappointment, depression and severe colds and influenza in the winter months made him unable to work for the major part of 1892. A curate looked after the parish. In a fit of religious despair he vowed to abandon secular poetry and to devote the rest of his life to the service of God. He and Matilda took a holiday in Ireland, where he renewed memories of Hopkins by visiting the Jesuit house in Dublin where Hopkins had died. Talking to the Jesuits there, Dixon realized the extent of Hopkins's loneliness. His fellow priests had sensed that Hopkins was out of the ordinary, but they had never understood the true nature of his poetic genius. It merely underscored Dixon's secret resolve to turn his back on the world.

Oddly enough, at this moment when he was renouncing hope of recognition, he became a focal point for a group of new young poets led by Bridges and including Laurence Binyon, Henry Newbold, H. B. Beeching and Mary Coleridge. They were fascinated by his connection with the Pre-Raphaelites, by his fastidious taste, his gentleness and his profound scholarship. Dixon was touched. It was another Brotherhood all over again.

Those early links were being snapped. William Morris died, and although Dixon had never understood or approved of Morris's socialism, he was saddened at his friend's death. Then it was the turn of Ned Burne-Jones, whose loss Dixon took very hard indeed. All art was lifeless now. 'All is but toys; renown and grace is dead,' he wrote to Bridges. Pembroke College, to his immense pleasure, awarded Dixon the honorary degree of doctor of divinity in 1899. He did not live much longer. The winter took its usual toll of him and in January 1900 he fell ill with a sharp attack of influenza which proved fatal.

Mary Coleridge wrote a memorial article, 'The Hermit of Warkworth', reminding her readers of his Pre-Raphaelite vision, which was sometimes obscure, sometimes absurd even, but always intense; she quoted:

For me, for me, two horses wait,
Two horses stand before my gate;

Their vast black plumes on high are cast,
Their black manes swing in the midnight blast,
Red sparkles from their eyes fly fast.

She included some of the nature poems admired by her generation.

Rise in their place the woods: the trees have cast,
Like earth to earth, their children: now they stand
Above the graves where lie, their very last . . .

There was the description of the pale moon:

Lo, there on high the unlighted moon is hung,
A cloud among the clouds . . .

Probably the gentle Canon's best loved lyric was the 'willow
poem':

The feathers of the willow
Are half of them grown yellow
    Above the swelling stream;
And ragged are the bushes,
And rusty now the rushes,
    And wild the clouded gleam.

The thistle now is older,
His stalk begins to moulder,
    His head is white as snow;
The branches all are barer,
The linnet's song is rarer,
    The robin pipeth now.

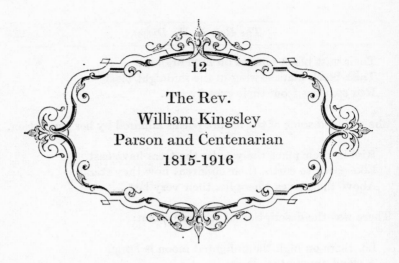

12

The Rev.
William Kingsley
Parson and Centenarian
1815-1916

Nineteenth-century Yorkshire was blessed with an abundance of colourful parsons. Canon J. C. Atkinson was vicar of a Yorkshire moorland parish for over fifty years, and became an antiquarian through his determination to uncover as much as possible of the history of his parish. Men like Atkinson became enthusiastic micro-patriots and built up a warm relationship with their parishioners, founded on mutual respect. In a like manner their sons often entered the Colonial Service and became junior District Commissioners in outlandish places, studying the language and anthropology of their charges and fighting the Civil Service loyally on their behalf.

Few Yorkshire parsons were more genial or more versatile than the Rev. William Kingsley, rector of South Kilvington from 1859 to 1916. For many years he held the title of 'England's oldest rector' and he was so spry that he did not engage a curate until after he had turned ninety. The village proudly celebrated his centenary in 1915, with him still in harness, although he was growing weaker and in the last year of his life was mainly confined to the rectory while his curate did virtually all the parish work.

Among his many friends were J. M. Turner and John Ruskin, but surprisingly enough Kingsley is now almost completely forgotten. His extreme longevity had the disadvantage that his widow was too old to undertake the customary pious biographical tribute (she outlived him by only fifteen months) and as they had no children to assume that task, he survived only in the memories of

Rev. W. Kingsley

To Miss Bell
    with best wishes
from those friends who made this drawing
of an old and valued friend

Two drawings of
the Rev. W. Kingsley

Canon R. W. Dixon

younger friends, and the blazing fame of Canon Charles Kingsley, which endured into the twentieth century, has quite outshone the softer light of the Yorkshire rector with the same surname.

William Kingsley was born in Berwick-on-Tweed in June 1815, a time when his father, a regular officer in the Army Pay Department, was occupied on the field of Waterloo. William Kingsley was proud of being a Northumbrian and proud of its culture, folk customs and local heroes, even though most of his adult life was spent in Cambridge or Yorkshire. At school he showed a normal boy's interest in machines and mechanical models, and he was befriended by a brilliant but unstable cousin of George Stephenson. Kingsley used to insist that this cousin was far more original and inventive than the famous 'Rocket' designer, but he lacked the perseverence needed to finalize ideas and rarely bothered to go further than to indicate preliminary sketches and models, although at the 1851 Exhibition in Hyde Park he exhibited an electric telegraph which he had invented some years previously. Young Kingsley became his willing and unpaid apprentice and was taught how to 'file flat', a dextrous feat in the days before mechanical planing machines. His patron was so impressed by the boy's natural aptitude that, when informed that Kingsley was going to Cambridge to enter Sydney Sussex College, he complained, 'It is wasting a smith.'

William Kingsley enjoyed his university studies, turned from mechanics to mathematics and was a wrangler in 1838. He took his M.A. in 1841 and, as the prerequisite to a university teaching career, became ordained in 1842, much to his father's annoyance because it signified a departure from the family tradition of military service. William argued cogently that he did not possess the robust physique needed for the rough and tumble of army life. Privately, he had already decided that the Army was far too constricting for someone with his remarkable bump of inquisitiveness. There was scarcely anything which did not interest him and he enjoyed turning his hand to all manner of pursuits. The last thing he wanted was to be fitted into a rigid mould.

Oddly enough, he was to become connected later with the Army for many years, but in a civilian capacity. The failures of the Crimean War forced the authorities to select their officer candidates more efficiently, and Kingsley was appointed an army examiner in technical drawing. He was also a visiting drawing master at

H

Woolwich Academy, where his most illustrious pupil was the Prince of Wales, an association recalled to him in 1915 when the prince, who by then had succeeded to the throne, sent Kingsley the usual royal telegram on his centenary.

It is now idle to speculate whether or not William Kingsley ever met his distant kinsman, Charles Kingsley, during those Cambridge years. The biographical devotions of Fanny Kingsley ensured that for decades Charles would be the only Kingsley popularly remembered, and even Charles's closest relatives—his brother Henry, the novelist; brother George, the doctor; and niece Mary, the traveller in West Africa—are barely permitted to share the stage with the Eversley rector. Both Kingsleys were at Cambridge at the same time, but their interests would most probably have kept them apart, and William was four years senior to Charles. The latter went to Magdalen College, then known as a 'fast' college, and in his first year thankfully threw over the traces in sheer exhilaration at leaving a strict Anglican home. The purely physical pursuits of wealthy young men at university meant more to young Charles Kingsley than the scholar's desk, while on the other hand William Kingsley had the academic mind and enjoyed learning for its own sake. Also his rather delicate health would have stopped any friendship with the hearties who were Charles Kingsley's friends at that time. In Charles Kingsley's second year, following his encounter with Fanny Grenfell, he altered his life style and joined a group of aspiring clergymen. Again, he was not likely to have met William Kingsley in such circles for the latter was not then considering a career as a parson, and took Holy Orders later on only so that he could teach in the university.

By the late 1860s, however, Charles Kingsley had become nationally famous and William Kingsley was an obscure country parson, whose wife was often plagued by well-meaning visitors asking if her husband were related to Charles. Loyal Mrs Kingsley had a tart rejoinder ready: 'You mean, is Charles Kingsley any relation to William?' So far as William Kingsley knew, his branch of the family and Charles Kingsley's had been connected in Devonshire up to the time of the Civil War, when William's branch supported the losing royalist side and went to Ireland afterwards, while Charles's branch fought on the parliamentarian side and remained in England, except for some who emigrated to America.

The paths of the two Kingsleys diverged after they took their degrees. Charles Kingsley was ordained and at once became a country curate. William Kingsley, greatly interested in Natural Science (which in the 1840s was as popular with advanced young thinkers as sociology and political science would be a century and more later), became a university examiner in that subject.

It seems that he did once make an effort to break out of the rut. He attended a lecture given by Dr Livingstone, and was so moved by the speaker that he offered himself as a medical missionary in Africa, only to be turned down on medical grounds. In addition to his indifferent health, Kingsley had become deaf following a fever which he contracted as a young man during a holiday in Munich. The deafness was progressive until he finally became stone deaf, a dreadful affliction for a sociable man with a great love of music.

He continued his studies at Cambridge and took his B.D. in 1848. Secluded in college, the political excitement of the 'Year of Revolutions' which altered the entire pattern of Charles Kingsley's life, passed William Kingsley by. He had discovered art, and he became a close friend of John Ruskin. For many years the two men were intimate. Kingsley would stay overnight with Ruskin when he went to London and Ruskin would stay at South Kilvington Rectory when he was in north Yorkshire. Kingsley did not have a high opinion of Ruskin's father, alleging that John Ruskin must have got his brains from his mother. Ruskin thought highly of Kingsley's taste and judgement in watercolours, especially of birds. Kingsley became a discriminating collector of paintings and drawings and, being of a most generous disposition, gave many away to friends.

Kingsley was a firm admirer of W. J. Turner and learned to paint rapid watercolours in the Turner manner and on the Turner scale. He possessed a number of Turners which for many years adorned the walls of South Kilvington Rectory. On one occasion, discussing with Turner some other painter, Kingsley suggested mildly that 'the want of power in a certain painter to depict what was not before him showed a want of genius' to which the great man replied emphatically, 'I know of no genius but the genius of hard work!'

Kingsley frequently despaired of the candidates he was called upon to examine for the Army. Once he added a note to his examination list to the effect that the Army chiefs could pick their men from either end of the list—'for they can none of 'em draw *or* paint'.

He was attached to the Civil Service as an outside examiner for fifty years, during which time he had frequent arguments with officialdom. His expense sheets in particular provoked dispute. One time he returned an item marked 'Porter 6*d*.' only to have an official rebuke telling him that 'liquid refreshment' could not be reimbursed. Kingsley explained that the item referred to the services of the man who had carried his bags at the railway station and inquired the correct language for describing such services in the future. Back came the proper phrase—'Portage, 6*d*.' Kingsley duly rewrote his expense sheet, received his 6*d*, and bided his time. When next he hired a cab he was happy to put it down on his expense sheet as 'Cabbage, 3*s*.6*d*.' in the entirely correct assumption that his masters would pay up and shut up.

He was an early pioneer in photography, not like Mrs Cameron pursuing an art form, but making use of the technique to photograph on to a block directly for engraving purposes. He was an amateur engraver of above average ability.

In the late 1850s he became engaged to Alicia Grant Wilkins, daughter of a successful Cambridge architect. Marriage meant the end of his university life, and he applied to his college for one of its country livings, and was appointed to South Kilvington, a mile or so north of Thirsk in North Yorkshire. This was a lucrative living which Sydney Sussex College had held since the early eighteenth century. The marriage took place in 1859, the year of his appointment, and the couple went to London for the honeymoon. There the new Mrs Kingsley suddenly died and the shocked widower took up his pastoral duties in Yorkshire in a mood very different from the one he had anticipated.

There was plenty of work to be done in South Kilvington. Kingsley found that the church, rectory and village alike were in a sorry state, with sanitary conditions so bad that health was constantly at risk. Improving the drainage was a practical task to which he immediately applied himself, with a success which was increasingly visible as the years went by. The problem of Dissenters hardly existed in South Kilvington, which had no chapel of its own. William Kingsley was a broadminded parson whose sermons and services were suitable for most brands of Protestantism. Really devout Dissenters had to walk into nearby Thirsk for their chapel.

The rectory was modernized inside and out, and its garden, fruit trees and greenhouses became district show pieces for Kingsley, like many country parsons, prided himself on being an up-to-date horticulturalist. His artless sense of humour was seen at work in the rectory grounds soon after he arrived, when he affixed a notice board to the back gate reading, 'Man-traps are set at night in these grounds'. He hoped by that device to deter the village lads who came round the back of the rectory courting the housemaids—the girls were certainly man-traps, he explained gleefully to his alarmed guests. The notice did not stop determined young men but it became part of village folklore and is still remembered with a chuckle by the old residents who recall the rector in his last years.

Five years after becoming a parson he married Octavia Barker, who was several years younger than Kingsley and the daughter of the rector of Thirkleby, a neighbouring village. She was a very suitable wife for him, not only because she had grown up in a country vicarage and thus knew all about the work and responsibilities of a parson's wife, but also because her sister was married to Tom Taylor, the dramatist and editor of *Punch*, and a former Professor of English literature at London University. He, too, had been at Cambridge but a year or so later than Kingsley. In 1846 he was admitted to the Bar and from 1850 until 1871 he was a civil servant, but his true love was the theatre and his job gave him enough leisure to be a successful freelance journalist and playwright. Like Kingsley, Taylor had been born in north-east England. The two men had much in common and became close friends.

The two sisters were both music lovers and Mrs Taylor was a gifted composer of light music. Kingsley was devoted to music, despite his deafness, and the rectory often echoed to the sounds of amateur musicians, some of them local, some guests. The village became famed for its choir, Mrs Kingsley taking a leading part. At one time a local family supplied four of the rectory housemaids, each girl a good singer, and these girls, with a brother and Mrs Kingsley, were the nucleus of the choir, and gave frequent concerts. There was also a good village orchestra which travelled round the district, and often performed in barns—sometimes with surprising results, like the occasion when a cow gave birth just as the orchestra came to the end of its piece, and the newborn calf bellowed unexpectedly. The audience laughed, to the bewilderment of the deaf rector who saw the merriment and turned in reproof to his neighbour, saying, 'Why are they laughing? I've heard that piece a hundred times and they played it just the same as always.'

The Kingsleys enjoyed entertaining and their home was often full of guests. The deaf rector would sit at table amid lively anecdotes and laughter, not a muscle moving, and at the end of each story little Mrs Kingsley would jump up from her seat and shout it into her husband's ear, when he would laugh in his turn and usually cap it with something amusing or interesting of his own. He never allowed his deafness to interfere with his enjoyment of every other faculty and he bore his condition with exemplary patience.

He was a keen fisherman who built his own rods and made his own flies. He had a wonderfully steady hand and in a note pencilled against an engraving of a Willow Wren in a fine 1800 edition of *Bewick's Birds*—Kingsley was a great lover of Bewick—he wrote: 'One day when I was fishing, a Willow Wren alighted on my rod, and examined every ring in hops. It spoke well for the steadiness of my hand.' Another pencilled remark in the Bewick was against the Cuckoo, mentioning that a north country word for Cuckoo was 'Gowk', which was also commonly applied to a stupid clumsy fellow. Kingsley's favourite example of its use was the bride at her wedding ceremony nudging the groom who seemed slow in making his responses, 'Say yes, ya Gowk!'

It was a cause of sadness to the Kingsleys that they had no children of their own. The rector was particularly fond of children and very patient with them. He enjoyed teaching and supervising in the school and in early summer he took the classes into the rectory hayfield where he fed the children gooseberry pie washed down with milk. Being rector and schoolmaster for so many years, Kingsley knew each child well, and their parents before them. Each season he bought quantities of tangerines as little gifts for the children, and at Christmas and Eastertime there were always presents of clothing for them, especially new trousers for the boys. His practical bent showed itself in his school organization, and he normally gained the support of the school inspector. Writing to a friend, he said:

I am trying to make 'object lessons' of some use, and have got the Inspector's leave to go my own way. My idea is for the children to know one thing pretty thoroughly before going to another, and about four in a year should be enough. I have been teaching them *Feet*, and find how little they observe by themselves. I

offered coppers for right answers to a very simple question, with
two days to look about, and got only one prizeman; so I gave
another and promised a bit of cane to all who did not answer
correctly, and I had no failures: so much for Solomon!

The course of 'Feet' included the wide differences in the feet of
ducks, sheep, flies and so forth.

In 1900 he wrote to the same friend about the 'New Code' being
introduced by the government into schools.

> . . . I shall be glad to have some talk with you about practical
> scholastics. I can easily supply the boys with spades; but where
> are they to get ground to dig? I can use some of the children
> to pick off gooseberry 'oobits', and do good in two ways, and if
> the boys learn to fight wasps, they will have got a good way
> towards fighting Boers. But then comes the difficulties of time
> tables.

He was as careful a teacher in his school as he was a careful
examiner for the Civil Service and the army, and he often complained that few people understood the mental worry of a serious
examiner placing candidates in competitive examinations which
might decide a candidate's entire future. He discovered that the
only way he could get his external examining done was to concen-
trate upon that and nothing else. He would take the work away on
his annual holiday in North Wales, where he was in considerable
demand as a visiting preacher. In a letter written in 1896 from
Capel Curig to the Rev. M. C. F. Morris of Nunburnholme he
said,

> I preached yesterday a sort of curse on the memory of Bishop
> Campbell, for encouraging the clergy to pull down the old simple
> Churches that fitted into the scenery like big stones, and re-
> placing them with flaunting meeting-houses. The people needed
> the old ones to remind them that their Church was as old as the
> hills, and not of the same date as dissent.

When he needed mental recreation he fished in the Welsh lakes
and rivers, the stream by South Kilvington being little more than

a beck. He loved boats and designed a number, mostly for inland waters but some as sea craft, and as he was an accomplished carpenter he built many boats himself. He had a large shed in the rectory garden which he used as a workshop. He possessed an array of fine tools for carpentry and wood carving and tempered them in the dining room fire. His boats had to be launched outside the village where there was sufficient depth of water. The rector tended to do everything on a lavish scale, including his boat building, and one boat, beautifully constructed, was unfortunately of such a size that when finished it was too big to go through the doors. The shed had to be partially demolished to let the boat out.

When Kingsley first went to South Kilvington the church had little to commend it apart from a fine view of the hills. It was a small, mean building whose fine oak beams and walls were washed white and it looked as much like a cowshed as like a church. The rector spent much of his money and more of his time beautifying its interior with wood carving. The great quantity of carving which remains in the church today represents only a fraction of the labour of love which occupied his years in the parish. The vanished carvings included some striking and intricate work at the back of the choir stalls, but the pews, pulpit, screen and a splendid chair remain in the church as witness to his skill. No one pew has the same design although all are based on bird, animal and plant motifs. His carvings were famous in his lifetime and many people visited the church to admire his art and marvel at his industry.

His love of music was also seen in his appreciation of organ music and his expertise in the matter of organ construction, but his experience when he built his own organ for the church was hardly felicitous. He made most of the parts himself and sent away to have the rest made. The huge contraption, which was totally out of proportion to the size of the church, was assembled under his supervision and when in place it filled the chancel, with pipes on one side and the massively carved organ jutting out on the other. It partially obscured the altar and dominated the interior to such an extent that many people actually felt uncomfortable inside. After the rector's death the village was impatient to have the gigantic organ dismantled and taken away, but had to wait until a church agreed to give it room.

Kingsley considered that many of the older organs possessed a better tone than the modern ones and he was fascinated by the mechanism of the old instruments. He remarked that the pneumatic action of the newer organs was unavoidably jerky, and said that '*legato* is the rule for organ playing . . . Old J. S. Bach had no pneumatics, and his music is full enough and melodic enough for an angel, though not for a demon.'

Village boys were pressed into service for working the bellows for the organ which, like its maker, had a fine and powerful tone. Sometimes there were mishaps. There was the day when the boy who was pumping the bellows decided that if he gave them some extra air the organ would keep going while he ran out to the sweet-shop for some sweets. Mindful of the rector's fierce reputation where the organ was concerned, the boy raced back across the churchyard without looking where he was going and ran smack into a gravestone. He knocked himself unconscious and was found when the organ stopped and investigations were made. The brother of that boy was taught to play the organ, which he did very well, and he developed a strongly proprietorial air towards the selection of hymns. One Sunday he remarked casually, 'I think we'll have "While Shepherds" today.' It was pointed out to him that it was the wrong season for that well-known hymn but the organist took no notice. 'I fancy "While Shepherds" today,' he insisted, and played it was.

South Kilvington was a fairly prosperous agricultural village where the main employment, apart from farming, was at a grist mill. The village knew a 'gentleman' when it saw one and their friendly, ingenious rector was certainly a 'gentleman'. He had long since outgrown his earlier poor health and had developed into a big-framed, imposing man with a full beard and a booming voice. Some of the children found his loud manner (probably due to his deafness) intimidating at first until they grew to know him better and to realize that more often than not he was teasing them. He and his wife could be relied upon to provide the traditional home-made meat soups during the hard winters, and the coal and blankets, not to mention bars of soap which were boiled up in the rectory.

In his latter years he turned increasingly to art, for his eyes did not give up like his ears and he possessed a fine collection of art books. He was generous in sharing his paintings and sketches with others. An old friend was Mrs Fawkes, whose collection of Turners at Farnley Hall was probably the largest single private collection in England, and on one of his visits there Kingsley took all his Turners 'for a pleasant sight for Mrs Fawkes'.

In the late 1890s the rector's friends urged him to engage a curate. Mrs Kingsley had become confined to a bath chair and the children made it their duty to keep her chair in good running order and to trundle her about the village. She had grown deaf, although not as deaf as her husband, and she could hear tolerably well when she used her ear trumpet. Kingsley agreed that a curate would be useful, reluctant though he was to take one on. As word was spread that the rector was looking for a curate a man presented himself promising to work free of charge. Kingsley felt suspicious of such altruism and declined the unusual offer. Later on he congratulated himself on his acumen because it seemed that another rector had been unable to resist the bargain and the curate had proved such a disaster to the parish that the rector had been driven to resign his benefice in order to rid himself and the parish of the man. Fortunately Kingsley could wait for the right applicant, and could afford to pay for him, and eventually an excellent young man arrived and was appointed.

The hundredth birthday of the Rev. William Kingsley was a notable occasion both in the parish and the neighbourhood. The local press was there in full force, Kingsley having provided copy for several years. The rector had not been well all that year and had rarely left his room, but his mind was always active and to the day of his death he enjoyed his daily game of cribbage. His wife, his most unflagging admirer, was deeply moved by the celebrations. She wrote to a friend:

He had a lovely birthday, and was unusually well that day. He began it with Holy Communion, in which the whole household partook by his bedside. Then a prettily illuminated Album, containing an address and the signatures of the whole parish, was presented to him, and he was very much pleased with it. A flag flew all day on the village green, and the evening bells sounded sweetly from Thirsk Church. Of the many letters, telegrams, presents, flowers, and attentions of every sort which flowed in all day I only allowed him to see a very limited quantity.

Among the letters he was shown was the one from the king,

written by Lord Stamfordham, and the one from the Archbishop of York and the one from the Master of Trinity.

He lived for a year after that birthday and died on 3 July 1916. His wife died in November 1917. They lie buried at the back of the church, still fondly remembered by the oldest residents of the village.

13

The Rev.
Sabine Baring-Gould
Squarson and Author
1834-1924

Among the industrious, widely published and even more widely
read authors of the latter half of the nineteenth century none was
better known than S. Baring-Gould, whose output was so prodigious as to suggest a factory rather than a man. His titles and subjects were amazingly diverse and although most reference books
called him a novelist it would be more accurate to describe him as
a popularizer and entertainer. Few parsons were as gifted as he,
yet the Church of England, flexible and welcoming as it was to
many, maintained a distinctly low profile when it came to Sabine
Baring-Gould. For instance, his religious views were too controversial, as he was of the second generation of the Tractarians, and
the Anglican Church still felt uneasy in the company of such
stormy petrels, believing that it had done its duty by offering them
shelter and further generosity was unnecessary. Thus Charles
Kingsley received less recognition from the Church than might
otherwise have been expected, and so did R. W. Dixon. Both those
men, like Baring-Gould, were idealists who wanted to see the
Church acknowledge a social as well as a religious function.

Nevertheless there were points of difference between Baring-
Gould and these other two parsons. The former was by birth a
squire, as well as parson, and his upbringing on the Continent left
its mark on his unorthodox opinions and tastes. But he resembled
Kingsley in writing songs which became nationally popular, and
thousands chorused 'Onward, Christian soldiers' and 'Widdecombe

Fair' without realizing that the songwriter was both a Dartmoor parson and a potboiling writer; and he resembled Dixon in writing monumental religious histories which testified to hours of solid and solitary toil.

Sabine Baring-Gould, born at Exeter on 28 January 1834, was the eldest child of two unusual people. His father was a cavalry officer in the private army of the East India Company who retired to his Devonshire estate only to become unendurably bored with the conversation and country pursuits of his fellow squires. Life in the country was clearly not for him. To make matters worse, the Devon squires were Tory to a man and Mr Baring-Gould was a confirmed Whig. His wife, daughter of an admiral, was a beautiful, sensitive woman who possessed some psychic gifts. She was perfectly prepared to fall in with her husband's eccentric plans for the family, and accordingly in 1837 Mr Baring-Gould let his historic manor house of Lew Trenchard to a tenant and took his wife and baby son off to Europe, travelling with servants and masses of baggage from one inviting spa to another.

Their son, Sabine, inherited good looks from both parents. He was a beautiful child who would become a handsome man and a distinguished patriarch. His earliest memories were of European towns and buildings. European Catholic art with an undercurrent of baroque and magic influenced the boy's early taste and for the rest of his life he infinitely preferred that to the bleaker art forms generated by Swiss Calvinism.

In 1844 Mr Baring-Gould took the family back to England so that his ten-year-old son might gain the benefit of an English education. The boy was enrolled in King's College, in the Strand, London, where he spent two thoroughly wretched years. His parents, who had rented a house in Warwickshire, then removed him from King's College and sent him to a Warwickshire school, where he was much happier, but he caught so many childish ailments that the doctor advised his father to take the lad to a warmer climate for the winter. Mr Baring-Gould needed no further persuasion and at once whisked his brood across the Channel. Thereafter, until he went to Cambridge, Sabine Baring-Gould's education would come from books, conversation, travel and experience. His mind was developed by massive reading and his memory strengthened through necessity, because without libraries and living an itinerant existence he was forced to rely on his memory

much more than he would have done had he had a normal education. As his books would later demonstrate, his memory was
infinitely capacious but not as infinitely trustworthy. In addition,
partly from his temperament and partly because of his mother's
interest in the miraculous, he developed a predilection for anything which was picturesque or dramatic.

He gave some indication of his character and intellectual
abilities when, as a boy of sixteen in Pau, he became aware of a
Roman mosaic pavement beneath a local farm and persuaded the
owner to let him organize an archaeological dig. We have an
account of those findings in a book he published in 1897.

In the year 1850 chance led me to the discovery of a Gallo-
Roman palace at Pont d'Oli (Pons Aulae) near Pau, in the south
of France. I was able to exhume the whole of the ruins, and to
bring to light one of the most extensive series of mosaic pave-
ments extant. The remains consisted of a mansion two hundred
feet long, paved throughout with mosaic; it was divided into
summer and winter apartments; the latter heated by means of
hypercausts, and of small size; the former very large, and opening on to a corridor above the river, once adorned with white
marble pillars, having capitals of the Corinthian order.

The principal room, 26 by 22 feet, boasted an elaborately
patterned pavement of circles and roses, with a huge cross which
measured nearly 20 feet by 13 feet, containing as a centre piece a
head of Neptune with his trident. Fish swam in the four legs of the
cross, and the superstitious French workers were so struck by the
resemblance to a crucifix that they crossed themselves and
exclaimed, 'C'est le bon Dieu, c'est Jésus!' They explained away
the trident as being the centurian's spear. Young Baring-Gould
attempted to persuade them that the design was pagan but he was
thwarted by the curé who said solemnly that the pavement had
been laid down in conscious prophecy of Christianity.[1]

The English boy, at sixteen, was already preparing the foun-
dations for his later studies of comparative myths which became
the basis of popular books. He was fascinated by the legend of the
cross, proving to his satisfaction and to the presumed interest of
his readers that the cross was a sacred Gallic sign, a hammer of
Thor, the symbol of the Buddha, a Phoenician sign for life restored

by rain and a symbol found in Italian excavations which long predated the Etruscans.

A year or so after the Pau excavation the Baring-Goulds returned to England. Lew Trenchard was still occupied by its tenant so until it fell vacant Mr Baring-Gould rented a house not far away, on Dartmoor, to which Sabine Baring-Gould was introduced for the first time. Its wild beauty and associations with history and magic made a deep appeal and he vowed to himself that when he inherited the estate he would make himself a custodian of Dartmoor, its myths and traditions.

He went to Clare College, Cambridge, in 1853, a handsome, dreamy youth who was both romantic and serious. He gravitated instinctively to the later Tractarian movement which had such a powerful dual attraction for the rebellious and the devout. He felt sure he possessed a call to enter the Church but his parents were so strongly opposed to the idea that in deference to their wishes he renounced it in favour of becoming a junior master at the Choir School of St Barnabas, Pimlico, although he remained there for a few months only. That church was made famous by three outstanding curates—the Rev. Charles F. Lowder, the Rev. A. H. Machonochie and the Rev. Bryan King. All three were Tractarians who introduced High Church rituals into their services and provoked scandalous riots in the church itself. In some quarters those men were regarded as martyrs, in others they were villains. Young Baring-Gould admired them greatly and longed to join them.

The Rev. Charles Lowder was an interesting man, a banker's son who had reacted against the comforts of the family home and burned with a zeal to take his High Church faith right into the heart of the London slums. Baring-Gould was anxious to assist him but did not see how he could do so, in view of his father's attitude. The most positive step he took at that time was to refuse to obey his father's wishes, that he should teach at Marlborough Grammar School where his uncle was headmaster, and to insist on teaching at a school of his own choice. This was the newly established Woodward School, which was run on strong Church principles. Baring-Gould taught there for a short period and then for eight happy and productive years he taught at its allied school, Hurstpierpoint, for a salary of twenty-five pounds a year and board. He became popular with the boys, not for any particular skill as a teacher but for his born talent for telling engrossing yarns.

After his mother died in 1863 Baring-Gould approached his father again on the matter of taking Holy Orders and this time his parent was more amenable. One reason was that neither of the two younger Baring-Gould sons was willing to be ordained and it had been for one of these boys that Mr Baring-Gould had been reserving the family living of Lew Trenchard. At the moment it was being kept warm by Mr Baring-Gould's brother. In those circumstances, therefore, he was prepared to change his mind and give his blessing to his eldest son.

Sabine Baring-Gould lost no time in studying for Holy Orders. He was ordained within the year and became curate to the Rev. John Sharpe, vicar of the small woollen and coalmining town of Horbury, near Wakefield, in Yorkshire. Sharpe was a quiet, tolerant bachelor who perceived a bold Messianic streak in Baring-Gould and smartly harnessed it by ordering him to open a mission at the roughest end of the town.

Baring-Gould was delighted. It was the sort of work which he had seen and admired at St Barnabas. The mission was called Horbury Brig and Baring-Gould used the premises as an adult night school, a Sunday school, a choir practice hall and an unofficial religious meeting house. The new curate, tall, handsome and dedicated, won his parishioners' hearts as much by his knack of telling a story as by his sermons. He liked them in return. Horbury was crammed with robust Yorkshire characters whom their curate would later portray in his books, men and women who enjoyed belting out emotional revivalist hymns, including the one their own curate wrote for them, 'Onward, Christian soldiers', set to a catchy tune by Sir Arthur Sullivan. It seems surprisingly militant, from a sensitive man like Baring-Gould, but its popularity was undeniable and it hit the mood of the Salvation Army, formed a few years later.

By composing hymns, Baring-Gould was following an old Tractarian tradition, copying the example of John Keble, John Henry Newman and John Mason Neale, as well as Low Church and revivalist preachers who concentrated on composing hymns which would enjoy mass appeal. Learned at Sunday school, sung again and again in adult life, many of those hymns became woven into the fabric of English community singing. A later Baring-Gould popular hymn, 'Through the Night of Doubt and Sorrow', was not original but a translation from a well-known Danish hymn.

Two years after arriving in Horbury, Sabine Baring-Gould astonished himself and everyone else by falling passionately in love with a beautiful, illiterate mill-girl of sixteen, Grace Taylor. She was exactly half his age.

He paid no attention to the difference in their social stations. Work at the mission had given him an insight into the lives and characters of mill-workers, and in his first novel, *Through Flood and Flame*, published in 1868 and partly autobiographical, he made the point that the rich had no monopoly of beauty and refinement. The determined lover ignored the well-meant and sensible objections to what the world might consider a misalliance, and he sent the girl to live with a family in York for a year or two so that she could acquire the education and social poise which would be needed when she became the squire's wife and had to take her place in Devonshire society. His plan was triumphantly successful. His barefoot mill-girl was transformed into a young woman of charm and distinction. The couple were married in May 1868 and their happy union lasted nearly fifty years.

Soon after his marriage Baring-Gould was appointed 'Perpetual Curate'—virtually vicar—of a hamlet in Swaledale called Dalton, more familiarly known in the locality as 'Dalton i't Muck'. He received a stipend of £150, to which his father added a like sum. Dalton was a country village made up of unquestioning and un-complaining farm labourers, a sad contrast from the lively men and women of Horbury Brig, and no amount of mission fervour was likely to stir up Dalton. If that were not disappointing enough, Baring-Gould was further plagued by an opinionated and inter-fering patroness, the Viscountess Downe, who, being the daughter of a bishop, believed that she had a divine right to pontificate about parish affairs.

The minister turned to his beautiful young wife for comfort and he occupied his leisure moments and kept his wits and his memory sharp by embarking upon an extremely ambitious literary project, nothing less than a semi-scientific answer to Charles Darwin and his evolutionary theory. Baring-Gould's book was entitled *The Origin and Development of Religious Belief* and it elaborated the theme that Christianity was true not because of some rather dubi-ous statements in the Bible, but because it corresponded to a basic human need.

This unusual and iconoclastic argument alarmed both the High and the Low Church factions and gave the author at once the reputation of being not only peculiar but potentially dangerous. Easy-going, middle-of-the-road Churchmen, who might in other circumstances have been inclined to be tolerant towards him, were offended by his critical Tractarian manner and since it was often those men who pulled the strings of promotion it is easy to imagine that when Baring-Gould's name cropped up during discussions about advancement it would be urbanely edged aside. Baring-Gould pretended not to care, but it needled him to be passed over, and his sharp tongue and barely concealed contempt for career clergy merely served to keep him for the rest of his life as a country parson and, very definitely from the Church point of view, nothing more than a country parson.

There is a revealing passage in his book of reminiscences when he described his half-brother, who had entered the Church[2], and was at one time Baring-Gould's curate before becoming a West Country parson. 'Being a man of exceptional gifts, mental and spiritual, no efforts were made by the successive bishops of Exeter to retain him in the diocese, where all favour is, or, at the time was, accorded to the flat-fish, one sided, one eyed, who flop about but do not swim or breast the wave. Some of these, as the sole, are very good eating, but the majority—the dabs—taste of the mud on which their lives are spent.' His half-brother, being no dab, was continually rejected by his bishop.

Nor was Baring-Gould helped in this matter of preferment by his incorrigible habit of telling stories against bishops.

Archbishop Tait was dining one evening at the house of the Duke of Westminster. During the meal his face became ghastly. Laying down his knife and fork by the plate, he said to himself in a suppressed voice: 'It has come to pass at last as I feared. I have been dreading, expecting, a stroke.'

'Console yourself, your Grace,' said the Duchess of Sutherland, who sat beside him. 'It is not *your* leg but *mine* that you have been pinching.'[3]

It is true that between his time at Dalton and his taking over the living of Lew Trenchard Baring-Gould was given promotion, but that occurred through the good offices of the prime minister, Mr Gladstone, and not through the benevolence of the Church.

Gladstone had been very impressed by Baring-Gould's answer to
Darwinism and, when the opportunity arose, he offered the parson
the crown living of East Mersea, Essex. The Baring-Goulds moved
in 1871 and remained at East Mersea for ten years, during which
time six children were born to them. Mr Baring-Gould died in 1872
and Sabine Baring-Gould inherited the Devonshire estate, and so
in theory he might have demanded the family living in addition,
but since the incumbent was his elderly uncle the new and
absentee squire left the rector to finish his days peacefully at
Lew Trenchard.

East Mersea is nine miles from Colchester. It was built on mud
flats which lay open to the sea, to the winds and to the towering
clouds. Baring-Gould rapidly took the measure of his new parish
and soon realized that its inhabitants were largely indifferent to
him. Indeed, many were Dissenters and actively hostile to Anglicans. The landscape was the uncompromising one described by
George Crabbe, an earlier parson. Baring-Gould used the countryside as the background for his melodramatic novel, *Mehalah*, a
powerful piece of writing which gained a few favourable notices.
He went on to try his hand at biography, choosing as his subject a
lately dead Devonshire parson and eccentric, the Rev. R. S.
Hawker of Morwenstow. The book was an overnight success and
Baring-Gould's name was made as a popular author.

Inhabitants of Morwenstow might complain of glaring in-
accuracies, caused by rapid writing and only a fortnight's research in
the village, since a rival biography was in progress and Baring-
Gould was anxious to publish first,[4] but the reading public loved
it. Modern critics have complained, and quite rightly, that Baring-
Gould was not a meticulous researcher, but whatever his short-
comings in that respect he managed to catch the spirit of Hawker,
and his lengthy digressions about folklore, wrecking and superstitions illustrated a new side of Baring-Gould.

But the one literary work which absorbed him for the remainder
of his time at East Mersea was nothing less than a sixteen-volume
collection of the lives of the saints, a project which he apparently
hoped would contribute to religious harmony but which, initially
at least, did not have that effect as the Roman Catholic Church
immediately placed it on the Index. The saintly compendium was
typical Baring-Gould, derived not from detailed study and checking in specialized libraries, which he could not visit in any case, but

originating from his bottomless ragbag of reading and recollection, and from information culled during a number of trips to the Continent, some of them undertaken with his family and some in company with another clergyman. These journeys were luxuries which he could afford once he had come into his Devonshire inheritance.

In 1881 his uncle, the Rev. Charles Baring-Gould, died and Sabine Baring-Gould was instituted to the living of Lew Trenchard. Henceforth until his death in 1924 he would devote himself to the expensive and loving restoration of his manor house, to his parish work, to loving care of the parish church, and to his immense literary output which paid for the first three preoccupations.

The village of Lew Trenchard comprised about three hundred souls, a compact village with a few outlying farms on Lew Down. The Gould family had owned the manor as early as the reign of Henry III but vicissitudes of fortune had seen it pass from their hands until the eighteenth century when a Margaret Gould married a rich Exeter merchant named Charles Baring. Sabine Baring-Gould considered it his pious and pleasing family duty to restore the manor house and the village to their former glory.

In manner, appearance and activity he was the squarson as much as he was the man of letters. He built model cottages, he threw open the manor house for school parties, and he followed the West Country custom of Harvest Festivals, rejoicing in the knowledge that Hawker had been one of the first country parsons to revive this old tradition.

Baring-Gould was not of that group which held that village parsons needed to bully their parishioners. He asserted that good parsons did not leave many memorials and that it was the delinquent clergyman who was longest remembered in the countryside. 'That our old country parsons were not, as a rule, a disreputable, drinking, neglectful set of men I believe, because so few traditions of their misconduct remain.' He thought highly of a former country parson who had visited the uncle of Baring-Gould's elderly coachman every day without fail for twenty years, when the old man had become bedridden, 'to see and read and pray with him every day, Sunday and weekday alike'.

Baring-Gould's parish visiting was conscientious but remarkably stately. He was driven by his coachman to the various cottages in the early mornings, and so as not to embarrass his people by taking them unawares, he made sure they always had advance notice of his coming. Duty done, he would return home to write for the rest of the day in the seclusion of his study, standing at a tall desk. He loved his house and the working conditions it provided.

Only one who, like myself, has the happiness to occupy a room with a six-light window, twelve feet wide and five feet high, through which the sun pours in and floods the whole room, whilst without the keen March wind is cutting, cold and cruel, can appreciate the blessedness of such a window, can tell the exhilarating effect it has on the spirits, how it lets the sun in, not only through the room, and on to one's book or paper, but into the very heart and soul as well.

Grace Baring-Gould lived up to her name and was a beautiful and dignified 'Lady of the Manor'. The rest of the children were born at Lew Trenchard. They had a large family, fifteen in all although a daughter died in infancy. Their father often appeared a trifle remote to his children. A famous story, probably apocryphal, but true in spirit, tells how the rector at a children's party held at the manor said indulgently to a pretty child, 'And whose little girl are you?' at which the child burst into tears and sobbed, 'Yours, Papa!' The children enjoyed a fairly free life in Devonshire and grew up to be vigorous and independent young people, excellent at all kinds of outdoor activities.

Many country parsons in the 1880s were antiquarians and social historians because their parish routines gave them ample opportunity for observation and deduction, and their educational background had given them a mildly academic taste. Most of them were cut off from interesting intellectual conversation once they took up their village outposts, and they derived great satisfaction in posting articles off to magazines, happily anticipating the correspondence which often resulted from appearance in print. Baring-Gould's antiquarian bent showed itself very strongly in the field of folk song collecting, a hobby which seems to have originated fortuitously as the result of a chance remark at a dinner party not long after he went to Lew Trenchard. Folk song collecting was quite the vogue at that time and he had a genial collaborator in K. A. Bussell, an Oxford don and one-time Vice-Principal of Brasenose College. The two men became friendly when the Bussells rented one of Baring-Gould's cottages for their holidays. A third companion in these ventures was another country parson, the Rev. Fleetwood Sheppard, of Thurscoe in Yorkshire.

Song-collecting proved very interesting and could be depended upon to give rise to unexpected incidents, and although in the interests of drawing-room gentility Baring-Gould usually bowdlerized the songs out of all recognition, he preserved the original words in his manuscripts which now repose in the Plymouth Reference Library. Baring-Gould's enthusiasm and success in popularizing Devon songs, especially hunting and drinking songs, led to more careful collecting later on by Cecil Sharpe and the Rev. Charles Marson, and to Baring-Gould's great satisfaction helped to save poems and songs which contained the beliefs, superstitions and recreations of a pre-industrial age. His most famous rescued song, 'Widdecombe Fair', is by a happy chance only very slightly at variance with the actual words as he took them down from the song-man.

Throughout the years he continued writing and turned his hand to so many different themes that it is impossible to distinguish any consistent thread, and we must conclude that he wrote partly from habit but mostly for money. From his first published work until 1920 he published 159 books. He wrote romances just as Sir Henry Rider Haggard and Sir Arthur Conan Doyle wrote romances, speed and versatility being keynotes of Baring-Gould's work. Only a few of his novels have survived: *Mehalah*, his most impressive story; *John Herring*, containing his best characterizations, and *The Broom Squire*, one of his last novels, published in 1896, and one of his best.

In all his novels, good or bad, the landscapes were lovingly and vividly pictured, contributing greatly to the value and interest of the book. He had no creative gift for character drawing, and had a tendency to choose as his main personages gloomy men who were forced to lead doom-driven lives. In view of his romantic marriage it is strange that his attitude to women should be distinctly ambivalent. He appeared both to fear and to despise their sexual power over men, and to conclude that in the majority of cases their influence was malign. This could hardly be part of his own experience, for the two women most important to him, his mother and his wife, were sensitive, passive women who allowed their husbands to dominate them.

He lived, as it were, at one remove from the common man in

spite of his happy marriage and large family. It proved quite impossible for the squarson to identify with the poor despite his genuine missionary instincts and his work at Horbury Brig and in his home village. His descriptions of men and women in scenes of poverty in his novels never rang true. He depicted them as carefully as he described the tors and marshes of Dartmoor but they remained mere puppets. Although industrious beyond the norm, and blessed with many gifts of the born writer, including the very special one of knowing how to hold an audience, Baring-Gould was never compelled to learn the humility of discipline and so he never produced more polished literary works which would have brought him within the ambit of serious critics. Among his many books were titles like *Book of Were-Wolves, In Troubadour Land, The Book of the Cevennes, A Book of Dartmoor, Cornish Characters and Strange Events, Songs and Ballads of Devon and Cornwall,* and *Song of the West.* He wrote innumerable articles for antiquarian and West Country magazines.

As a popular writer he gave much pleasure to general readers who liked to read travel books, especially about Europe and the West Country, in the days before paid holidays and foreign package tours were commonplace. His numerous books on the West Country in all its aspects, written with a sense of fun and decidedly from the heart, popularized that lovely region and helped to make it a magnet for holiday-makers. Baring-Gould was a past master at recounting anecdotes and he particularly enjoyed writing about eccentrics, past and present.

His wife died in 1916 at the age of sixty-six, by which time the children had grown up and left home, and Baring-Gould lived on at Lew Trenchard, lonely, arthritic, and writing compulsively. Most of his friends were either dead or, like himself, practically housebound by ill-health. In 1906 he had had the curious experience of reading his own obituaries as a result of a mistaken report of his death, and their kindly tone had surprised him pleasantly. That at least had been gratifying. In 1918 Clare College honoured its former student by bestowing upon him an honorary fellowship, and that too was very gratifying. His beloved West Country recognized and honoured him as a patriotic son by electing him President of the Devonshire Association, and a President of the Royal Institution of Cornwall.

Sabine Baring-Gould died in 1924, after living through the Firs

World War and its subsequent upheavals without allowing many of them to affect him or to despoil the living museum of Lew Trenchard. He had written two volumes of reminiscences and planned a third, but he became too infirm to complete that last volume, so effectively his recollections ended at the year 1894. The result was that Sabine Baring-Gould, perhaps more truly than he knew, remained essentially a nineteenth-century writer and a Victorian country parson.

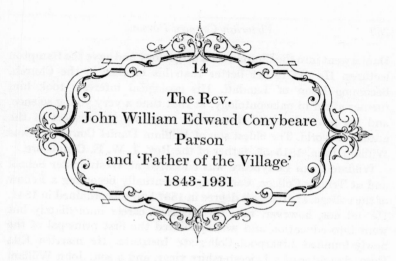

14

The Rev.
John William Edward Conybeare
Parson
and 'Father of the Village'
1843-1931

In most villages the parson was exactly what his title implied, and a life of service to his parishioners gave that sense of purpose which made a country vicar's life rewarding in a very special way. The Rev. J. W. E. Conybeare was just a parson for many years, although he retired in late middle age and spent his last years as a freelance writer. Eventually he left the Anglican Church and became a Roman Catholic convert.

He had followed an old family tradition when he became a parson. The Conybeares were originally Huguenots who fled from France during the persecution and settled in the West Country where they joined the Church of England. Successive generations became clergymen, their most eminent divine being John Conybeare, 1692–1755, an Exeter vicar who became a Bishop of Bristol. The clerical bent continued in the family and that bishop's son became a rector, remembered mainly on account of his two remarkable sons, John Josias and William Daniel.

John Josias was educated at Oxford, entered the Church and became a Somerset vicar with an interest in poetry and geology. In 1812 he was appointed professor of poetry at Oxford and from 1817 onwards he lectured and published papers on geology, speaking to the Royal and to the Geological Societies, specializing on the geology of Somerset and the West Country. Just before his death he delivered the Bampton lectures.

His younger brother, Willliam Daniel, pursued a similar career but in nearly all respects he far outshone John Josias. William

Daniel went into the Church, took up geology and gave the Bampton lectures. He did rather better than his brother in the Church, becoming Dean of Landaff. His geological interests took him further afield to palaeontology, at that time a very young science, and his researches and discoveries won him the respect of the academic world. The eldest son of William Daniel Conybeare was William John, 1815–57, father of the Rev. J. W. E. Conybeare.

William John Conybeare was educated at Westminster School and at Trinity College, Cambridge, eventually becoming a Fellow of the college. He took his degree in 1837 and was ordained in 1841. He did not, however, take up a clerical career immediately but went into education and was appointed the first principal of the newly-founded Liverpool Collegiate Institute. He married Ella Rose, daughter of a Leicestershire vicar, and a son, John William Edward (called Edward by the family), was born in 1843. Another son, Bruce, died at the age of five. W. J. Conybeare was not a robust man and in 1848 ill-health forced him to resign from the Institute. His friend and co-author of a number of books, the Rev. J. S. Howson (later to become Dean of Chester), succeeded him as head of the Institute. Conybeare took over his father's living at Axminster in Devonshire in the hope that a country parson's duties would be light enough for his diminishing strength.

This hope did not materialize and in 1854 Conybeare resigned. The family moved to Weybridge in Surrey, where Mrs Conybeare's brother, the Rev. Edward Rose, was a parish priest, and a last child, Grace, was born to the Conybeares. William Conybeare lived for only two more years and his death was a sad blow for his father, the Dean, who after attending his son's funeral went to the home of another son, suffered a stroke, and died shortly afterwards. Thus young Edward Conybeare, at the impressionable age of twelve, lost both father and grandfather within a brief space of time. The result was that he became older than his years, feeling that he must assume all the responsibilities proper to the head of a family, in order to look after a baby sister to whom he felt more of an uncle than a brother, to comfort a grieving mother, and to prove worthy of a most distinguished family background. It was a remarkably heavy burden for so young a boy.

Edward Conybeare's education up to that point had been thoroughly atypical. He had frequently accompanied his father on trips to the Continent where he acquired a taste for mountain climbing. Several years at Eton as a colleger gave him a self-assurance which Cambridge University polished thereafter. The mountaineering he had enjoyed as a child with his father was transmogrified at university into impressive roof climbing. He was admitted to Trinity College in 1862, became a Scholar in 1865, took his B.A. in 1866, was ordained deacon in 1868, received his M.A. degree in 1869 and was admitted as priest in the Anglican Church in 1869. As an undergraduate he had taught at the Jesus Lane Sunday School, and he followed his uncle's example in supporting the English Catholic Union.

He went as curate first to Staines and then to West Molesey; both parishes were close enough to Weybridge for him to be near his mother and young sister. Although he had adopted the clerical profession it was no secret that economic need and family tradition had dictated the course, not a sense of vocation, although he enjoyed the pastoral side of his ministry. He had the temperament of a versatile scholar, lively and imaginative, and his dearest hope was to follow in his father's footsteps and become a Cambridge don. If, however, he failed to gain a Trinity Fellowship, he expected that his college would offer him one of its several livings around the university, so that he would still be able to share in the academic life of Cambridge. In some measure this occurred, for in 1871 he was appointed to the Trinity living of Barrington, some seven miles south of Cambridge, but the living fell far short of what he had wanted and although for years he hoped his many friends and acquaintances would put him in the running for better things, he obtained neither the coveted Fellowship nor a more convenient parish.

Lesser men than he had succeeded in these modest aims, as he well knew, and the knowledge embittered him. Of course, his religious views did not help matters along, for the ruling Cambridge circles, and Trinity in particular, were imbued with Cromwellian fervour and Low Church Evangelical ideals, while Conybeare leaned to the ecumenical position of the English Church Union. He longed for one single Church; and his perfect solution was for the Roman Church to join the English one. He regretted the Pope's directive that English priests could not be taken on as Roman priests, which he rightly interpreted as meaning that if an English parson went over to Rome, himself for instance, then all his years as an English parish priest could count for nothing in Roman eyes.

If that clash of views were not enough to place a permanently black mark against him, Conybeare had a quick, acid tongue which did not endear him to the Cambridge élite. When he wrote in his diary about attending a gathering of 'sundry desiccated dons' we may be sure that it was an opinion which did not remain buried in his private journal but which surfaced to public view.

His diaries were commenced in 1857 and continued until 1925, when failing sight forced him to abandon them, by which time he had not only resigned from his living, but had become a Catholic. His handwriting, clear and ornate in the early volumes, became crabbed and difficult as his eyes failed him and in old age he was almost blind. The diaries make it clear that Conybeare was no humdrum clergyman whose vision was limited by the boundaries of his parish. Like Parson Armstrong of East Dereham in Norfolk, Conybeare commented on everything which took his attention. Thus in February 1869 he travelled on the newly-opened Metropolitan Line over Westminster Bridge and wrote enthusiastically, 'Travelled luxuriously to St Pancras the New Midland Station which has cost £5,000,000.'

His life as a country parson really began when he went to Barrington. That village was interesting for a number of reasons, not least for its wonderful village green of twenty-seven acres, bisected by an ancient causeway called the Church Path, which Conybeare reckoned to be at least a thousand years old. The causeway had once been pebbled but in Conybeare's day it was overgrown with turf. Rent from the Causeway Meadow had for centuries been used for the maintenance of the causeway, but at some date in the nineteenth century the Causeway Meadow had been taken over by an unscrupulous churchwarden who had stolen parish documents stored in the church. Conybeare visited the church before his installation and did not like what he saw. 'Nothing seems to have been done between 1627 (when bells were given, now all smashed up) and Thrupp whose revival Whiting has let drop again: all he could do.'

The bells referred to in that diary entry had been cast by one Miles Grey and donated in the reign of James I. During the Civil War the stained glass windows were broken by the Roundheads. In 1670 work began on restoring the church and silver plate was donated in 1680. Barrington Church was reasonably well looked after for the next century, but the régime of the Rev. W. Finch, a

Fellow of Trinity College who was appointed to the living in 1770, was nothing less than disastrous. He held the living for sixty-five years, and during twenty-five of those years he also held two other livings. There was no celebration of Holy Communion in Barrington Church for twenty-five years. Sunday afternoon services were held every three weeks, but only if the vicar considered there was a congregation present worthy of his time.

He would ride to the top of the hill and the clerk would signal to him from the bottom whether there was likely to be a congregation or no. If not, Mr Finch would ride away. If there were only children, he would give them sweets and send them home.[1]

The church bells were nevertheless unfailingly rung every Sunday morning at 9 a.m., the ancient hour for High Mass as ordered in the First Prayer Book.

After years of decay the living was sequestered and the Rev. Michael Gibbs, a young Fellow of Caius, appointed curate. He dubbed the village 'Barren-town' but he was brimful of zeal and rode regularly from Cambridge to get matters in order. The main church door was rehung and closed, to the disgust of the villagers. 'Where will our cattle go in the winter?' they demanded. Gibbs held confirmation classes, celebrated Holy Communion and insisted that in the winter months the villagers should bring candles in their lanterns which were secured in holes which Gibbs bored in the pews. He himself read from the pulpit by a candle fixed in a hole, and the first time he lit the candle with a Lucifer match the congregation was petrified with fright.

Edward Conybeare was as amazed by the corporate village sense of the past as he was appalled by the rehabilitation task which confronted him. 'Things awfully gone to rack. Wondrous stories from Oment of past history of Barrington. Delapidation work begun in house. Hung pictures,' he recorded in January 1872. One of the old stories which fascinated both him and his wife[2] was told by Thomas Chapman, to the effect that in years gone by a fairy cart came at night to take any persons not rightly belonging to Barrington Churchyard and those corpses would be buried five miles away at Shingay. At that time the story sounded like sheer rigmarole to the Conybeares but much later a leaden seal of the Knights Hospitallers was found at Shingay and taken to Cony-

beare for identification. Through this it became clear that there
was once a House at Shingay whose Knights Hospitallers claimed
the right to give Christian burial to persons forbidden it. So
Chapman's fairy cart must have been the wheeled bier of the
Knights Hospitallers taking corpses away under cover of darkness.

Conybeare, who took his antiquarian interests very seriously,
began steps to repair the church. It was partly twelfth century and
partly fourteenth, and an earlier vicar, the Rev. Matthew Robinson, a Fellow of Trinity, had actually sold the ancient carved oak
screen and the fourteenth century benches in the side aisles to
raise money for church restoration, but being disappointed in the
proceeds of sale he had halted any further destruction, for which
Conybeare gave many thanks. His aim was to repair the church
rather than to restore it. The Miles Grey bells were located, recast
and rehung. Conybeare was thrilled. It was the first time for fifty
years that three sound bells had been heard in the village, and a
large wooden panel was put up in the church to commemorate the
occasion and also to clarify the regulations which Conybeare
enforced strictly to ensure that the bellringers behaved with proper
decorum.

His first full year at Barrington was exhausting and the diary
was full of phrases like 'Tired and down'; 'Trying day'; 'Seedy'. He
was a hypochondriac who suffered miserably from neuralgia and
headaches, the last undoubtedly due to eyestrain as well as to
emotional stress and overwork. School examinations used to bring
on psychosomatic illnesses and the strain of university examinations was so severe that he collapsed and was awarded an aegrotat
degree. In addition to winning people back into the church,
Conybeare had to work hard to get order restored in the school. He
wrote off for texts and pictures from the National Society, then
wiped the dust off the school registers which had been started by
the energetic Gibbs in 1838 but had not been kept after 1842.
Within weeks the new vicar had organized a choir concert in the
school and raised £5 4s. 6d., a very worthy result which pleased
him although a raging toothache prevented him from attending
the concert.

He worked hard to make his first Good Friday in Barrington an
important occasion and was pleased to count 105 at the morning
service, even though sixty were schoolchildren and therefore a
captive audience. He remained, quietly contemplative, in the

church until the next service at 2 p.m. when about 170 attended, mostly working men who came straight from work in the fields and left their tools outside at the church door. There were 120 at the evening service and he felt, with justice, that it was an entirely satisfactory state of affairs in a village of about 800 inhabitants where the Dissenting spirit was very strong, and where Dissenting employers deliberately kept their men at work all day on the Anglican festivals to prevent their going to church.

Dissent had first taken firm hold of Barrington during those long years of Anglican neglect, and by the time the Conybeares were in Barrington most of the better-off and more respectable inhabitants were Dissenters. The dominant Coleman family, which owned a cement works, had been Dissenters for 200 years, and it had been a Coleman who donated the site for the Dissenters chapel, set up square and solid in 1854. It had replaced the older meeting place built in the reign of Charles II as a consequence of the Five Mile Act, Barrington being just over that limit from Cambridge. The Coleman heir, a lame boy of seventeen, surprised Conybeare one day by calling at the vicarage with the request that he should be baptized into the Anglican Church. Conybeare tactfully hinted that the boy should first consult his family, and the lad's doughty old aunt, hearing the news, objected most strongly. When the boy attempted to quote St Paul to support his wish, the old lady retorted, 'His name wasn't Coleman!' But the boy won his point in the end and joined the Anglicans.

The Barrington Dissenters did not cause any trouble for Conybeare. They quickly recognized his interest in the village as a whole, his readiness to help everyone, especially the men in times of unemployment, and they appreciated his learning. Unlike many Anglican parsons, Conybeare was on reasonably social terms with the Dissenting minister, and sometimes attended religious meetings in the chapel.

Meanwhile the vicarage was repaired, painted and furnished, fit for a bride, and soon young Mrs Conybeare came to the village and quickly became a favourite. She was by everyone's standards a beautiful young woman and years later she made village history when her husband, a pioneer cyclist, affixed a large seat to the front of his machine so that he could ride round the countryside with his dainty wife perched precariously in front of him. The vicarage was fairly modern, having been built in 1842 on an orchard site donated by Squire Bendyshe, whose estate was adjacent to the church. The vicarage had a fine flower garden, a walled kitchen garden and lawns sloping down to the river. Conybeare, who loved children, gave the children permission to play freely in the rectory garden. They never took liberties and made it their particular playground on Sunday afternoons after catechism in church.

The vicar kept in close touch with his Cambridge friends, going into the city several times a week, on horseback, on bicycle, on foot, sometimes taking the train there and walking home. His friends used similar means of transport and in summer they often arrived by boat. There was plenty of tea and talk on the vicarage lawn. Oscar Browning and Professor Waldstein would gallop up on the most obstreperous horses; Conybeare's cousins, George, W. and R. Macaulay, and their sons, would come; F. W. Myer; Dr Aldis Wright; Dr Parry; Dr M. R. James; A. C. Benson with his brother, Hugh; Walter Morley Fletcher; the massive J. K. Stephen, his shoes nearly dropping off his feet, with his sister who became principal of Newnham College, Anne Clough, the first principal of Newnham, and sometimes Rose Kingsley visited them.

The most important man in the village was Squire Bendyshe who lived at Barrington Hall. He was in Holy Orders and had actually served as a curate in several parishes although he had never been a vicar. He was a very shy bachelor and had succeeded rather surprisingly to the estate which was large but encumbered by inheritances to his sisters. Bendyshe was generous towards the parish charities but miserly in his private life. His garden was neglected, his house filthy, his beard unkempt, his clothes thread-bare. Yet he was a well-spoken man with a cultivated mind and an obsessive sense of family which constrained him to take notice only of old county families. He regarded most of the aristocracy as upstarts. Bendyshes had owned land in Barrington for 500 years but they looked back to Bendyshe Hall near Saffron Walden as their real home. That house was mortgaged to the monks of Rad-winter so that the Bendyshes could lend money for Edward III to besiege the town of Calais. The commercially-minded monks foreclosed on the mortgage and the Bendyshes had to live thence-forth on their Cambridge estate.

The Conybeares treated the squire with some degree of care, humouring his little whims for the sake of the village as a whole. His snobbishness was illustrated by a strange incident concerning

Pencil drawing of the Rev. Sabine Baring-Gould

The Rev. Sabine Baring-Gould on his morning round

The Rev. J. W. E. Conybeare with the bellringers of Barrington Church

his widowed sister-in-law, Mrs Nelson Bendyshe, who lived at Margate. (The Nelson was for Horatio Nelson, Bendyshe's great-uncle.) One day the squire told Conybeare that he wanted him to officiate at the lady's funeral. 'Sorry to hear she's died,' said the vicar, and was surprised when the squire replied, 'Oh, she hasn't, but my other brother thinks she cannot live long; to be sure he's a very impatient man but hearing that you were shortly going away for your sister's wedding[3] I wanted to make arrangements in case of your absence.' Conybeare said he would be leaving on the following Wednesday. 'Then I think we may fix the funeral for Tuesday,' decided the squire, and went away, his mind at ease.

The lady, however, had other ideas and, not dying at the stipu-lated time, precipitated the very situation which Bendyshe had tried to avoid, namely having to employ a substitute clergyman. The squire consulted the vicar once again. Conybeare merely suggested the name of a neighbouring clergyman and was aston-ished when the squire raised objections. 'I hardly like to say it, but you know some of our neighbours are self-made men, in fact the sons of tradesmen, and I should not like one such to take the funeral of my sister-in-law. We know ladies are so very particular in these matters,' he said stiffly. Conybeare next offered a clergyman whose father had been a professional man and to this the squire agreed. Conybeare went to his sister's wedding, the Bendyshe lady died and the funeral day was set. On the day before the ceremony the substitute clergyman broke his arm, and Conybeare being still absent, the dismayed squire had to go through the charade once more. He finally discovered close by the ordained son of a beneficed clergyman and propriety was observed.

The Conybeares greatly disliked snobbishness of any kind but they learned to live with it since the gentry contributed generously to local charities and it would not have done to offend them un-necessarily. Mrs Conybeare recalled an incident which occurred when the village labourers had been locked out by the farmers during a long industrial dispute. The vicar and his wife sympath-ized with the men and Mrs Conybeare, while discussing the matter with the lady of one of the grand houses, realized from the tone of the conversation that her companion strongly disapproved of the labourers. The vicar's wife hurriedly changed the subject to the new Holman Hunt painting, *The Shadow of Death*, which showed Christ in the workshop at Nazareth. Her companion confessed she

I

had seen the painting at the exhibition in London and condemned it. 'I do not like having forced upon me that our Lord was a working man and his Mother a peasant woman,' she explained frostily.

Barrington School was something of a problem for Conybeare. His first thought was a complete reorganization and he began by dismissing all existing teachers and hiring new ones. At first that seemed successful. 'Wondrous and instantaneous change in discipline,' he noted. But the new schoolmistress quailed before the mammoth and unexpected task of getting the registers into order and she resigned 'incontinently and of disgust'. In 1879 the school came partly under the control of the School Board and the day was arranged so that four and a quarter hours were devoted to secular teaching and paid for by the Board, and the other three-quarters of an hour daily was religious teaching, undertaken jointly by the vicar and the teachers, and paid for by Conybeare alone. It was an admirable arrangement which relieved the Board of part of the burden of payment and it lasted until the Conybeares left Barrington.

From the very beginning of his pastoral duties, Conybeare wanted to encourage village involvement and community celebrations. Ascension Day 1872 was his first true success and the diary showed his satisfaction. 'Great day. All school to church, and treat in aft. Tea on lawn, and games. Sack racing and swing boat hired from village. Feast now on. Band marched us back to church in grand style. Congregations $140 + 155 + 235 = 500$, much largest yet.'

The Ascension Day festival became a highlight of the Barrington spring and everyone participated in it. For weeks beforehand all the cottages were newly papered, painted and whitewashed outside. Daughters returned from their places as servants in the big houses, merry-go-rounds and booths for sweets and coconuts were erected on the green. Everyone had fun and it was very rarely that any unfortunate accident occurred.

In early autumn the important community activity was gleaning, which at Barrington survived until the end of the century. The school closed for six or seven weeks to allow the children to accompany their mothers to the fields. Everyone looked forward to gleaning time as to a period of bracing relaxation which brought in some money, rather as the London East Enders looked forward to hop picking in Kent. Nobody was ever allowed to steal a march on the others and mothers with very young children were specially helped. It was forbidden to start gleaning before 8.30 a.m. at which time a bell was rung at the church. About sixty women of all ages, with their children, set out, each woman carrying a cotton sheet to hold the wheat. The gleaners went to whichever field was known to be ready for gleaning. The furthest fields were a mile away and indeed closer to the next village of Orwell than to Barrington, but there were strict unwritten laws on gleaning and no Orwell woman would have dreamed of gleaning corn from Barrington fields.

Then towards noon this company would troop homeward; each woman carrying her spoils, not as drawn by artists in a graceful sheaf; but all wrapped up in the sheet tied together at the four corners, a great clumsy heavy bundle; yet how graceful those women looked as they stepped along with firm upright carriage, their bundles poised on their head, one hand steadying the bundle, while the other held a bonnet or hat. After dinner, out they trooped again and the prettiest scene was when the company of gleaners returned toward sundown, in the light of the setting September sun. Thus were brought home wheat, barley, beans. £4 was sometimes gathered by a good gleaner. Part was sold to pay the rent (due at the old Michaelmas, October 11), part was used for fowls, part supplied the family with bread. A gleaning loaf was sometimes given to us, only the sweeter for being somewhat gritty. But flour became cheap; machines raked the stubble-fields bare, and towards the close of the century the zeal for gleaning began to wane.

I remember once congratulating a woman on the cheapness of bread and flour. 'It's too cheap for us poor people,' rejoined she. 'My father used to say that bread ought never to be under 6*d.* a loaf—the 4 lb loaf—' This was true, for wages rose and fell with the price of flour, and when wheat was low the farmers could only afford to employ the minimum of labourers at the minimum wage.[4]

Conybeare always organized a special Gleaners' Tea as a village celebration to follow the traditional Harvest Festival. Tuesday 4 November 1879 was typical.

Busy day again. First up to see about river by Vicarage Close, wh. Smith wants cleaning. In to Cambridge by 12 train to E.C.U. Committee—they having elected me to represent Branch at London meeting on 13th. Home by 4. With Mrs Wortham to Gleaners Tea, which passed off brilliantly. From 5–10.30. Mrs Wallis and Miss Porter helped & the Squire made himself vastly agreeable. Band came 6.30. Dancing till 8, when put up platform and seated room for Cambridge Youths, who gave good entertainment (esp. Terence Portmanteaufish!). They were two hours late again and on way back drove into slurry pit and did not get out till midnight.

The vicar was an active man who crammed a myriad of activities into his day and it was a joy to him in January 1876 when he first made 'practical use of a bicycle'. The family went by carriage as usual and the vicar raced by them on his machine. The bicycle increased his mobility, permitting him to go into Cambridge five or six times a week. He met all his friends, attended church organizational meetings in the town and kept abreast of the latest scientific marvels. 'Friday May 24, 1878 . . . Clarke Maxwell on telephones . . . C.M.W. lecturer, but experiments interesting, esp. microphone, by wh. a watch could be heard ticking all over the Senate House.' In June 1878 he purchased the very latest bicycle— 'a Coventry Club, a sweet machine weighing only 36 lb.' That November he 'saw for first time electric light, curiously blue and gold, the very ideal of "light without love" '.

In spite of the Church not being his vocation he took all his pastoral duties very seriously and was proud of his village nickname as 'Father of the village'. One of his duties was to uphold morality—'Dec. 10, 1874. Excommunicated Holder for refusing to repent of shameful assault on Mrs Titmarsh.'—but later Holder was restored to favour and employed digging ditches for the vicar. Conybeare worried greatly when his parishioners were in trouble. 'Grievous news of Forsters who have bailiffs in house.' In July 1879, during the agricultural depression, he wrote, 'J.W. utterly cut up, having had to reduce all his men to 10/– for single & 15/– for married men per week. They mostly get 30/– & 40/–. But not a man threw up, times being so fearfully bad.' Another entry, about the same time, ran: 'Startling advertisement in Chronicle of sale of whole Prime property over their heads by mortgagees. E.P. professes to know nothing about it !'

The Primes, like the Colemans, were leading Dissenters, but they ranked as relative strangers, having lived in Barrington no more than a hundred years. They had recently started a cement works at the southern end of the village but the project failed almost from the start and was bought cheaply by a Mr Wallis, a newcomer, who proved more grasping than Edward Prime and did not possess the saving grace of being Barrington born. In December 1882 a dispute over pay and conditions reached such a pitch that his workers attacked Wallis, flung him into a ditch and beat him until the blood flowed. Wallis flourished his walking stick and displayed a concealed sword blade, which sight made his workers feel they had been justified in their attacks and they proceeded to chase him home. Wallis flung himself inside, with an angry mob threatening to break down his front door and drag him outside. One of the villagers ran to Conybeare for help, the vicar rushed over and stationed himself in front of Wallis's door to declare that the villagers would enter the house only over their parson's prone body. That had the desired effect of dispersing the crowd, and during the night Wallis and his wife secretly left Barrington, never to return.

The following day, when the vicar and family were at midday dinner, they heard a loud noise. The same group which had attacked Wallis was outside the vicarage windows, armed with flags, tin kettles and sticks. Mrs Conybeare felt alarmed, for the gardener had gone home for dinner, her son was only eleven years old, and the vicar was the only man in the house. Conybeare ordered his wife and son upstairs for safety, then went outside, locking his front door behind him. He stood facing the men, a priestly figure in cassock and skull cap, and at once realized that the rather fearsome impedimenta which the villagers carried were arms of peace and celebration. They wished to thank him for his intervention in the Wallis business, and having done so, burst rather incongruously into the Christmas carol 'God rest you merry gentlemen' before going home. Wallis laid charges against the villagers and there was a court case, but only the ringleaders were convicted, and they received lighter sentences than would have been the case without Conybeare's mediation.

The vicar was often asked to assist discreetly in awkward situations, such as the time when Cambridge, a wheelwright who owned several cottages, was ordered by the sanitary authorities to repair his drains. He applied to the vicar for advice, explaining that he did not object to carrying out the repair but was afraid his friends, who were also property owners in a small way, would accuse him of being 'too modern'. Cambridge's solution was to stage a public demonstration in which he would appear reluctant to obey the order and Conybeare was to insist sternly that he had to comply.

'So you, Sir, come down and blow out at me about it, and I'll blow out at you, but don't you take no notice, sir, of what I say.'

At the pre-arranged hour, Conybeare strolled down to the cottage and gazed pensively at the offending ditch.

'You'll be getting into trouble about that ditch,' he remarked to Cambridge in a very loud voice.

'Don't care nothing for you nor for any one else,' replied Cambridge in an equally loud voice, adding in a hushed aside, 'Don't you take no notice, sir, don't you take no notice.'

When Cambridge deemed the public altercation had lasted long enough for him to pose as an independent man forced against his will to improve his property, he yielded and in due course the ditch was cleaned up.

Barrington abounded in village personalities. One was Daniel Dacura, of Celtic stock, a descendant of those men who had fled to the Fens when the Saxons conquered Britain. He had a proper respect for death and when told of any neighbour who had recently died would raise his hat reverently and say, 'God rest his soul.' Another personality was Mr Coates, yeoman farmer and coprolite pit foreman, a handsome man who had taught himself to read and write when he was courting his wife. It happened that he began by trusting a friend to write love letters to the girl on his behalf and then found that the friend was wooing the girl himself. Coates was a strong Radical in politics but respected Conybeare, who was certainly not a Radical, and instructed his gang of coprolite diggers not to swear when they were working near the vicarage. On his deathbed he called for Conybeare to administer the Sacrament.

Another character was John Munns, a Wesleyan, who wrote poetry and played the fiddle at village celebrations. He was very friendly with the Conybeares and bequeathed them his fiddle which had come into his possession from a bankrupt employer. When Mrs Conybeare cleaned it she found an old label saying

'Antonius Stradivarius Cremonensis faciebat anno 17 . . . A†S.'
The instrument was beautifully varnished and inlaid and had a
lovely tone. The Conybeares traced its history back for a hundred
years and hoped it was a genuine Strad, but nobody ever confirmed
it.

The village was in many ways a self-contained community.
Illness was something which concerned the entire village and it was
seldom that a district nurse was called in from outside. The doctor
lived three or four miles away but he was not sent for except in
direst emergency. The women nursed their families through long
illnesses and all showed boundless care and tenderness. Babies
were brought into the world by elderly self-trained midwives with
centuries of traditional knowledge supporting them. Only once
during the time that the Conybeares were in the village did a young
mother die in childbirth and the villagers were aghast. Such a thing
had not happened for fifty-two years.

The Conybeares, like so many other Victorian professional
families, were interested in local archaeology and around Barrington, chiefly as a result of the coprolite diggings, antiquities were
common. Sharks' teeth by the bushel, called by the villagers
'Birds' beaks'; fossil sea urchins, which the villagers called 'fairy
loaves'; fossilized bones of elephants, rhinoceros and hyenas;
carved deer horns; flint axe-heads, also jadeite and bronze axe-
heads. There were coins from the days of the Roman occupation
and Conybeare began a collection in the vicarage which became
locally famous and was constantly added to by villagers bringing
him coins and other curios which they reckoned would interest
him. There were also Anglo Saxon coins, and there was great
excitement on the day when a child brought in a papal bulla dating
from about 1416.

The coin which impressed the vicar most was a large defaced
bronze one, brought to him about 1893, and which for years he
could not decipher. Just after the war, and long after he had left
Barrington, another coin was given him from a collection which
had been brought to England from Palestine in the 1870s. The two
coins were identical, and were Ptolemaic coins from the Middle
East.

Another discovery resulting from the coprolite excavations was
an Anglo Saxon cemetery where a number of skeletons were
exhumed, each male wearing a necklace of amber or coloured glass

and a bronze brooch, often gilded. Their plaid coverings had long since decayed. The female skeletons were buried beside a bone or clay spindle.

All these interesting finds stimulated the vicar to write articles on local history and geography, and to his surprise and gratification the articles found a ready market. He had resigned himself to the fact that he would never become a Cambridge don, and he began to devote an increasing amount of time to freelance writing where his energy and his inexhaustible interest in human affairs both past and present could be put to profitable use. Another advantage of literary activities was that they did not interfere with his work as 'Father of the village'.

When living and working conditions were bad the vicar was always ready to help. During the hard winter of 1893 he raised over a hundred pounds to help relieve poverty in the village. When the coprolite diggings were worked out he obtained permission from the squire to use the old workings to sink artesian wells for the village. The work, supervised by Conybeare who acted as civil engineer, took several weeks and employed a large group of men. Three wells were sunk in the grounds of Barrington Hall, producing three perennial springs for the village, and these were incorporated into a drinking-water fountain on the green, a boon for a village with no piped mains water. The grateful villagers subscribed to an inscription on the fountain to commemorate the work of Edward Conybeare.

He tried to keep the villagers involved at every level with Church matters. In 1890 he decided to have a metal screen made for the church to replace the ancient wooden one which had been removed about a hundred years earlier. He wrote in his diary on 27 October 1890: 'To tea at Newton where learnt rudiments of Venetian ironwork from Harold Hurrell for possible boys' class.' Within a fortnight he had started a class for boys and young men, about ten in number, in Venetian iron work and before Christmas the screen was finished and installed. It was a period of widespread unemployment and Conybeare hoped by his class to teach a new and perhaps profitable skill to his pupils.

He was an early and enthusiastic photographer, pressing his family into service as subjects. Probably no local children had their photographs taken as frequently as did the Conybeare children. He loved children and enjoyed teaching in the school.

His lessons were not confined to religious topics, and he read literary classics like the novels of Walter Scott to his classes.

In 1898 Conybeare resigned the living. He had been in Barrington for twenty-six years. His five children had been born there, but now they were grown up and at the start of their own careers. He was in his mid-fifties, not too late to change direction, and his literary prospects were more than encouraging. Macmillans had accepted one or two books and were interested in others, and he had gained a reasonable reputation as a local historian.

The Conybeares returned to Cambridge, taking a small house, where they lived quietly and Edward Conybeare spent his next thirty years as a hard-working author. Their elder daughter, as lovely as her mother, grew up to be one of the toasts of the Cambridge colleges.

Notes

Chapter 1
1. A. Tindal Hart, *The Country Priest in English History*, Phoenix House, London, 1959, p. 19.
2. C. K. Francis Brown, *A History of the English Clergy 1800–1900*, The Faith Press, London, 1953, p. 129 (footnote).
3. A. Tindal Hart and Edward Carpenter, *The Nineteenth Century Country Parson*, Wilding & Son, Shrewsbury, 1954, p. xxviii.
4. Anthony Trollope, *Clergymen of the Church of England*, Chapman & Hall, London, 1866.
5. John H. Overton, *The English Church in the Nineteenth century. 1800–1833*, Longmans Green, London, 1894, p. 130.
6. Dr C. K. F. Brown says that some advowsons were traded in the famous Garraway's Coffee House, where the shares of the South Sea Company had been bought and sold.
7. Owen Chadwick, *Victorian Miniature*, Hodder & Stoughton, London, 1960, p. 177.
8. Dean Hole, *Then and Now*, Hutchinson, London, 1902.
9. A. Tindal Hart and Edward Carpenter, *The Nineteenth Century Country Parson*, Wilding & Son, Shrewsbury, 1954, p. 30.
10. Richard Jeffries, *Hodge and His Masters*, Faber & Faber, London, 1946, p. 269.

Chapter 2
My thanks are due to the County Archivist, Essex County Council, for information about the Rev. Joseph Arkwright and 'Parson Fane'. Also to the Area Librarian, Devon County Library, Exeter.

See E. W. L. Davies, *Memoirs of the Rev. John Russell and his out-of-door life*, Chatto & Windus, London, 1902; Eleanor Kerr, *Hunting passion: the life and times of the Reverend John Russell*, Herbert Jenkins, London, 1963; and S. Baring-Gould *Devonshire characters and strange events*, John Lane, London, 1908.

Thanks are also due to the Archivist, Devon Public Record Office, Exeter, for permission to work on the Chichester Diary. Photos are by permission of Exeter University. My thanks to the Rev. A. H. Jones of The Rectory, Drewsteignton.

My thanks also to William A. Hornby of St Michael's-on-Wyre for letting me see the diaries of his great grandfather, the Rev. William Hornby of St Michael's-on-Wyre, Lancashire.

For work on the Landor section I have used various lives of Walter Savage Landor, including *Savage Landor*, by Malcolm Elwin, Macmillans, New York, 1941, and I am indebted to two books by Eric Partridge: a memoir of the Rev. Robert Eyres Landor, London, 1927; and *Selections from Robert Landor*, ed. Eric Partridge, Fanfrolico Press, London, 1927. I would like to acknowledge with gratitude the help and interest of Mr J. F. I. Comins of Birlingham.

Material for the Cunningham section has been drawn from diaries and information kindly supplied by the diarist's grand-daughter, Miss Rosalind Fynes-Clinton, M.B.E., M.A., of Reading, Berks, for which I am grateful.

The material for the Miller section has been drawn largely from his article, 'Village Tyrant', in the *Nineteenth Century*, 1893; and for Ellman, see W. Robertson Nicoll, *A Bookman's Letters*, Hodder & Stoughton, London, 1913, and *The Recollections of a Sussex Parson* by the Rev. Edward Boys Ellman, 1912.

Chapter 3

I am especially indebted to members of the family of the Rev. O. Pickard-Cambridge including Mrs Pickard-Cambridge, of Ringwood; Miss R. Pickard-Cambridge of Wareham; and Col. and Mrs Lane of Bloxworth. I should also like to record thanks to Francis Dalton, former curator of the Dorset County Museum, and to Dr W. S. Bristowe; also to present staff members of the Dorset County Museum and the Record Office and the Reference Library at Dorchester.

1. Letter from Dr W. S. Bristowe, of Battle, Sussex.
2. Incident told to R. F. Dalton by one of the sons of O. Pickard-Cambridge, and corroborated by his grand-daughter, Miss R. Pickard-Cambridge.
3. Rev. M. C. F. Morris, *Yorkshire Reminiscences*, Oxford University Press, 1922, pp. 223–5.
4. When, around 1970, repairs were again made to the church (financed by Mrs Lane, a descendant of O. P.-C.) and that same organ had to be shored up because of subsidence, the builders found a glass bottle buried under the wall, containing a note saying that O. P.-C. had donated the organ. A paragraph was added to this note, stating that a century later another member of the family had restored the foundation. Then the bottle was resealed and reburied. The organ still sounds sweetly, but it is no longer played by the vicar's wife.
5. There is another link between Hardy and Bloxworth. Both Hardy and O. P.-C. were friends and admirers of William Barnes and wrote memorials of him for the Dorset learned societies.
6. G. Kitson Clark, *The Making of Victorian England*, Methuen, 1973, p. 62.
7. His collection and his fine library of Arachnological literature was

bequeathed to the University Museum at Oxford, a gift which the Hope Professor of Zoology described as the greatest contribution to systematic zoology that the University had ever received by one gift.

Chapter 4

My interest in the Rev. Patrick Brontë was first aroused through a short book, *The Father of the Brontës—His Life and Work at Dewsbury and Hartshead*, by W. W. Yates, Fred R. Spark & Son, Leeds, 1897; then by Annette B. Hopkins's book, *The Father of the Brontës*, John Hopkins University Press, Baltimore, 1958. A monumental and extremely readable book which has helped me to understand the subject is *A Man of Sorrow. The Life, Letters and Times of the Rev. Patrick Brontë* by John Lock and Canon W. T. Dixon, Nelson, 1965. Readers who wish to learn more of Brontë can do no better than read this last book.

I would like to express deep appreciation to Gillian Hughes who read the chapter and made some useful suggestions which have been incorporated.

1. For the sake of simplicity I have used the form Brontë throughout, although Patrick Brontë first spelled his surname Brunty, then Brontē, then Bronté, and adopted Brontë only after his daughters had made that form famous.
2. Quoted in A. B. Hopkins, *Elizabeth Gaskell*, John Lehmann, London, 1952, p. 187.
3. The spelling of Branty was later changed to Brontë.
4. See A. B. Hopkins, *The Father of the Brontës*, John Hopkins University Press, Baltimore, 1958, p. 47.
5. The Rev. William Grimshaw, born in 1708, became Perpetual Curate of Haworth in 1742. He brought about almost single-handed, a great religious revival in Haworth and during his incumbency all the great Wesleyans preached in Haworth Church. By 1763 Grimshaw ranked third among the Wesleyans, after John Wesley and Charles Wesley. He was a man of strong character and blunt speech.
6. Charlotte, a lynx-eyed child with a genius for coming to conclusions, made Cowan Bridge the model for Lowood School in *Jane Eyre*, exaggerating almost everything except the 'black marble' Calvinism of its founder, the Rev. William Carus Wilson.
7. J. Lock and W. E. Dixon, *A Man of Sorrow*, Nelson, London, 1965, p. 309.

Chapter 5

I should like to express thanks to the Rev. John F. G. Griffin of Little Glemham, who gave me some interesting information about Farnham Church and who also gave me some leads on other aspects connected with Benhall and Mitford.

The chief source of information about Mitford is in *Sylvanus Redivivus* by Mrs Houston, London, 1889. There is an obituary in the *Gentleman's*

Magazine, July 1859, and an entry in the *Dictionary of National Biography.* References to him can be found in contemporary books, including *Recollections of the Table Talk of Samuel Rogers,* ed. A. Dyce, Edward Moxon, London, 1856. His Will is on file at Somerset House and his papers and commonplace books are in the Manuscript Room of the British Library, London.
1. Benhall Parsonage has since been sold.
2. Mitford's commonplace books and recollection consist almost entirely of notes, records and information such as any working writer might accumulate. In the Manuscript Room, British Library.
3. *Gentleman's Magazine,* July 1833.
4. Lewis Melville, *The Life & Letters of William Beckford,* Heinemann, 1910, p. 111.
See also 'Suffolk's Forgotten Scholar', by C. E. Heanley, *East Anglian Magazine,* March–May, 1937.

Chapter 6
I am very grateful to Mrs Jocelyn Gilbert of Paris and to Miss Phyllida Chewett of Watford for telling me about their great-grandfather, the Rev. T. T. Lewis, and especially to Miss Chewett for letting me see family letters, diary extracts and other accounts of Lewis and his family.
    I am also indebted to the City Librarian, Hereford, and the Librarian, Ross-on-Wye, for information and articles kindly supplied me.
1. Family letters.
2. Address of the Rev. T. T. Lewis as retiring President of the Woolhope Naturalists' Field Club, 1854.

Chapter 7
I would like to thank the staff of the Dorchester Central Reference Library and the curator of the Dorchester Museum. Among the published books which I have drawn upon for this chapter are:

Giles Dugdale, *William Barnes of Dorset,* Cassell, London, 1953. Lucy Baxter ('Leader Scott'), *The Life of William Barnes, Poet and Philologist,* Macmillan, London, 1887. 'William Barnes', 1939, in E. M. Forster, *Two Cheers for Democracy,* Edward Arnold, London, 1951. Geoffrey Grigson, *Selected Poems of William Barnes,* Routledge, London, William Barnes, *Collected Poems.*

    In the dialect poems which I have quoted I have omitted the phonetic signs which Barnes included to indicate pronunciation. Students of Barnes's poetry should however study the collections and note the signs.
1. Thomas Hardy, in the obituary he wrote for the *Athenaeum,* gave Barnes's birthdate as 1800 but the Barnes family always believed it to be 1801. It is unlikely that the christening would have been postponed for a whole year, although John Keble knew of many late christenings.

See Giles Dugdale, *William Barnes of Dorset*, Cassell, London, 1953, p. 8.
2. Lucy Baxter, *The Life of William Barnes, Poet and Philologist*, Macmillan, London, 1887, p. 26.
3. Ibid. p. 28.
4. He became surgeon to the royal family and was knighted.
5. Sir Frederick Treves, *Highways and Byways in Dorset*, Macmillan, London, pp. 356–7.
6. The statute was afterwards removed, but at one time St John's College had as many as 78 ten-year students on its books, studying for their B.D.
7. Quoted in Giles Dugdale, *William Barnes of Dorset*, p. 134.
8. The clotes were yellow waterlilies.
9. Lucy Baxter, *The Life of William Barnes*, p. 121.
10. One man walked nine miles there and nine miles home.
11. These daughters were Laura and Isobel. Isobel was a widow, having married a clergyman who died soon after the wedding, and she returned to live with her father. The Barnes children were all adult by that time. Lucy was a governess in Italy with ambitions to become a writer. Julia was in Italy, studying to be an operatic singer. Egbert was an engineer, married with children. William was in his last year at Cambridge, planning to enter the Church.
12. Blue veined cheese, the famous blue vinney of Dorset.
13. There is an early exception to this, a piece of anti-Chartist writing which apparently Barnes in later life regretted having written.
14. See introduction to *Selected Poems of William Barnes*, by Geoffrey Grigson, Routledge, London, p. 7. Also see essay on Barnes in *Two Cheers for Democracy*, by E. M. Forster.

Chapter 8
I have drawn mainly on James Spedding's article in *Nineteenth Century*, September 1879, pp. 461–80: and on *Memoirs of the Tennysons*, H. D. Rawnsley, Maclehouse & Sons, 1900; *The Tennysons. Background to Genius*, Sir Charles Tennyson and Hope Dyson, Macmillan, London, 1974; *Life of Alfred Tennyson*, Charles Tennyson, Macmillan, London 1949; and the *Collected Sonnets*, Charles Tennyson Turner, C. Kegan Paul & Co., London, 1880.

The church at Grasby is as grey and windswept as in his time; the school he built is still standing.
1. Charles Tennyson, *Life of Alfred Tennyson*, Macmillan, London, 1949, p. 128.

Chapter 9
My thanks are especially due to Mr C. T. O. Prosser and to Frederick Grice who read this chapter and gave me timely advice; also to the other members and friends of The Kilvert Society. Many of the details in this chapter were researched by the above individuals and I am appreciative of their good work over many years, which has made my

task that much easier. I am also indebted to the Estate of Mr F. R. Fletcher, the editor, for permission to quote from *Kilvert's Diary*.

1. Account from *Recollections*, written by the Rev. Robert Kilvert, son of the coach-builder and father of the diarist, and published by The Kilvert Society.
2. The Rev. Francis Kilvert of Claverton Lodge, uncle of the diarist.
3. The Rev. Robert Kilvert, father of the diarist.
4. The Rev. Edward Kilvert, uncle of the diarist.
5. *Kilvert's Diary*, Vol. I, ed. William Plomer, Jonathan Cape, London, 1940, p. 258.
6. Frederick Grice, *Francis Kilvert, Priest and Diarist*, The Kilvert Society, 1975. Kilvert and the Church.
7. *Kilvert's Diary*, Vol. I, p. 95. It is a touch worthy of Stanley Spencer.
8. A nephew recalled Kilvert as possessing the boundless energy and warm friendly responses of a Newfoundland puppy.
9. *Kilvert's Diary*, Vol. I, pp. 36–7.
10. Lord Alfred Tennyson also had defective vision, a shortsightedness which made his sight abnormally keen within a certain distance. Kilvert seems to have had a similar kind of sight.
11. *Kilvert's Diary*, Vol. I, p. 139.
12. *Kilvert's Diary*, Vol. I, p. 238.
13. *Kilvert's Diary*, Vol. I, pp. 308–9.
14. *Kilvert's Diary*, Vol. II, ed. Dr William Plomer, Jonathan Cape, London, 1939. pp. 37–8.
15. *Kilvert's Diary*, Vol. II, p. 126.
16. *Kilvert's Diary*, Vol. III, ed. Dr William Plomer, Jonathan Cape, London, 1940, p. 107.
17. *Kilvert's Diary*, Vol. III, p. 223.

Chapter 10
The main source of information about S.G.O., apart from the *Dictionary of Nationary Biography*, obituaries, reference books and mentions in contemporary books, is *The Life and Letters of S.G.O.*, ed. Arnold White, 2 vols., Griffith, Farran, Okeden & Welsh, London, 1891.

My thanks are due to Humphrey Gifford, J.P. of Durweston, Dorset, for assistance in drawing upon his recollections of his father's knowledge of S.G.O.: and to David Muspratt, Curator of the Muniment Room at the Working Men's College, London.

1. *Politics for the People*, John Parker, London, 1848, p. 37.
2. *Politics for the People*, John Parker, London, 1848, pp. 88–9.
3. *The Life and Letters of S.G.O.*, ed. Arnold White, Vol. I., p. 189.

Chapter 11
I should like to express thanks to the Rev. Stephen Scott Huxley, Vicar of United Benefice of Warkworth and Acklington, for information and for assistance in procuring photographs.

In addition to the books on the early Pre-Raphaelites and books by Robert Bridges, I have relied particularly upon Dr James Sambrook's *A Poet Hidden*, The Athlone Press, London, 1962. His title seemed especially appropriate when I visited the exhibition of 250 years of Warkworth history, mounted in Warkworth Church by the Local Record Office, and was struck by the cursory mention of Dixon in that exhibition. The poet receives far better-deserved treatment in the guide to Warkworth Parish Church.

1. From 'Memorials of Burne-Jones', i. 74, quoted in James Sambrook, *A Poet Hidden*, The Athlone Press, 1962, p. 123

2. He was to become headmaster of the United Services College at Westward Ho!, the original of 'the Prooshian Bates' in Rudyard Kipling's *Stalky & Co.*

Also see 'The Last Hermit of Warkwarth', Mary Coleridge, *Northern Counties Magazine*; and 'Pages from a Private Diary', H. C. Beeching, *Cornhill Magazine*, March 1898, p. 390.

Chapter 12

My attention was drawn to the Rev. William Kingsley by a chapter in *Yorkshire Reminiscences* by the Rev. M. C. F. Morris, Oxford University Press, 1922. I discovered several references to him in lives of John Ruskin, and some articles from Yorkshire newspapers of the time. However the military colleges where he taught art or examined in that subject and the Civil Service Commission, for which he was an examiner in drawing for many years, now have no record of him.

My thanks are due to the Rev. Ian J. Tomlinson, of Thirsk, for information and help in procuring photographs, and also to Mr and Mrs Rymer of South Kilvington, North Yorkshire, who recall Kingsley in his last years and also Mrs Kingsley.

Chapter 13

The reader who wishes to know more of this interesting man is referred to *Onward Christian Soldier* by William Purcell, Longmans, Green & Co., London, 1957, which has been invaluable in the writing of this chapter. Extensive browsing through Sabine Baring-Gould's actual published books will give the true flavour of the man.

1. S. Baring-Gould, *Curious Myths of the Middle Ages*, Longmans, Green, London, 1897.

2. Mr Baring-Gould senior remarried after his first wife's death and had a second family.

3. Stories from S. Baring-Gould, *Further Reminiscences 1864–1894*, John Lane, London, 1925.

4. Information supplied by Canon J. H. Adams, of St Agnes, Cornwall, to whom I am indebted for many fascinating details about country parsons, as well as the activities of Baring-Gould in Morwenstow and further details about the Rev. R. S. Hawker. The Andrews family in

Baring-Gould's first edition of his life of Hawker was clearly recognized in the village as being the Adams family, and Canon Adams's grandfather threatened a libel suit to ensure proper changes in the second edition. Baring-Gould apologized, explaining that his publishers were hustling him to get his book out before the rival biography which was being written by F. G. Lee.

Chapter 14

My thanks are due to Miss Frances M. McCormick, of Trumpington, Cambridge, and grand-daughter of the Rev. J. W. E. Conybeare, for permission to make use of her grandfather's diaries; to the Rev. J. Breay of Shepreth Vicarage; to the staff of Cambridge County Public Record Office for giving me access to Mrs Conybeare's recollections of Barrington; to the librarian of Trinity College, Cambridge.

J. W. E. Conybeare was the author of: *La Morte d'Arthur, Roman Britain, Alfred in the Chronicles, Rides Around Cambridge, Highways and Byways,* etc.

1. From Mrs Conybeare's *Recollections of Barrington*; Typescript in Cambridge County Public Record Office.

Mr Finch did not set much store by Barrington's stern injunction, cut in stone opposite the vestry door:

> Lo fol how the day goth
> Cast foly now to the cok
> Ryht sone tydeth the wroth
> It ys almast XII of the clok

2. She had been a Frances Cropper of Kendal. The Croppers were of Quaker stock, and her grandfather was a leading campaigner in the anti-slavery campaign. Her father became an M.P. Conybeare liked and admired his father-in-law and referred to him as 'Father' in the diaries.

3. Grace Conybeare married her cousin, George Macaulay, a master at Rugby School.

4. From Mrs Conybeare's recollections. There was a brief resurgence of gleaning in Barrington during the First World War.

Bibliography

Further books consulted and not specifically referred to in the notes to chapters

ADDISON, WILLIAM, *The English Country Parson* (Dent, London, 1947).

ARMSTRONG, REV. BENJAMIN JOHN, *A Norfolk Diary*, ed. Armstrong, H. B. J. (Harrop, London, 1949).

ATKINSON, J. C., *Forty Years in a Moorland Parish* (Macmillan, London, 1907).

BAKER, W. P., *The English Village* (Oxford University Press, 1953).

BARING-GOULD, S., *Old Country Life* (Methuen, London, 1913).

BARING-GOULD, S., *The Vicar of Morwenstow* (Methuen, London, 1903).

BRENDON, PIERS, *Hawker of Morwenstow* (Jonathan Cape, London, 1975).

BRIDGES, ROBERT, *Poems of the Rev. Richard Watson Dixon* (Smith, Elder & Co., London, 1909).

BRIDGES, ROBERT, *Three Friends* (Oxford University Press, 1932).

CHURCH, R. W., *Life and Letters of Dean Church* (Macmillan, London, 1894).

COLLINGWOOD, STUART DODGSON, *Life and Letters of Lewis Carroll* (Fisher Unwin, London, 1898).

COLLINGWOOD, W. G., *Life and Letters of John Ruskin* (Methuen, London, 1893).

DENISON, HENRY PHIPPS, *Seventy Two Years' Church Recollections* (Robert Scott, London, 1925).

DENNIS, ROBERT NATHANIEL, *Extracts from Diaries, 1845–1869*, ed. Mullins, W. H. and Ticehurst, N. F. (Witherby, London, 1952).

DITCHFIELD, P. H., *The Old Time Parson* (Methuen, London, 1908).

DOLLING, REV. R. R., *Ten Years in a Portsmouth Slum* (Sonnenschein, London, 1896).

FLETCHER, J. S., *Memorials of a Yorkshire Parish* (John Lane, London, 1917).

GREEN, F. E., *The Tyranny of the Countryside* (T. Fisher Unwin, London, 1913).

HARE, AUGUSTUS J. C., *Story of My Life* (George Allen, London, 1896–1900).

HEARL, TREVOR W., *William Barnes, the Schoolmaster* (Longmans, Dorchester, 1966).

HOLE, S. R., *Memories of Dean Hole* (Arnold, London, 1893).

HORSLEY, J. W., *I Remember* (Wells, Gardner, Darton & Co., London, 1911).

HUDSON, DEREK, *Lewis Carroll* (Constable, London, 1954).

JONES, DR, *Dorset Worthies 1* (Dorset County Museum, Dorchester, 1962).

KEBBELL, T. E., 'The Country Parson as he was, and as he is', *Blackwoods Magazine*, Vol. 142, September, 1887.

LEVY, WILLIAM TURNER, *William Barnes, the Man and the Poems* (Longmans, Dorchester, 1960).

MARSON, CHARLES LATIMER, *Village Silhouettes* (Society of SS. Peter and Paul, London, 1914).

MASSINGHAM, H. J., *The English Countryman* (B. T. Batsford, London, 1942).

MEREWETHER, DEAN JOHN, *Diary of a Dean. An Examination of Silbury Hill* (George Bell, London, 1851).

NEWSOME, DAVID, *Godliness and Good Learning* (Murray, London, 1961).

PELLING, HENRY, *Popular Politics and Society in Late Victorian Britain* (Macmillan, London, 1968).

QUEKETT, REV. WILLIAM, *My Sayings and Doings* (Kegan Paul Trench & Co., London, 1888).

QUILLER-COUCH, SIR ARTHUR, *The Poet as Citizen* (Cambridge University Press, 1934).

RAVEN, C. E., *Christian Socialism: 1848–1854* (Macmillan, London, 1920).

ROWSE, A. L., *The English Spirit* (Macmillan, London, 1944).

RUSKIN, JOHN, *The Diaries of John Ruskin*, ed. Evans, Joan and Whitehouse, J. H. (Clarendon Press, Oxford, 1958).

SPRINGHALL, MARION, *Labouring Life in Norfolk Villages, 1834–1914* (Allen & Unwin, London, 1936).

THOMPSON, FLORA, *Lark Rise to Candleford* (Oxford University Press, 1946).

WICKHAM, E. R., *Church and People in an Industrial City* (Lutterworth Press, London, 1969).

WILLIAMS, ISAAC, *Autobiography*, ed. Prevost, The Ven. Sir George (Longmans, London, 1892).

WINGFIELD-STRATFORD, ESME, *This Was a Man* (Robert Hale, London, 1949).

WOODWARD, E. L., *The Age of Reform: 1815–1870* (Clarendon Press, Oxford, 1938).

YOUNG, G. M., *Victorian England: Portrait of an Age* (Oxford University Press, London, 1936).

Index

The reign of Queen Victoria witnessed 'the golden summer of the parson's progress'. Brenda Colloms begins her new book with a brief historical outline of the status – social and economic – of the cleric since Chaucer's day, culminating in the high noon of his prosperity in the latter part of the nineteenth century when 'the priest and his patron had in many cases been at the same school and university, and a much larger proportion of the clergy than previously belonged to the higher grades of society'. This more stable period at the parsonage sheltered and encouraged an immense flowering of talent: the budding naturalist, scientist, poet, artist, eccentric – and black sheep – prospered and developed in the atmosphere of ordered calm and comparative leisure. The lives of some of the most vivid of these marvellously individualistic characters are the subject of this book.

Amongst others included are Charles Tennyson Turner, the sonneteer; John Mitford, Editor of the *Gentleman's Magazine*; William Barnes, vigorous defender of the Dorset tongue; Octavius Pickard-Cambridge, who became an expert on spiders, and whose work is still valued and relevant in scientific circles today; Patrick Brontë, father of the Brontë sisters; and Francis Kilvert who recorded country life in the matchless prose of his diary as he went 'villaging'. The variety of experience and the achievements of the Victorian country parson were astonishing; they added colour and vigour to the Victorian scene.